Folsom, Cal.

Smo   th l

SMOKE THE DONKEY

SMOKE
THE DONKEY

A Marine's Unlikely Friend

CATE FOLSOM

Foreword by Lt. Gen. Robert R. Ruark

Potomac Books
An imprint of the University of Nebraska Press

Library of Congress Cataloging-in-Publication Data

Names: Folsom, Cate, author.
Title: Smoke the donkey: a marine's unlikely friend /
Cate Folsom; foreword
by Lt. Gen. Robert R. Ruark.
Description: Lincoln: Potomac Books, 2016.
Identifiers: LCCN 2015040302
ISBN 9781612348117 (cloth: alk. paper)
ISBN 9781612348414 (epub)
ISBN 9781612348421 (mobi)
ISBN 9781612348438 (pdf)
Subjects: LCSH: Donkeys—Iraq. | Folsom, John D. | Iraq War,
2003–2011—Personal narratives, American.
Classification: LCC SF361.3.172 F65 2016 | DDC 636.1/82—dc23
LC record available at http://lccn.loc.gov/2015040302

Set in Scala OT by M. Scheer.

To the unsung heroes, the logisticians,
be they Marines, soldiers, sailors, or airmen,
without whom battles could not be fought nor wars won

Contents

Illustrations

Foreword

LT. GEN. ROBERT R. RUARK, USMC

The first things a student of war learns is to never underestimate your opponent and plan for the unexpected. Too often we apply this axiom only to actual fighting. In the midst of a counterinsurgency campaign in al-Anbar Province, Iraq, from 2008 to 2009, I made that mistake, which is really what this book is all about.

As a brand-new brigadier general I was fully aware of the need to be careful of what you say to Marines, who can take an offhand comment seriously. However, I made a remark that became the impetus for not only the capture of Smoke but also, in some indirect way, his effect on the world, as Cate Folsom notes in her book.

When the I Marine Expeditionary Force (MEF) (Forward) of twenty-five thousand arrived in al-Anbar in January 2008, we viewed our predecessors' success as having moved the football to the ten-yard line. Our job was to take it to the end zone. Ultimately, we wanted to return al-Anbar to the Iraqis. Our logistics mission was considerable. Our predecessors had established outposts at 147 locations across a province the size of North Carolina. These all had to be resupplied, and while the convoys were out, we still had to guard our primary bases.

"Out of sight and out of mind": this was our guidance regarding the Iraqi populace from Maj. Gen. John Kelly, our I MEF (Forward) commander. We stayed off the roads during business hours, and our convoys often numbered five to ten per night for all 365 days of our tour. When the leading tribal sheiks asked General Kelly in early 2008 to begin removing several heavily guarded checkpoints between Ramadi, Fallujah, and Baghdad to promote commerce and trade, we put forth maximum efforts to clear the roads. Eventually, tactical vehicles became part of normal Iraqi traffic.

Make no mistake, al-Anbar was still dangerous, the main weapon of choice being the roadside improvised explosive device. Other threats included small, well-armed insurgents striking to inflict maximum casualties, suicide bombers at large gatherings, and the occasional rocket attacks. Our Explosive Ordnance Disposal Company handled hundreds of calls from I MEF to render safe bombs, rockets, arms caches, weapons, and so on. It was a more complex atmosphere than full-scale combat in many ways, certainly no time to become complacent.

In my capacity as the commanding general of First Marine Logistics Group my day began with an ops-intel update to cover the last night's events, upcoming combat operations, and the latest threat intelligence. After one ops-intel I showed Marine Col. John Folsom a video taken by our Taqaddum Base Defense Force of an Iraqi donkey that had strayed onto our airbase yet eluded capture by multiple Marines. The video was shot by cameras mounted nearly eighty feet high. It portrayed a donkey that wasn't particularly fast . . . it was just quicker than any Marine trying to snatch it. The video had been sped up and played to the Benny Hill theme song "Yakety Sax," all of which got the roaring approval of the Operations Center's personnel. Had our hardened Base Defense Force really been unable to capture a stray animal?

My offhand comment that the video "was funny" and "we should have our own donkey" was something I truly underestimated in terms of its perception by Marines. In my attempt to inject a little humor, I misunderstood the long-term impact.

In reality it was John Folsom's interpretation that I underestimated. We had not met before his arrival at Taqaddum in summer 2008. But I instantly knew from meeting John, a reserve colonel, that he was serious minded and always up for a challenge. I just didn't imagine it would be this sort of challenge. The sheer amount of responsibility of being "mayor" of Taqaddum was burdensome enough, involving significant interaction with combat and combat support units, contractors, the Iraqi Army, animal control, a fire department, a base police force, a security force, and so on. Taking time to capture and host a wandering donkey, undersized by our U.S. standards, was unheard of . . . or so I thought.

John proved me wrong. While the capture of the donkey didn't necessarily surprise me, the aftermath did. Once Smoke was approved as a "therapy animal," he gained an entirely new status. As the months passed, Smoke became a star attraction for all visitors, from the secretary of the Navy, to the commandant of the Marine Corps, to the Philadelphia Eagles cheerleaders, to professional golfers, wrestlers, and football and baseball players. Yet that was never anyone's intent. It just happened and created a legend in the process.

Why did Smoke become such a hit?

First, I think Marines related well to Smoke. Stubbornness is not a trait unique to donkeys and mules. Marine leaders do not take "no" for an answer when it means compromising the mission, and the capture of Smoke evolved from this. John Folsom interpreted my comment that "we should have our own donkey" as an order that was passed to Sgt. Juan Garcia, who made it happen.

Second, Marines had warm feelings about Smoke. Quite frankly, he conjured visions of home for many. The sight of Smoke with a blanket draped around him that read "Kick Ass" under our unit logo at a 9/11 event made me laugh harder than anything else that year. Smoke's presence made home seem reachable, that we could return to family, friends, pets, and normal routines. He also showed another side to our organization, our mission, and our people. We could be human. We could treat indigenous animals as we do at home. We could care . . . and we did.

Third, I sanctioned Smoke. With all the stressors of a combat tour, visiting a fully sanctioned "therapy animal" became a highlight for any resident or visitor at Taqaddum. People literally went out of their way to visit, feed, or exercise Smoke. And I suppose I exploited it as much as anyone. To visit Colonel Folsom and his donkey was a treat for any tour group or dignitary, and we had a plethora during our thirteen months there. John would often lead off with his base mayor's brief, showing the challenges of running a city and airbase of eight thousand people, and then close with a visit to the base's official mascot, Smoke. That visit would steal the show and reveal a unique aspect of life at Taqaddum.

Fourth, John Folsom sincerely saw into my psyche. He sensed that the mere mention of Smoke brought a twinkle to my eye, a relaxation of any conversation, and the onset of laughter. To this day I laugh when I think of the impact of Smoke. I cannot explain why I traveled one hundred miles to visit him in 2011 when John brought him to U.S. soil. Perhaps I knew his journey was a logistics miracle and admired it. Perhaps I could learn more about the people's lives that Smoke touched. Perhaps I had never seen or met anyone like John Folsom and had to personally witness his own "logistics miracle." Perhaps it was the memory of the Officer's Mess Night we held at the mess hall just before we redeployed in January 2009, where a chorus turned the lyrics of Kenny Rogers's "Three Times a Lady" into "Yes he's once, twice, three times a donkey . . . I loooooovvvvvvveeeeee youuuuuuuuuu," to the unbridled laughter of over one hundred officers.

Finally, the last thing in the world I imagined after a combat tour was writing a foreword for a story about an indigenous therapy animal. I would much rather discuss Corps' very successful role in accomplishing its combat mission, which contributed to a safer, more secure al-Anbar Province. But that story has already been written. What hasn't been told is the story of the impact of one undersized donkey both here and abroad and of one Marine colonel's quest to share that impact with countless admirers in the United States through his own extraordinary efforts.

Acknowledgments

So many people have helped bring this book to life. My research began by mining John's wonderful recollections of his time with Smoke in Iraq and the long trail of emails he exchanged with everyone he contacted or heard from as he brought Smoke to America. But it wasn't until I expanded my search, tracking down dozens of those who were involved in Smoke's life, that I could truly do justice to the little donkey's story. In all three-dozen people were interviewed, either in person, by telephone, or by email.

Veterinarians and USDA officials provided valuable expertise and insight into animal import regulations and equine health issues: Army Col. Anthony Bostick, who vaccinated Smoke in Iraq; Dr. Kenneth Davis, Dr. Jason Koopman, and Dr. Dale Weinmann, who worked together at the Animal Import Center; Dr. Michael Thomassen, who treated Smoke for colic; Dr. Bruce Brodersen, who conducted Smoke's necropsy; and Donita Eickholt with the National Veterinary Services Laboratories, who worked so diligently to help John with animal testing procedures.

Military officers shared their recollections, including Marine Corps Maj. Gen. Juan Ayala; Marine Corps Lt. Gen. Robert Ruark; retired Army Lt. Gen. John Sylvester; Marine Corps Col. Patrick McCarthy; Navy Capt. Joseph Penta; Marine Corps Maj. Steve Castora; Marine Corps Staff Sgts. Juan Garcia and Steven Saitta Jr.; and Sgt. James McGarr. On the diplomatic front Ambassador Doug Silliman was kind enough to respond to my questions, and retired Lt. Col. Lloyd Freeman and Lt. Col. Daniel Barnard were quite generous with their time.

The professionals who helped when Smoke was stranded in

Turkey were invaluable: Paul Weygand, Heike Schmitz, and Dr. Andrea Göbel shared documents and knowledge, and Paul and Heike were extremely patient in explaining the complexities of equine transportation issues.

Debbie Nash and Army Lt. Col. Robert L. Ditchey II shared their memories of Smoke's visits to Virginia, the Pentagon, and New York. Smoke's horse-set friends in Nebraska helped explain what a prey animal can offer in understanding humans, how important equine therapy can be, and why they all got such a kick out of Smoke: Lisa Roskens, Gale Faltin, Karman De Luca, Mary Lou Chapek, Sharon Robino-West, Lissa Sutton, Sara Weiss, Kelly O'Brien, and of course Brenda Sheets. Pam Wiese and Gale shared stories about the night Smoke was honored by the Nebraska Humane Society, which was also generous with its support after Smoke's death.

The current executive director of the Society for the Prevention of Cruelty to Animals International (SPCAI), Meredith Ayan, and communications director, Stephanie Scott, dug through financial records, emails, and photo archives to help deepen my understanding of their organization's mighty undertaking in delivering Smoke to New York. They also graciously allowed use of the detailed blog written by Terri Crisp. Then there was Isaam. This Iraqi expatriate not only helped John to contact and communicate with the sheik and the donkey wranglers but also offered me his thoughtful insights into the attitudes of his countrymen.

My special thanks and gratitude go to George Edmonson, a retired editor with *USA Today*, the *Omaha World-Herald*, and the *Atlanta Journal-Constitution*, who gamely agreed to be my consulting editor. George, with his impeccable eye for narrative, helped me find my voice and coached me in how to shift from writing a chronology to crafting a story.

Many others offered anecdotes about Smoke through emails, blogs, and other correspondence. I thank them all.

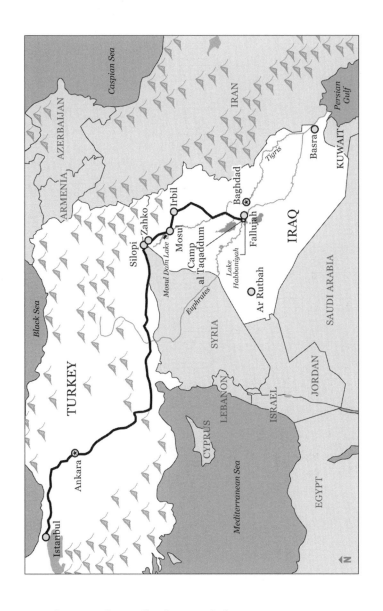

Smoke's route from Fallujah to Istanbul. COURTESY OF MATT HANEY.

Prologue

The lean, middle-aged passenger with the rugged face and no-nonsense look sat in the departure lounge at John F. Kennedy International Airport, his passport in hand. It was blue, the mark of a tourist. For once his travel didn't require an official government passport, the dark brown one affirming that "the Bearer Is Abroad on an Official Assignment for the United States Government." This was the beginning of yet another journey in a long string of journeys to foreign lands over the course of his fifty-seven years, but for the first time in many years the trip was unofficial. He was sitting there in this utilitarian chair in this equally utilitarian air terminal, ignoring the drone of endless public address messages, because of an email he had received four days earlier, back home in Omaha, Nebraska.

"How soon do you think you could get to Istanbul?" his contact had pressed him. The urgent tone wasn't lost on recently retired Marine Col. John Folsom. It puzzled him, though, because the international operation had been going relatively smoothly as of late. But he didn't argue. He accepted that his involvement was necessary and made his plans. Most of the major airlines flew into Ataturk International Airport, on the southern tip of Istanbul, just inland from the Sea of Marmara: Delta, United, Air Canada, KLM Turkish Airlines, and Lufthansa, plus at least a dozen more. But given the last-minute nature of the trip his options were fewer than usual. Lufthansa had the lowest fare, so he booked it.

He had been given little time to prepare. Thankfully, for no particular reason he had renewed his civilian passport several weeks earlier. As he waited to board, he thumbed through the blank pages. It struck him how a passport in some ways is like a diary—with blank pages waiting to be filled with visas, entry stamps, and exit stamps. Once filled, the pages would form a story about his experiences and adventures. He was sure this trip would give him one worth telling and retelling. He played it out in his mind, confident of how it would end.

Yet his confidence was mixed with a few doubts. He had never met Terri, his contact, in person and hadn't known her before this mission began. They had talked, of course—a few international phone calls, a couple of Skype calls, and a blizzard of emails—but that was all.

He had taken the necessary steps to ensure his safety, checking the "warden messages" on the U.S. State Department website for Americans traveling abroad. He looked, specifically, for warnings about any Islamist threats against U.S. citizens. Although Turkey was a U.S. ally and generally safe for Americans, some Islamist elements were disenchanted with Turkey's overall secular government. Taking out a retired Marine Corps officer would definitely make a political statement—and the news. But he saw only petty street crimes in the travel warnings, no cause for concern.

He thought back to a trip he had taken to Manila in February 2002 to attend a counterterrorism conference. At the time the Moro National Liberation Front, a political organization fighting for the right to secede, was intent on killing a senior U.S. military officer. Any senior military officer would do. The U.S. embassy took the threat so seriously that when John, a lieutenant colonel at the time, stepped outside the Manila International Airport, a "hard car" was waiting to pick him up. Bulletproof and bomb resistant, this black Suburban afforded a measure of safety on his drive to a well-guarded hotel.

This time around he had no official sponsorship or protection, although the U.S. State Department was involved behind the scenes. He expected to be away only a few days. He simply needed to meet Terri in Istanbul, effect the handoff, and return home. Maybe he would spend a few hours in the city's Grand

Bazaar and pick up some souvenirs. He wasn't worried about his safety, confident he could rely on his military training and common sense to avoid problems. He knew the drill: Avoid demonstrations. Stick to open public areas, areas with lots of tourists. Avoid being surrounded by a crowd. Don't accept packages from strangers. Don't talk politics or religion.

He checked his watch: 4:30 p.m. About an hour and a half remained before Lufthansa 411 would depart for Munich. It was time to activate his international phone and make his way to the gate. Settling into his seat in coach, he thought to himself that it seemed like first class.

As Lufthansa 411 tracked north and east from New York, he watched the East Coast disappear below the horizon. "Feet wet" as Newfoundland slipped away, thirty-six thousand feet below the Airbus 340. It was 8:30. The pilots would have signed off by now with the controllers at Gander Center, he thought. They winged their way over the North Atlantic. He made out a faint, reddish glow low on the northwestern horizon in the blackness of night. It was a reminder that summer was coming and with it the midnight sun. He curled up next to the window and thought back to the other trips he had made above the North Atlantic, on his way to deployments to Afghanistan and Iraq. He fell asleep listening to the hum of the four giant Rolls Royce turbofans and thinking back to the beginning, back to when this adventure had started.

1.

The Bray Heard Round the World

The harsh sound broke over the Iraqi desert like an out-of-tune bugle, jarring him awake early one Sunday in August 2008.

"Heehaw, heehaw, heehaw!"

"What the . . . ?" John muttered to himself.

Suspended in that state of half awareness that comes in the moments between asleep and awake, he knew he wasn't dreaming, but was that really a donkey braying outside his quarters?

It certainly wasn't one of the typical sounds of Camp al Taqaddum. The colonel's quarters were just north of the camp's runways, along the taxiway. Throughout the day and night Purple Fox CH-46 helicopters flew in and out. There were early mornings—"zero dark thirty," as they were called—when a special operations helicopter would appear, three hundred feet from his quarters. These were UH-60 Blackhawks, which staged on the taxiway, far from the rest of the camp. The crews waited in the middle of the night, engines running and rotors engaged, until they were called in for a raid as part of a task force so secretive that even its designation was classified. The distinctive, thudding roar of the helicopter rotors cut the quiet of the night. Not that it was ever truly quiet: all the power needed for camp operations came from generators, and their growling drone could be heard everywhere.

Still, that braying noise was distinctive, and it roused John from his last dregs of sleep. As commandant of Camp al Taqaddum John would already have been on duty for hours on any other day of the week, attending briefings, inspecting the base, and overseeing the projects his Marines did to ensure that life support systems on the base were in working order. If a generator blew up, or a sewage lagoon overflowed, or part of the camp's electrical system needed to be rewired, John's crew was on the job, and so was he.

But on Sundays he granted his staff—and himself—a half day off, barring emergencies. His crew had been reporting to work by 5 or 6 a.m., seven days a week, and they worked long hours. The load was beginning to wear them down and was damaging morale. He wanted to make sure they had time for themselves, time to relax, time to write letters or emails home to family or to attend religious services. So he instituted a new policy: on Sundays, short of an emergency, only a skeletal crew must report before noon.

So he was still in the rack, long past sunrise. This morning, startled by the brays, he hopped out of bed, shoved on his flip-flops, and walked outside. There, tied to a scrawny eucalyptus tree with a hemp rope, stood the donkey that, unbeknownst to him at the time, would change his life. "Well, well, look what we have here," John told the donkey.

"Heehaw, heehaw, heehaw!"

John sized up his braying visitor. The donkey must be young, he guessed, judging by its size—it stood no more than three feet tall at the shoulder. It was a male donkey, a jack, and had an intelligent look, the colonel thought. Its coloring was slate gray, and it was sleek, probably because of the Iraqi climate and the intense summer heat.

The donkey was terribly thin, unlike the well-fed versions he had seen over the years in the States, with their barrel-like mid-sections. What struck him as remarkable was the pronounced black cross on the donkey's back. The horizontal line extended the width of his back and into his shoulders. The vertical line stretched from the donkey's mane all the way to the base of his tail.

The donkey looked like a living Eeyore, but without a ribbon tied to his tail. He had a plaintive look—not pathetic but friendly. He showed no fear at being tied up to a tree in a strange place. The donkey held his head down as he peered up at the colonel with kind of a "here I am" look.

Little did the donkey know that the man peering back at him was a sucker for animals. What he saw was a man of medium height with a lean, muscular build and a booming voice. His thinning salt-and-pepper hair was closely trimmed in a regulation Marine cut. His all-business, Marine-issued olive-green T-shirt clashed with his navy-and-garish-yellow SpongeBob pajama bottoms. The pants had been a gift from his two children—all three were avid fans of the naïve underwater doofus.

John grinned as he looked over the donkey. He had been around animals, especially dogs, for as long as he could remember, starting with Snooks, a beagle pup he had been given for Christmas as a toddler. Young Johnny had been the kind of boy whom strays always seemed to follow home. As an adult he couldn't pass an injured bird or rabbit without taking it in and trying to nurse it back to health. He encouraged his children to take in pets and projects—from salamanders and hamsters to goldfish and garter snakes. Nothing too exotic, but enough to finally prompt a household rule: a two-species limit at any given time.

True, John hadn't grown up on a farm or spent much time with horses or other livestock. But he had great confidence in his ability to master any situation. So when he saw those big expressive dark brown eyes looking at him plaintively, there was only one thing to do. He reached out and scratched the donkey's head. *Looks like I've got myself a donkey,* he thought to himself.

He had no idea of the significance of the moment. He had no way of knowing this was the beginning of a beautiful and highly unlikely friendship, one that would last for years, defy war and distance, overcome bureaucratic hurdles, and ultimately create an international celebrity out of the little donkey with the black cross on his back.

Several weeks earlier, on July 10, 2008, a massive Air Force c-130 cargo plane had rolled onto a runway at Camp al Taqaddum, carrying supplies and troops. The supplies were stowed on pallets in the back half of the plane. In the front section soldiers and Marines were squeezed into four rows of red web seating that ran lengthwise through the plane. They were like military-issue sardines, crammed into a giant, flying aluminum can. One row of troops faced another, sitting side-by-side in their camouflaged uniforms and Kevlar vests, knee-to-knee with the opposite row. No reclining seats here, no flight attendants with beverage carts and peanuts.

John was too senior to be one of those wedged into the web seating. As a courtesy to him as senior officer and a pilot, the aircraft commander had invited him to spend the flight in the "front office," the cockpit. He was on his way to an assignment with the First Marine Logistics Group (MLG). Stateside the First MLG was based in Camp Pendleton, California. In Iraq the First MLG had taken over the operation of the sprawling Camp al Taqaddum back in February. But the camp commandant had been reassigned as chief of staff, and John was called up to replace him, one of thousands of U.S. Reserve and National Guard members deployed to the war zone when active-duty troops became stretched thin.

John was well prepared for the work. It was far from his first deployment, even though all but six of his twenty-eight years in the Marine Corps had been spent as a reserve officer—a "weekend warrior." But between the 9/11 bombings in 2001 and the summer of 2008 John had been separated from his family a total of thirty-eight months to serve the Marine Corps mission.

During an earlier deployment to Iraq, from February 2005 to February 2006, he had initially been assigned as the Second Marine Aircraft Wing (Forward) liaison officer to II Marine Expeditionary Force (Forward). In October 2005 he was sent to Camp Korean Village, an isolated post at ar Rutbah in western Iraq, near the borders of Jordan and Syria. There he was the air boss, the senior officer with the Second Marine Aircraft Wing. He coordinated the efforts of the light attack helicopter detachment—HMLA-167—made up of two Marine AH-1W Cobras and a UH-1N Huey gunship, which were used for close air support. He also coordinated the activities of a detachment from a Marine support squadron, MWSS-372, which ran airfield operations, communications, and weather forecasting.

Two Army UH-60 Blackhawks from the 571st Air Ambulance Company were based at Korean Village. They were used for the medical evacuation of casualties in southwestern Iraq. In his four months there John and the Marines in his command center oversaw forty-eight medevac missions. His team was small but capable. After returning home, when friends and acquaintances asked about his experiences, he told them he had had too few assets: people, helicopters, and, most important, time. But he worked hard to make the best possible use of those at his disposal. His Bronze Star citation summed it up: "Colonel Folsom's extraordinary performance under dynamic and challenging conditions directly contributed to the ability of the Wing to successfully execute all of its missions in the Korean Village–Rutbah region and along the Syrian border."

But a lot had changed since 2005. And this time around, instead of running a small, isolated airfield, he would head the unit running Camp al Taqaddum. This massive air base was near Fallujah, a once-embattled city about forty miles west of Baghdad. Al Taqaddum had changed hands a number of times. The British had built it in 1952 as an extension of their nearby Royal Air Force Station Habbaniyah. Al Taqaddum was built on a plateau to handle the long-range and jet aircraft developed after World War II.

The British withdrew in May 1959, after the July 1958 Revolution, leaving the base to the Iraqi Air Force. Then in March 2003 the United States led a military coalition that launched Operation Iraqi Freedom. The U.S. Army took over the air base and renamed it Forward Operating Base Ridgway. That summer U.S. officials were staggered when they discovered Russian MiG-25 fighter jets and Su-25 ground attack jets, buried here and there across the base. A handful of old Il-28 Russian Beagles were parked near a dining facility. The bombers stood as silent monuments to the base's Cold War past.

The name changed again in 2004, when I Marine Expeditionary Force took charge of operations in al-Anbar Province. Forward Operating Base Ridgway, named for Army Maj. Gen. Matthew Ridgway of World War II and Korean War fame, became

Camp al Taqaddum as the Marine Corps sought to show respect for local culture.

By 2008, when John returned to Iraq, U.S. forces had turned the corner in al-Anbar. Combat operations were still under way, and casualties were still being transported regularly to the surgical unit at the base. But gone were the continual rocket attacks launched at Camp al Taqaddum that had marked the colonel's 2005 deployment.

John was surprised at how quiet the camp was this time around. The only gunfire he heard was the occasional ceremonial shots into the air to mark weddings and special occasions in the small nearby town of Habbaniyah. The colonel would describe the change several weeks later, in a posting he made on *You Served*, a military news blog.

> The Invisible Success
> August 25, 2008
>
> When I landed at Camp Al Taqaddum, Iraq on July 10th to assume the duties as an assistant chief of staff for the 1st Marine Logistics Group and camp commandant, I found myself in a much different environment than I remembered from over three years ago.
>
> Throughout much of 2005 Camp Al Taqaddum ("TQ") was frequently targeted with indirect fire as were many of the camps in al-Anbar Province.
>
> "TQ" hasn't had a rocket fired at it in over a year.
>
> Three years ago in the daily operations-intelligence briefings at II Marine Expeditionary Force (Forward), we heard a recap of the previous day's indirect fire attacks, reports of improvised explosive device (IEDs, as you all know) and small arms fire engagements.
>
> The IED incidents briefed in our morning ops-intel briefs are far fewer in number and are more likely directed at Iraqi security forces than U.S. personnel. In the six weeks that I have been here I can recall only one incident of a deliberate attack on one of our outposts.

In October of 2005 I was sent to the edge of al-Anbar, near the Syrian and Jordanian borders, as the Air Boss at Camp Korean Village. Requests for urgent MEDEVACS were frequent. We often heard the detonation of IEDS and sometimes could see the smoke from a burning vehicle that had been hit. We were rocketed once in awhile for good measure. . . .

On the trip from Camp Pendleton to "TQ" I met a young first lieutenant from the 11th Marines, one of our four artillery regiments in our Corps. This was his first deployment and, as you would expect, [he] was quite excited.

He and I talked for a while. I told him that I hoped that he did not ever fire a single round in a fire mission. He looked at me in a way that I would have to describe as a combination of disbelief and disappointment. I explained that if he were to have a fire mission that means something bad has happened to us: we were hit with indirect fire or a unit was in contact. . . .

That isn't to tell you that there's not combat operations in al-Anbar or that young Marines are no longer being wounded or killed. It's that the level of violence is down considerably and is so because of the service and sacrifice of those who were here on previous deployments.

Our Marines, Sailors, Soldiers and Airmen are doing legendary work at "TQ" to support Operation "Iraqi Freedom." I am especially proud to support them as their camp commandant.

Semper Fidelis!

Colonel John D. Folsom, USMCR

Camp al Taqaddum provided logistics support for combat operations and several helicopter squadrons. Russian cargo planes belonging to private contractors also landed regularly to drop off supplies. The camp was a major air hub, and it was the first stop for thousands of troops who were deployed to Iraq. Marines, soldiers, airmen, sailors, and civilian contractors called Camp al Taqaddum home. Sometimes as many as twelve thousand were based there, creating a good-sized town on the bleak landscape.

John's job was akin to being the town mayor. He was in charge of infrastructure needs on the base. He had carpenters, engineers, electrical crews, and more. They looked after generators, repaired air-conditioning units, kept the lights on and the water running, and worked with the private contractors. It was a big job. One of the largest military bases in Iraq, Camp al Taqaddum covered twenty-four square miles. There were reinforced concrete aircraft hangars, a medical unit, living quarters, offices, recreational facilities, and support buildings.

It was just a month later, on August 24, 2008, when John awoke to the braying of that donkey. The sight of a stray donkey surprised John—but didn't shock him. After all, he was the one who had instructed his staff a few weeks earlier to be on the lookout for just such a critter. It wasn't unusual to find stray or native animals roaming the camp. The staff had encountered striped hyenas, golden jackals, desert foxes, raptors, and other animals. Including donkeys.

Although they aren't native to the country, donkeys have long lived in Iraq. Poor Iraqi farmers rely on them as work animals, but they aren't highly valued, so their owners don't bother to keep them sheltered. Since Iraqi farms aren't fenced, the donkeys roam, eating what they can scavenge. The little donkey that had landed on John's doorstep that Sunday had probably wandered onto the vast camp hunting for food.

John's quest for a donkey had been inspired by his commanding general, Brig. Gen. Robert Ruark. One day not long after John had settled into his new job on the base, he was visiting the headquarters building for the First Marine Logistics Group. The building was dubbed the Dark Tower because it was darker in color than the air wing headquarters next door—the Light Tower. The Dark Tower housed offices for Ruark and his staff.

John walked over from his Base Operations Section for meetings or whenever he needed to talk to the staff there. Three times a week designated staff would gather for "ops-intel" briefings. After one of these 8 a.m. meetings John lingered to talk to the general.

"Hey, I've got something really funny to show you," Ruark told him, and he walked over to his computer.

John stood by the desk as the general clicked on a video that had been floating around the base. It starred a donkey that had strayed onto Camp al Taqaddum. The episode had been captured by Base Defense Operations Center (BDOC) security cameras, which were mounted on tall poles around the camp. A BDOC camera immortalized the predicament of several Marines chasing the donkey around and around, trying to capture the animal and remove it from camp.

Some of the Marines were on foot, others in trucks. They ran and drove this way and that as the donkey ran, then wheeled and dodged, staying just out of reach as it galloped along roads and over earthen berms. The vehicles kicked up huge clouds of dust as the Marines drove along the dusty roads.

Someone had copied this surveillance footage, cranked up the speed, and overlaid it with *The Benny Hill Show*'s frenetic theme song, "Yakety Sax," a 1963 recording by saxophonist Boots Randolph. The video eventually was labeled "Herbert the Donkey." It became a YouTube phenomenon, in addition to being a big hit with the general, who thought it was hilarious. "The next time there's a donkey on the base, you ought to catch it," he told John.

It wasn't that Ruark was particularly fond of donkeys. He simply thought that catching one was a funny idea. Marines have a distinct sense of humor, especially when it comes to animals. Ruark once regaled John with a story from his days as a first lieutenant. During a 1985 deployment to the Western Pacific his battalion held a mess night—a formal dinner—at the Officers Club at Naval Air Station Cubi Point, at Naval Base Subic Bay. At one point the president of the mess gave an order to "parade the beef," which ordinarily signals the club stewards to carry out platters of roast beef. Instead out trotted beef on the hoof: a two-thousand-pound water buffalo, which proceeded to "crap all over the floor of the club," Ruark told John. The room erupted in laughter, and the water buffalo incident became legendary in the Marine Corps.

So the idea that the general would suggest rounding up a donkey wasn't entirely out of the blue. And while it was really little more than an off-hand suggestion by Ruark, John had been trained to believe that a suggestion from a general was as good as an order. Besides, he agreed that having a donkey around could be fun.

Later that day John ran into Sgt. Juan Garcia, the roadmaster of Camp al Taqaddum. It was Garcia's job to make sure that traffic regulations were obeyed and that speed limits were enforced. He also supervised the Iraqi workers who were allowed on base to do work. This was a big responsibility. Garcia had the assignment because he could be trusted to make sure it was done correctly. He was also well liked because of his demeanor. Garcia was tough, but in a quiet way. He wasn't mean-tough, but he was resolute-tough. Garcia got things done, and he didn't need much in the way of supervision. John told him about the donkey video and repeated what the general had said. "The next time you find a donkey wandering around," the colonel told the sergeant, "catch it."

Garcia didn't ask questions. There was no "Are you kidding me?" or "Why would you want me to catch a donkey?" "Yes, Sir," Garcia said, and that was that.

Weeks passed. John, focused on keeping the camp infrastructure in good shape, forgot all about the incident. He never asked the sergeant how the donkey search was going, and the subject didn't come up again with the general. But when John walked outside on that morning of August 24, he knew exactly what had happened. Sergeant Garcia had captured a donkey.

Several hours earlier a corporal had knocked on the door of Garcia's quarters in the bos cell, the Base Operations Section. Garcia and some of the junior Marines lived in this sturdy but simple plywood structure, decorated with the kind of posters that twentysomethings appreciate. Their decor was not unlike the World War II pinups of Betty Grable and the Vargas Girls, but for this generation it was rock stars and scantily clad NFL cheerleaders, who handed out publicity posters when they toured the war zone.

It was early, and the knocking woke Garcia. He opened the door to the corporal, who announced, "There's a donkey on base."

"Why are you bothering me?" Garcia said in the haze of sleep. "Animal control isn't my job."

"I know. We called KBR Vector Control. But they said they didn't deal with donkeys," the corporal told him. "And they said to notify you."

Garcia was alert enough by now to remember those instructions he had received weeks earlier. *Oh, yeah*, he thought to himself. *Colonel Folsom wants a donkey.*

Back when John had told the sergeant to capture a donkey, Garcia first suspected he was joking. But after realizing the colonel was serious, he had responded in his usual fashion: Receive the command. Make a big kick left. And execute. For a while after that he had kept his eyes open for a donkey as he patrolled the base perimeter. But no luck, and he eventually stopped thinking about it.

Now this corporal was at the door, and Garcia's mission was clear. The twenty-three-year-old sergeant pulled himself out of bed, dressed, and headed over to Entry Control Point 2. One of the two camp entrances, this control point was at the south end of the vast base, where tactical and commercial vehicles waited before joining convoys to travel on or off the base. There, in the dirt parking lot for tactical vehicles, stood a scrawny donkey, looking around warily.

Garcia was determined to catch him and recruited several Marines to help. A handful came over from Entry Control Point 2. Three others answered his summons from the Provost Marshal Office—the military police. None of them had any equipment that might be useful, not even a rope, but that didn't stop them. They just kept chasing the donkey that didn't want to be caught, in a scene reminiscent of the earlier donkey chase. Cue "Yakety Sax."

Garcia started off by driving his truck around and around, chasing the little animal, hoping to wear it out. But that clearly wasn't working, and there was traffic on the road. So Garcia turned his roadmaster truck sideways to create a roadblock and flipped on his emergency lights. He diverted two of the Marines, posting them as guards to keep traffic away. The others continued the chase in their vehicles. Garcia continued the pursuit on foot, as the donkey ran and ran, wheeling and dodging, along roads, over berms, back and forth, on and on.

A couple of donkey-chasing hours later two developments occurred: The donkey began to wear out. And Garcia found a rope. He saw it hanging off a seven-ton truck and quickly appropriated it. Then he crept close enough to the donkey to throw the rope over his neck. Game over.

Now Garcia found himself with a donkey, but he was miles away from the Base Operations Section, where Colonel Folsom was still sleeping. A forced march began, with Garcia pulling the animal down the road. The donkey put up with it for a while. And then he didn't. The 200-pound critter stopped. The 150-pound sergeant pulled. And pulled again. And pulled harder. Nothing.

Then Garcia had an idea. If this had been a cartoon, a light bulb would have popped up above his head. If you can't pull a donkey, he reasoned, what about pushing? He marched to the rear. BAM! Donkey hoof to the ribs! Sergeant to the ground! Garcia was furious.

With Garcia on the ground, gasping for breath, the donkey saw his opportunity. He started to run—but the sergeant still had the rope in his hand. Ribs aching, Garcia held on as tightly as he could and gulped down some air. Finally, the donkey gave up. Garcia had won this battle. The march continued. Another Marine drove the roadmaster truck down the camp road, moving slowly to alert other vehicles. The sergeant followed on foot. The donkey resisted the rope at every step but reluctantly accepted Garcia as the boss. Garcia thought the two-mile walk would never end, but finally, the colonel's donkey was delivered.

John's first order of business was finding some donkey-friendly food. The problem: the entire camp was a barren landscape—mile upon mile of mostly dirt. Camp al Taqaddum is situated above the Euphrates River valley, on a desert plateau. No grass and few plants grow in the dry soil, other than scattered clumps of tamarisk and eucalyptus trees. The area doesn't benefit from the vast supply of fresh water stored in nearby Lake Habbaniyah. Deep, rough canyons cut the plateau in jagged ridges, stretching down to the lake.

The canyon walls are honeycombed with small dens. These are home to the top of the food chain: striped hyenas. These nasty-looking creatures survive mostly by scavenging their food, although they are vicious fighters and will occasionally kill their prey or even attack people. Skulls and bones litter the entrances of their dens.

Plants have it tough here. Once the spring rains end, the skies remain cloudless until fall. Unless you count the dust clouds. These billow in on the *shamal* winds—strong, northwesterly winds that accompany cold fronts. The winds pick up dust and sand particles from miles away, sending them rolling over the countryside. The sight made John think of a Martian landscape. This flying red dust can cut visibility to one hundred yards or less. The siltlike particles, as fine as talcum powder, get into everything from engines to buildings to eyes and nostrils. The dust storms can last for hours. Anyone who can stay inside does, and those who have to drive somewhere turn on their headlights to cut through the red fog.

The dry landscape is also prone to giant dust devils. At least once a week John saw a dust devil kick up, spinning dirt and sand into a giant column that grew up to one thousand feet high, meandering around the desert floor. Heat also inhibits plant growth around Camp al Taqaddum. During the summer months temperatures barely dip into the mid-80s at night. By 9:00 in the morning, it's typically 90 degrees. The highs routinely hit 110 degrees and can spike to 120.

Without lush vegetation for the donkey to graze on, John decided to see what he could rummage up at the dining facility. He changed from his SpongeBob PJs into his uniform and walked over to the large building, with two cafeteria lines and row after row of tables and chairs. The place was busy and noisy, as usual. He grabbed some breakfast for himself and collected a handful of apples for the donkey. After scrounging around, he found an Igloo cooler and filled it with water. The donkey's breakfast was served.

John walked across the compound to his office and told a few Marines about his new donkey. Word quickly spread. Staff Sgt. Matthew Shelato, who worked in the Public Affairs Office, offered to take the donkey for a walk around the compound. One person after another stopped by. The donkey was a novelty, and many of these visitors, eager for some news to send home, posed for photos.

Later that day John took a closer look at the stray. He noticed what looked to be cuts and abrasions on the donkey's legs, just above his hooves. Maybe he had gotten tangled in the razor wire used along the camp's exterior fence line. John talked things over with a few people who stopped by to meet the donkey. "I'm worried that this could get serious if it's not treated," he told them. "I'll have to get Penta to look him over."

Cmdr. Joseph Penta was the group surgeon. That Monday, the day after the donkey's capture, Penta was in his office when Navy Lt. Prasad Diwadkar, the environmental health officer on the colonel's staff, strolled in, laughing. "What's so funny?" Penta demanded.

"Guess what?" the lieutenant asked, still laughing. "You have to give a donkey a medical exam!"

"What are you talking about?" Penta demanded.

Diwadkar told him the story of Colonel Folsom's donkey.

Diwadkar had been on hand when the colonel had talked about wanting Penta's professional advice for the donkey.

"That's crazy," Penta said. "What do I know about animal physiology? I didn't even grow up on a farm!"

As group surgeon for the First Marine Logistics Group, Penta was Brigadier General Ruark's senior medical adviser for logistics issues. He was certainly not a veterinarian. "How am I going to get out of this one?" he wondered and started pondering his options.

He remembered seeing a shack across base, the one with a sign announcing it as the Veterinarian Services Office. Penta had often walked past it without giving it much thought. But it had his attention now. Penta headed for the little shack. Sure enough, two U.S. Army vet techs were on duty. "Colonel Folsom has a donkey that needs to be examined," the surgeon told them. "Can you take care of that?"

They shook their heads. "No way, Sir," came the reply. "We only do food inspections."

Penta left, unimpressed. Muttering under his breath exactly what he thought about the Army, he realized he was trapped. He headed over to Base Operations Section with a medical corpsman, thinking dark thoughts. *What if the donkey kicks me?* he thought to himself. *What if somebody decides, "Looks pretty bad, Doc, better put him down"?*

But when Penta got to Colonel Folsom's office and finally took a look at the donkey, he relaxed. "This isn't bad," he diagnosed. "These are just scrapes. They've gotten dirt in them, and the wounds might be a little infected."

The surgeon cleaned the wounds and declared the donkey good to go. To his relief the animal didn't kick him. Penta decided the little donkey was cool—quite striking looking, in fact, between his black stripe and his small size. He and his corpsman posed for a photo with their patient. The little donkey had gained another fan.

2.

Hiding a Donkey in Plain Sight

Donkeys love apples—and this little donkey had all he could eat that first day at Camp al Taqaddum. Visitor after visitor dropped by with an apple for the latest recruit. But apples weren't practical for a daily diet. On the other hand, the chow hall didn't exactly cater to donkeys. There was a salad bar, but definitely no hay on the buffet. So John improvised. He looked up the manager at the dining facility. "I'm looking for food scraps—anything a donkey could eat," he explained. "Do you have any old bread you're going to throw out?"

"Sure," the manager replied. He told his staff to fill a plastic garbage bag with the stale hamburger and hot dog buns that were headed for the trash.

Then John rummaged around and found an old embarkation box. These green, wooden containers, about four-by-two-by-two feet, originally were used to ship military supplies. Perfect for repurposing as a feed bin. John filled it with some of the buns, and dinner was served. It wasn't a traditional donkey dinner. But take away the soybean oil, the yeast, the high-fructose corn syrup, the calcium stearoyl lactylate, the calcium sulfate, and the dozen or so other ingredients in a bag of buns, and what's left is a mouthful of grain. The donkey gobbled it up.

John still wasn't satisfied. He knew he had to find a better food supply for the long term if the donkey was to thrive. Still, this was Iraq, in the middle of a war zone. It wasn't as if an American in uniform could just tool into Fallujah and ask around for the local feed store.

He knew of someone who could, though: a young Iraqi merchant who ran a shop at Camp al Taqaddum made regular trips into town to buy supplies. John dropped in on him one day and made inquiries. The shop owner said yes, he knew of a local farmer who grew alfalfa. They negotiated a price for the hay, and the merchant agreed to bring back a supply the next time he made a run to town.

When the first batch arrived, John was thrilled. So was the donkey. John filled the old shipping box with fresh hay and let the hungry donkey go at it. The colonel stood off to the side, back by the donkey's tail, watching him and thinking how the box filled with hay reminded him of a manger. It was a satisfying, reflective moment.

Until the donkey did, well, what donkeys do. He picked up his hind leg and kicked. It wasn't that he was mad at the colonel. His kick was donkey speak for, "Back off, buddy!" This was his first real meal in some time, and he wasn't about to share it. He had no way of knowing that John had absolutely no interest in fresh alfalfa hay, and he wasn't taking any chances.

John dodged the kick. But he wasn't going to put up with that nonsense. Back when the donkey had first shown up, John had scoured the Internet for advice and advisers. Among the contacts he made was Crystal Ward, a donkey breeder in Placerville, California, who ran the Ass-Pen Ranch. She trained and boarded equines and was a competition judge in a number of donkey, horse, and mule organizations. John asked for some wisdom about donkeys, and they traded a few emails.

Among other things Crystal told John that donkeys are highly intelligent and very trainable. If they misbehave, she told him, they must be corrected. And fast. If a donkey makes the wrong move, she said, better react within eight seconds or forget about it, because after that the donkey won't connect the discipline with the behavior. Sometimes, Crystal told him, these animals respond to a certain amount of physical force. Not a beating, but a stern rap. She advised him to keep something on hand to teach the donkey a lesson if needed.

So John dropped by the exchange—the base store—and shopped around for a donkey behavior modification tool. Suddenly he spotted a yellow plastic baseball bat, the kind kids use for whiffle ball. Really? In a military exchange? In the middle of a war zone? John was baffled about why the exchange stocked a whiffle ball set. But he was happy to find it—the bat looked perfectly suited for his purpose.

He had taken to carrying it around whenever he spent time with the donkey. Today, when the donkey kicked, it was time to play ball. Without a word John grabbed the bat. Swat! It wasn't an I-want-to-hurt-you swat; it was a single, I-mean-business swat, right across the offending body part: the donkey's left rear haunches. Lesson learned. It was the only time the donkey tried to kick him—at least during meal times.

In the evenings, after the Marines had wrapped up their work duties, they were ready to relax. The camp's carpenters had built a wooden deck on the back of the BOS headquarters, complete with a railing and a roof for some shade. The deck was furnished with chairs, a few tables, even an outdoor grill. The Marines spent their off time there, drinking their near beer, cooking a burger, having a smoke, and swapping stories.

The donkey was one of the regulars. During the day John tethered him to a eucalyptus tree outside his office. The donkey's rope was long enough to let him walk around but not long enough to allow for mischief. After regular duty hours the colonel took him over to the deck, tied him there, and let him hang out with the guys.

One night, about a week after the donkey arrived, they were on the deck, as usual. One Marine was relaxing by the edge of the deck, smoking a cigarette. Between puffs he rested his arm on the railing. Suddenly, the donkey walked up, leaned over, and snatched the cigarette from his hand. He calmly chewed up the whole thing—paper, filter, burning tobacco, and all.

The Marines roared. Who ever heard of a donkey eating a cigarette? Especially a lighted one! As much as they got a kick out of the donkey's attraction to cigarettes, John put the kibosh on smokes for snacks. But the cigarette episode was long remembered. And it did more than give young Marines another story to swap. It gave them the much-needed inspiration for a moniker for this as-yet-unnamed animal:

Goodbye, "Donkey." Hello, Smoke.

Smoke was soon a star. Everyone knew where he hung out, and they stopped by often to pet him, bring him a snack, or take him for a walk. Occasionally, he got loose and went exploring. But not for long. The calls rolled in on the BOS headquarters "trouble line."

"I'm calling to report a Smoke sighting," the caller would say and give the location. "Come and get him."

Sergeant Garcia drove over in his roadmaster truck, tied Smoke's rope to the bumper, and headed slowly back to BOS headquarters, dragging the burro behind him.

At other times Smoke did more than walk by—he dropped in for a visit. The doors on the camp buildings featured levers, not knobs. It didn't take Smoke long to figure out how to push down on a lever with his muzzle and open the door. He strolled in and passed the time of day until the Marines on duty ratted him out. Some offices kept a community candy dish out. Smoke knew just which ones those were.

With Smoke's growing popularity came something of a dilemma. Among the directives establishing rules and regulations for military life is a document titled General Order Number 1 or, more specifically, General Order Number 1B, issued March 13, 2006, by Gen. John P. Abizaid, commanding officer of U.S. Central Command.

This six-page document lays out "Prohibited Activities for U.S. Department of Defense Personnel Present within the United States Central Command (USCENTCOM) Area of Responsibility (AOR)." You know the military and its acronyms. And the AOR of USCENTCOM includes Iraq. Much of the order focuses on prohibiting or restricting certain activities that might violate local laws or offend local customs in countries where CENTCOM forces are operating. For example, no privately owned firearms, ammunition, or explosives are allowed in designated areas. Non-

Muslims are barred from entering a mosque or any other place of significance to the Islamic religion, unless military authorities direct otherwise or unless military authorities and the host nation approve it.

Sexually explicit materials aren't allowed anywhere. Neither is gambling. Archaeological artifacts and national treasures are strictly protected. Alcohol is off limits in Iraq, as well as in Kuwait, Saudi Arabia, Afghanistan, and Pakistan. And then there is the animal rule.

General Order Number 1B, section 2, part j, prohibits "adopting as pets or mascots, caring for, or feeding any type of domestic or wild animal." And according to General Order Number 1B, violations are subject to possible "criminal prosecution or adverse administrative action."

So the Marines at Camp al Taqaddum had a delicate problem. Marines, soldiers, sailors, and airmen were forbidden from keeping pets, and units could not have mascots. Yet it was widely known that the First MLG had a donkey on the camp.

Still, several days after Smoke arrived, he received a house call from one of the top U.S. veterinarians in the country. At the time Lt. Col. Anthony Bostick was commander of the Forty-third Medical Detachment Veterinary Service, stationed in Balad, north of Baghdad. The U.S. Army Veterinary Corps had personnel spread out at seventeen locations throughout the war zone. That included the two vet techs who had so disappointed Commander Penta when Smoke first arrived.

Bostick's duties included making regular rounds to visit his troops and see how things were going. During one such tour he dropped in at Camp al Taqaddum. The vet techs were quick to mention the donkey to their boss. "We need some help here," they told him.

Bostick knew he had a sensitive situation on his hands. Under General Order Number 1, of course, it's no mascots allowed. But job one for the Army Veterinary Corps is keeping the troops healthy.

"We're restricted on what we can do with these strays," Bostick told John. "We don't want to promote anything against General Order Number 1, but our job is to make sure soldiers, sailors, Marines, and airmen don't get sick. If these animals are going to be on post, we need to take care of them."

There had been cases of troops taking in stray dogs—and then finding out the dogs were rabid after they bit someone. And it wasn't just dogs that could carry rabies. Any mammal could—even some of the local cattle were carriers. There was no way of knowing up front which animals were healthy and which weren't.

So when Bostick heard about John's donkey, he felt obliged to examine it, give it the proper vaccinations, and deworm it. Name notwithstanding, the Veterinary Corps' primary function in Iraq was not to care for live animals but to inspect food and water supplies and storage methods, to ensure that troops had a healthy food source.

A secondary mission was to provide health care to the many working dogs stationed throughout the country—bomb-sniffing dogs and other service canines trained to help provide security and perform other tasks.

Bostick's unit tended to all the service dogs in the war zone— not only those in all the U.S. service branches but also any dogs assigned to other international forces in Iraq. The United States had the only military veterinarians deployed to the country at that time.

Donkeys and other large animals rarely got onto the bases. Bostick had personally heard about only one other donkey that had infiltrated a base, and that was at Balad, maybe ten months earlier. It had simply wandered through the front gate—and, unlike Smoke, it was escorted right out again. Herbert the Donkey's fame apparently hadn't made it to Balad yet.

When Bostick made his house call on Smoke, he restricted his role to making sure the donkey was healthy. He knew that concern about rabies was the main reason for the mascot restriction in General Order Number 1. Smoke, he figured, was a great donkey and a big morale booster—he was part of the team. And that was how the contraband donkey received his seal of good health. Straight from the top.

But General Order Number 1 continued to nag at John, even after the donkey had a clean bill of health. He figured the commander of the Multi-National Corps–Iraq had bigger fish to fry than worrying about a donkey being kept by a bunch of Marines at Camp al Taqaddum. Still, how do you keep a two-hundred-pound donkey in plain sight, without violating CENTCOM regulations and without drawing complaints? John could just imagine the grousing: "Hey, look at them, they have a donkey. So how come I can't have a puppy?"

The solution arrived one day, to his surprise, in an unsolicited email from Navy Capt. Michael Hoffer, an ear-nose-and-throat specialist at the Surgical Company. Along with his ENT specialty Hoffer was also known as an expert in mild traumatic brain injury (TBI), which had become a signature injury in the Iraq War.

Hoffer had put his mind to work on the problem and drafted a two-page memo on the value of keeping Smoke the Donkey as a therapy animal. He described the mental health benefits the donkey provided, detailed how the animal was a needed morale booster, and reviewed how he benefited the command as a service animal. Rather than simply being a pet or mascot, Hoffer opined, Smoke had a job, a role in decreasing "combat stress." It might have been a little tongue-in-cheek, but it was a serious memo. In any case Hoffer's commentary was definitely something to keep in the files, in case anyone ever made an issue of Smoke.

No one ever did, though. In fact, Smoke was sometimes a topic of high-level discussions. John's boss, Brigadier General Ruark, took part in a daily video teleconference with other senior commanders of Multi-National Corps–Iraq for a Battle Update Assessment. The various commanders provided information and discussed combat operations. One day Smoke had gotten loose and was wandering around the camp. His escape was reported up the chain—and warranted a mention during the Battle Update Assessment. Everyone laughed. The senior commanders all knew just who Smoke was. And no one mentioned General Order Number 1.

The anniversary of the 9/11 attacks fell a few weeks after Smoke came to live at Camp al Taqaddum. The camp marked the date by staging a Freedom Walk. The idea was to gather everyone together to commemorate those who had lost their lives in the terrorist attacks of September 11, 2001. And Smoke helped to lead the way. He was loaded into an old blue Air Force step van and taken to the starting point of the walk. Smoke was dressed in style for the occasion.

John had visited a concessionaire on base, a man who could design and sew embroidered items. John commissioned him to embroider the First MLG crest onto a small red blanket. The crest, divided in four squares, displays the numeral 1, superimposed with "MLG"; the eagle-globe-and-anchor Marine Corps insignia; a fighting lion; and a symbol of waves, roads, and air. Across the top: "1st Marine Logistics Group." Along the bottom: "Victory Through Logistics."

The blanket also carried another motto, one the colonel devised to recognize the work of the First MLG. Logistics Marines don't get a lot of public credit. But there's a saying in the military: amateurs talk tactics, but professionals talk logistics. The point is that without logistics teams supplying troops with the food, supplies, and other support they need to survive and fight, they can't perform combat operations. The colonel's motto reflected the hustle it took to get the job done: "Kick Ass."

So there was Smoke, with his "Kick Ass" blanket. He and his lucky escort for the day, Sgt. Lonnie Forrest, together led hundreds of sailors, soldiers, airmen, and Marines on their Freedom Walk.

John returned to the concessionaire later with a new request: a uniform for Smoke. He took along a camouflage uniform shirt, size large. At John's instruction the Sri Lankan tailor removed the collar and sleeves, sewed the armholes closed, and stitched "Smoke" on a name tag. The shirt hung neatly over the donkey's shoulders. Smoke the Donkey, reporting for duty, Sir.

This donkey had a penchant for play. And that led John to develop little games for Smoke's exercise and entertainment. A favorite was "king of the hill." Although Camp al Taqaddum is predominantly flat, the Iraqis had covered a number of their military structures with earth for camouflage and protection. These earthen bunkers also created gently sloping hills of sorts.

The post office hill was one of the bigger ones. When the colonel and the donkey arrived at the post office, John let Smoke loose. The donkey charged up the hill as though he were a cavalry horse. Sometimes he heehawed all the way to the top. After arriving at the crest, he stopped and surveyed his domain, scanning the horizon in one direction and then the other, ears erect and back straight. Satisfied, he took off again, charging down the other side of the slope. Smoke loved this game.

Other times John and Smoke walked along a base road near the big runway until they reached the remnants of the former Iraqi Air Force base. The Americans didn't use this part of the base, where large, concrete, reinforced aircraft hangars still stood. The hangars, also covered with earth, were perfect for a round of hide-and-seek. While Smoke ran up the hill, John hid, slipping behind a nearby building. When Smoke reached the top, he turned to look for John. If he couldn't see him, the donkey started braying until John came out of hiding. Then Smoke galloped down the hill to his friend.

Smoke also loved his independence. Sometimes when it was time to stop playing and have his lead rope put back on, he stayed out of reach until he was ready—or until John pulled out his trump card: a snack. Smoke was a sucker for a treat.

On some walks they headed for a closed compound where old tires, abandoned equipment, trucks, and other machinery had been parked, a kind of junkyard. But it was fenced in, so it provided Smoke with a play area of several acres. With only one way in and one way out, he couldn't do one of his escape tricks.

Once John removed his rope, Smoke took off, running and running, in a wide, sweeping circle. He turned to the left, then ran down a little trail and made another big, sweeping turn. He pricked up his ears as he ran, heehawing all the way. After making his last big loop, Smoke made a beeline for John, galloping at top speed. He rushed up, then put on the brakes at the last second and came to a halt right in front of him. Then he looked up, as if seeking approval.

"Smoke, go do it again! Go run!" John urged him.

And Smoke took off again, repeating his circuit, running, heehawing, then galloping back with a swish of his tail. These were happy days for the little donkey.

John couldn't keep Smoke on a rope forever, but he didn't have the authority to order anyone to build an enclosure. He had a great staff and knew they could build anything. It was just a matter of somebody giving them an idea. One day John was sitting on the deck, smoking a cigar and drinking a near beer. He was looking across to the area where Smoke was tied up under a eucalyptus tree. "Boy, it sure would be nice if Smoke had a corral," John said, reflecting.

A day or two later he walked outside and found five or six Marines with an augur, drilling holes in the ground and pounding in fence posts. Before he knew it, there was a professionally made corral, with a latched gate.

"Wow, this is great!" John told the corporal in charge of the project. "Where did you come up with that lumber?"

"Easy," the corporal told him with a grin. "The Seabees took care of us!"

Translation: like any resourceful Marines they had driven over to the Construction Battalion, nicknamed the Seabees. This unit had all the building materials they could want. They wheeled and dealed for some scrap lumber, a couple of gate hinges, a latch, and everything else they needed. Now Smoke had a bang-up corral to call home.

Sometime in September the Iraqi merchant at Camp al Taqaddum told the colonel he couldn't keep making trips into Fallujah for hay.

"But don't worry," he said. "I will make arrangements. You can pick up the hay at another store."

That was the Iraqi store over at East Camp Habbaniyah, just north of Camp al Taqaddum. East Camp was home to an Iraqi Army unit commanded by Brig. Gen. Ali Haider Abdul Hameed. At the time West Camp Habbaniyah was the base for the First Battalion, Second Marine Regiment, although later that year the camp would be turned over to the Iraqi military.

The gravel road leading north from Camp al Taqaddum passed over the important Alternate Supply Route Michigan. ASR Michigan was a code name for Highway 10. The major east-west road links Baghdad with the Syrian border, passing the infamous Abu Ghraib prison and cutting through the middle of Fallujah and Ramadi along the way. At the height of the war the highway was considered one of the five deadliest routes in al-Anbar Province because of IED attacks. Just north of ASR Michigan the gravel road crossed an overflow canal that diverted water from the vast Lake Habbaniyah into the Euphrates River.

When the East Camp store owner had hay in stock, he sent word to Camp al Taqaddum. The next time John made a run to West Camp Habbaniyah, he and his driver would make a side trip to East Camp and the Iraqi store.

The store was filthy. It was in a small, rundown building, with plenty of windows but no air conditioning to combat the brutal heat of an Iraqi summer. The store had a small café, as well, with a counter open to the kitchen. Flies crawled around on a large sheet of baklava-type pastry, left sitting in the open. A few Iraqi civilians sat at tables in the café area, smoking and visiting. John looked past the filth and the flies, bought his hay, and left.

Once the alfalfa harvest ended, feeding Smoke again became a challenge. John came up with the idea of harvesting the reeds that grew along the edges of Lake Habbaniyah. Every day or two he and whoever volunteered to help him would drive the blue step van to the lake and spend a half hour or more cutting reeds. Only the leaves were edible, not the long stalks, so it took a lot of reeds to get a small amount of feed. To supplement the reeds, John again resorted to dining hall leftovers. He discovered that donkeys, or at least this donkey, really liked bagels—especially

Hiding a Donkey in Plain Sight

frozen bagels. They were crunchy, cold, and more substantial than white bread and hamburger buns.

All the time it took to find food for Smoke began to be a strain. John worked long days to oversee the running of the camp. You never knew when a power outage, fire, or other emergency would pop up. While Smoke's fan base remained strong, the novelty of having a donkey around was fading, and the offers of help, whether cutting reeds or taking Smoke for a walk, began to drop off.

So John was willing to listen in early October, when a Navy lieutenant from the combat stress office made a pitch. This office was where troops could go if they were struggling with mental health issues, whether depression or post-traumatic stress disorder or any other emotional issue. "I've got a great idea," the lieutenant told John. "We'd really like to have Smoke move over to the combat stress office."

After all, she reasoned, he was a therapy animal. He could help take the edge off for troops suffering from combat-induced stress, give them something to smile about. And having Smoke right there at the office might get some people to walk in the front door who had been reluctant to seek help. She assured John that she and her staff, a couple of petty officers, would be happy to take over the donkey's care. "We've got a corral built for him and everything," she said.

So John agreed, and off went Smoke to his new home. The change of scenery had one bonus from the donkey's vantage point. The combat stress office was next to Staff Sergeant Shelato's small tomato garden. Shelato, who had taken Smoke for a walk on his first day in camp, was quite proud of his tomato garden and tended it carefully. And Smoke was appreciative: he raided the tomato plants whenever he could. Not that he bothered waiting for the tomatoes to ripen. It was the pungent leaves that he loved. It's difficult to say whether Shelato was ever able to harvest a tomato during Smoke's stay.

3.

Life as a Fobbit

Smoke's social life continued to thrive after his change of address. Friends still dropped by to see him in his new home outside the entrance to the combat stress office. They still brought treats or stopped to say hello and scratch his head. All went well for about two weeks. Then the lieutenant at the combat stress office decided the arrangement wasn't working out quite how she had envisioned. Back she went to Colonel Folsom. Smoke, she said, was certainly popular. "That's the problem," she told John. "He's too popular."

Smoke, she said, was drawing a crowd. She was concerned that people needing therapy would be embarrassed by the idea of Smoke's fan club seeing them going inside the combat stress office, and they would stay away.

John didn't quite buy the story. He suspected that Smoke created too much stress of another type—for the lieutenant and her staff, who realized by now how much time and work the little donkey took. Smoke needed a couple of walks a day. His corral needed cleaning. And there was the ever-present chore of finding food for him. John figured the staff didn't want to deal with all that work. Oh, well. Smoke's corral back at the BOS cell was better for him, anyway—more space to stretch his legs. So back he went.

Some of the emotional struggles that U.S. troops suffered from during the war in Iraq had nothing to do with the stress of battle. Certainly the members of the First MLG faced danger when they deployed outside the confines of the base. They were responsible for moving food, fuel, ammunition, and parts to combat units throughout the theater. Convoys traveling the open roads faced the daily risk of IEDs and other threats. The logistics group also provided explosive ordnance disposal, finding and detonating roadside bombs. Maintenance contact teams routinely traveled off base to conduct repairs. In other words, as the scarlet-and-gold sign on top of a maintenance Humvee proclaimed, with typical Marine humor, "We Fix Your Broke $H*T."

But while most of the First MLG provided combat service support "outside the wire," many had to remain behind. These were the unsung heroes of the war. They included everyone who made up the medical, electrical, maintenance, supply, administrative, fiscal, postal, and other military occupational specialties often unrelated to direct combat. Their primary assignment—combat service support—was important. Marines talk about the three B's of logistics: beans, bullets, and bandages. Without them you can't fight a war. But the work wasn't exciting or glamorous, and it wouldn't yield dramatic war stories to tell in the years to come. Nor would Steven Spielberg or Clint Eastwood make a movie about a young lance corporal whose MOS, or job description, was to change the oil on a Humvee or work in a supply warehouse. Many craved a more exciting assignment. Whenever there was a call for volunteers to provide a service such as convoy security duty outside the wire or extra security around the base perimeter, the Marines at Camp al Taqaddum stepped up. John always had to turn people down for these potentially dangerous assignments because so many had volunteered.

Marines whose duties required them to stay "inside the wire" at a FOB, or Forward Operating Base, were known derogatorily as Fobbits. It was a play on J. R. R. Tolkien's hobbits, those fictional creatures with large hairy feet who live under the ground. These Marines were just as capable of proving their mettle in combat as those assigned to a rifle company—yet many never had the opportunity. Instead they bloomed where they were planted, as the saying goes. And where they were planted was inside the wire at a FOB.

But things were pretty quiet in al-Anbar Province in 2008—

although there were still IED blasts on the roads, few expected an attack on the camp with rockets, mortars, or vehicle-borne explosive devices. Instead, the Fobbits' enemy was the grinding monotony of camp life. They worked twelve- to fourteen-hour days, seven days a week—there was no such thing as a week-end in the war zone. Their daily routine was to work, eat, go to the gym, call home, check out the Internet, hit the rack, and repeat. Some Marines called it "Groundhog Day." Each day was pretty much like the day before, and tomorrow would be pretty much like today.

Pentagon leadership did what it could to help with morale. The troops, for example, were amazingly well fed—better than in any previous generation of warfighters. Private contractors spent millions of dollars on food: fresh pies, expertly sliced roast beef, custom-made omelets, fresh fruit and vegetables, and just about any flavor of ice cream produced by Baskin-Robbins. Huge decorated cakes were whipped up for holidays and other spe-cial occasions.

U.S. Army Maj. Gen. Kenneth Dowd, the logistics director at Central Command, once regaled Brigadier General Ruark with a story as they ate at a Camp al Taqaddum chow hall. Dowd told Ruark he had been eating lunch one day with his boss, Adm. William J. Fallon, commander of U.S. Central Command, at one of the better chow halls in Iraq. The topic of conversation was how to cut the costs of war. Fallon turned to Dowd at one point. "Really, do we need Baskin-Robbins in the mess halls?" the admiral demanded.

"Sir, they're in combat!" shot back Dowd, a veteran of multi-ple Middle East tours. And that was the end of that.

The takeaway was clear to Ruark: the military literally couldn't do enough for those at war. But the all-you-could-eat food and Internet access reminded John of what Capt. Benjamin Willard observes in *Apocalypse Now*, when Kilgore "turned the LZ into a beach party," complete with steaks and beer, but "the more they tried to make it just like home, the more they made every-body miss it."

Marines, sailors, and soldiers were often left to wonder and worry about their family, friends, and life back home. For single troops a deployment meant spending months away from a girlfriend or boyfriend, sometimes watching tenuous relationships deteriorate from halfway across the world, unable to control their destiny. For parents it meant a year away from growing children, missing birthdays and anniversaries, unable to help with homework or cheer at Little League games, not there to fix the broken washing machine or discipline a rebellious teenager.

This is where Smoke came into the picture. The little donkey provided a distraction and a much-needed break in camp routine. He was a morale booster on four legs. Smoke made people smile or even laugh—sometimes at John's expense. Take the PowerPoint slide that popped up during an ops-intel briefing one day. The slide informed the staff of a new secret weapon.

There, with the U.S. flag as the backdrop, was a photograph of John, gazing off into the horizon, flanked by his troops: a row of Photoshopped donkeys, standing at attention in flak jackets, their ears poking neatly out of camouflage helmets. John laughed along with everyone in the room as he read the slide:

READY FOR BATTLE

A new breed of Warrior!
Coming to a base near you.
Specifically trained to sniff out weaknesses in base perimeters.
Lives off the land.
Eludes captors for hours.
Twice as many feet as a human!
Superb hearing.
Fuzzy and Cuddly.

John didn't mind the ribbing. In fact, he reminded the jokesters of the popular *M*A*S*H* television series. "Colonel Potter had his horse," he told them. "Colonel Folsom has his donkey."

While life on the FOB wasn't generally exciting, there was the occasional fire at the trash dump. And sometimes huts burned down. Fire was always a concern, given the prevalence of extension cords and the potential for overloading circuits. Keeping fire hazards at a minimum was a key concern for John's crew. At one point John received some unintended help with fire prevention. But it nearly backfired—even on Smoke.

At one point Folsom was informed that a civilian firm had a contract to apply insulation foam at U.S. installations throughout the country. Others had turned down the offer because it created extra work for them, so John got heavy pressure to allow the contractors onto Camp al Taqaddum. He agreed and soon had reason to be glad. Many troops were housed in Southwest Asia huts, known as SWA huts. A few days after one of these sixteen-by-thirty-two-foot buildings was foamed, it happened to catch fire. With these wooden huts built in tight configurations, a fire in one could spread quickly to every hut nearby. Thanks to the insulation foam, though, this fire was contained to that single—and thankfully unoccupied—hut.

That impressed John, and he soon had the contractors foaming everything that didn't move. Word spread to other FOBs about this wonder foam, and camps that had initially turned down the work now wanted it. One day John heard from an Army staff sergeant at Camp Victory, the Multi-National Corps–Iraq headquarters in Baghdad. Her office was overseeing the foaming contract, and she wanted him to wrap up the operation—now.

"Not so fast," Folsom told her. "Under our contract we were guaranteed a certain number of square feet of foam, and that hasn't been applied yet. These guys aren't going anywhere until they finish up here."

The staff sergeant told her command that Colonel Folsom was being uncooperative. And she had another complaint, which John found out about from Col. Patrick McCarthy, an old Marine Corps friend. McCarthy was the senior liaison officer for logistics and engineering for I Marine Expeditionary Force to Multi-National Corps–Iraq, where the staff sergeant worked. McCarthy called John one day after word of the foaming fuss reached his ears. "Hey, John!" he started in. "What's this I hear about foaming Smoke's manger?"

"Foaming his manger? What are you talking about?" John replied, baffled.

"I was in a staff meeting the other day, and this staff sergeant told the c-4 staff that Colonel Folsom was going have his donkey's manger sprayed. I sat there, and I thought, 'Manger? Manger?'" McCarthy told him. "'Oh, she must mean his stable!'"

John told McCarthy that, of course, he had no intention of foaming either the food trough or the stable. They both had a good laugh about the "manger foaming." Whether or not the staff sergeant's superiors took the story seriously was never clear, but no one else brought it up with John. The foam contractors completed their work, and life at the fob moved on.

John did a lot of walking around to make sure everything was in order and to consider potential improvements. Once Smoke arrived, he often joined the camp commandant on many of these walks. John came to realize that Smoke had a serious role to play at Camp al Taqaddum. Just as the Fobbits provided combat service support to the grunts in the field, Smoke provided noncombat service support to the Fobbits. He sort of formed his own mrw unit—morale, recreation, and welfare. He wasn't a hero working outside the wire. But in a small way Smoke contributed to Operation Iraqi Freedom.

Not everyone at Camp al Taqaddum was stationed there. Many troops were simply passing through on the way to somewhere else. Cpl. Steven Saitta Jr. bumped into Smoke when he flew through Camp tq. As part of Marine Corps Tactical Systems Support Activity, or mctssa, his four-member unit provided technical support throughout al-Anbar Province.

Saitta and a buddy had just left the chow hall when they noticed Smoke in his corral. They were used to seeing dogs or the occasional cat on military installations. But a donkey? The young animal lovers asked around for the back story about Smoke. And they were smitten. There was something comforting, Saitta thought, about encountering animals in the middle of a war zone. He and his friend made a point of stopping to visit Smoke after every meal during their two-day stay.

Marines who were assigned to Camp al Taqaddum got to know Smoke pretty well. For them Smoke became an important way to connect with family. Deployments take a toll on families. And even when soldiers are home between deployments, there are disruptions, such as travel for training deployments. During nearly nine years of combat operations in Iraq many U.S. troops were deployed more than once. They were called up for six months or twelve months at a time, sometimes longer. Staying in contact with family during such long absences was important.

Combat leave helped a bit, but that was only for two weeks, including travel time. From their base soldiers would get a helicopter ride to Baghdad International Airport. Then they would hop a c-130 to Ali al Salem Air Base, just over the Iraqi border in Kuwait. But before they could catch a "freedom bird" to the States they would have to be processed. It wasn't easy, and it always took a great deal of time. Weapons and combat gear were stored in a warehouse. Soldiers went through customs, where they and their remaining gear were inspected for contraband. After that they were kept in a holding facility, complete with razor wire, until their charter flights departed Kuwait International Airport for Frankfurt, Germany, or Atlanta or Dallas. From those airports they traveled home at their own expense. Then they had to factor in time at the end of leave to make the reverse trip.

Beyond combat leave families had few ways to keep in touch— although modern technology certainly made it much easier than in earlier wars. Email was fast, and digital photos could be attached. Not all soldiers had access to their own computers, however, and while the military provided Internet cafés stocked with computers, there were always more soldiers who wanted to use computers than there were computers available.

As John and Smoke took their daily walks, people invariably stopped to say hello, pet the donkey, and pose for photographs.

Life as a Fobbit

His photos and exploits became the stuff of emails, phone calls, and letters back home. Smoke turned out to be a great conversation piece.

"Guess what?" soldiers could say. "Smoke is so smart, he knows how to open the doors on our buildings. He walked right into someone's office today, just to visit and look for a candy dish!" Or, "I went to see Smoke today and took him some carrots, and he really likes those." Or, "Smoke escaped today, and Sergeant Garcia had to chase after him and take him home!"

Families got such a kick out of Smoke that they sent him presents. Lt. Col. Steven Simmons, the deputy operations officer for First MLG, was among those who told family back home about Smoke. His wife, Laura, loved hearing about the donkey. She decided to give him a present. So she pulled out her sewing machine and made him a special blanket. On one side was the emblem of the Democratic National Committee, complete with the image of a donkey and a motto: "Democrats make better lovers. Who ever heard of a nice piece of elephant?" Even John, a die-hard Republican, thought that was pretty funny.

Donkey lovers sent Smoke horse treats or mailed books to John about donkey care and training. One day the mail call brought Smoke another special gift: a red pony halter. The grandfather of one of the civilian contractors had sent it along after hearing about the donkey. Smoke loved his halter. Whenever John brought it out, the donkey bobbed his head up and down. Smoke knew that halter meant playtime.

Children became enthralled with the donkey. Some sent cards and letters directly to Smoke. Many were familiar with Disney's *Shrek* movies. They addressed their cards and letters to "Smoke the Donkey," or even "Shrek's Donkey," in care of Colonel Folsom, at the APO address for the First Marine Logistics Group in Iraq. The post office took it from there.

4.

Changing of the Guard

Early autumn progressed into late autumn, which meant the winter rains were coming. About 90 percent of Iraq's rain falls between November and April. And donkeys don't like to get wet. Once again John found himself on the smoking deck, chewing on a cigar and talking about how rain and donkeys don't mix. He looked over at Smoke's well-built corral.

"Wouldn't it be nice if Smoke had a way to get out of the weather?" he mused, speaking to no one in particular.

His young, can-do Marines sitting nearby were listening. Next thing he knew, there they were in Smoke's corral with a few sheets of plywood and some power tools. The donkey soon had a smart little A-frame, with a wooden floor and walls, perfect to slip into when the weather turned wet and windy.

Smoke wasn't the only resident of al-Anbar Province that John took under his wing. The countryside around Camp al Taqaddum was a testament to the grinding poverty that gripped much of Iraq. John got a close-up look at rural Iraqis' lifestyle one day when he and other members of the First MLG, including some engineers, visited a village. They were installing a water treatment system for the local residents. It was the nearest village to the camp and lay along the east shore of Lake Habbaniyah. The village consisted of a dozen ancient-looking houses built of stone, with mud for mortar. Aside from a few junked cars and the incongruous sight of satellite dishes scattered here and there, John thought, a visitor might have thought this was a village from the days of Nebuchadnezzar.

Children quickly gathered to watch the Americans. John noticed that only one child had a toy: a boy who had fashioned some wire into two wheels, attached to a wire stick. He pushed the contraption along in the dirt for his fun. John had an inspiration. He decided to launch Operation "Toy Story." When he returned to camp, he put out the word through his email lists back home. He described the village and talked about the children he had seen. These kids have nothing, he told his email followers. Let's do something for them. If you send us some toys, we will distribute them. His followers loved the idea. They mailed hundreds of toys, games, and dolls. The Marines soon became very popular in this and other nearby villages.

Then there was Operation "pb&j." John noticed that the base exchange had to throw out packaged food once it reached its "sell by" date, even though the food was still edible. He persuaded the exchange manager to donate the discards to the locals. So the Marines periodically loaded up box after box of soup, cookies, jam, and peanut butter and hauled the groceries to the little village —which is how some Iraqi children came to discover Girl Scout cookies.

When he found out that scrap lumber was burned after being discarded from building projects at the camp, he approached the governing coalition in Ramadi. He proposed giving the local sheik any goods that were legally appropriate for Iraqi use—as long as "security conditions" remained favorable. In other words, if a roadside bomb erupted, the deal was off. Obtaining the lumber was a big incentive for the sheik, whose *wasta*, or influence, relied on his ability to provide for his people.

John's main work, of course, was to look out for the safety and well-being of everyone on camp. One day, while he and Smoke were making their rounds, John stopped by a small shop that sold dvds, power cords, and power converters. It was popular, but there was a problem: the goods were bootlegged. That meant the merchant could undercut prices at the base exchange. Now this was the same shopkeeper who had initially helped John procure supplies of hay for Smoke, and he liked the young man. But when the operator of the exchange complained about the unfair competition, John took action. "You have to stop selling these things," he told the shopkeeper.

"Why?" the shopkeeper demanded.

John explained that selling bootleg DVDs violated U.S. copyright laws and that the substandard power converters and power cords created a fire hazard. "Either get rid of these illegal products, or get off Camp al Taqaddum," the colonel told him.

While he couldn't condone the sales of inferior products, he was reluctant to take away the young man's livelihood. The Americans were trying to promote local economic development. In a small way having an Iraqi shopkeeper on base helped with that.

"I have an idea for you," he told the young man. "This war has brought a lot of young Americans to your country who will never see any more of Iraq than Camp al Taqaddum. That's a shame. But you could help change that."

He pointed out a vacant building nearby that was known as the greenhouse. Long and narrow, it had glass walls and a glass ceiling. John speculated it might have been a restaurant at one time because it had the remains of a brick oven inside.

"Why don't you clean up the greenhouse and serve tea?" he suggested. "You could serve chai to the soldiers. And you could offer hookahs, maybe serve Iraqi food. Give them a taste of Iraqi culture."

The enterprising young man liked the idea. He set to work cleaning up the building. He bought tables, chairs, and hookahs, used for smoking flavored tobacco. He also created a small kitchen.

John and Smoke watched his progress during their daily walks. Then came the grand finale—from Smoke's perspective. A big truck pulled up one day with a load of sod. Workers laid out roll after roll of fragrant green grass—right in the middle of the desert. Two plots of donkey food, twenty feet long by twenty feet wide. How the merchant finagled the grass transaction was a mystery to John, nor did he know what kind of deal the young merchant had struck to arrange for a contractor to routinely water the only stretch of grass on the entire camp.

The teahouse became an instant hit. John dropped by occasionally for a cup of chai and a smoke. But the shopkeeper refused to take his money. One day the interpreter caught up with the colonel. "When you go to the teahouse, you must not pay for the tea," the interpreter told him.

"Why not?" John asked. "I want to pay like everybody else does."

"This brings dishonor on him," the interpreter explained. "He sees you as a benefactor. He considers you as he would a sheik, because you have given him your guidance. He is making a better living now than he did before. If you accept money, you are not his guest, you are his customer. This is a big distinction."

John never tried to pay for his tea again. In the end the episode was a win-win-win. He had halted the sale of illegal goods. A local entrepreneur was launched on a respectable career path that also introduced Iraqi culture to Americans on the camp. And Smoke could now dine in style on that well-watered sod. After that the teahouse was part of the regular circuit for the colonel and the donkey.

While Smoke surely was the largest stray taken in by U.S. military personnel in Iraq, he was far from the only one. Making pets out of local animals became a way to cope with being far from home, friends, and loved ones. Many soldiers and Marines took in wanderers—mostly dogs and cats. But not always.

Several years earlier, in December 2005, when John was the air boss at Camp Korean Village, near the Syrian and Jordanian borders, his Marines caught a reddish-brown field mouse as it explored his office. They dubbed him Little Dude, housed him in a two-liter pop bottle—air holes added—and fed him crackers. It was a short-lived relationship. A day or two later someone uncorked the bottle to drop in some cracker crumbs, and Little Dude saw his opportunity. The mouse made an amazingly accurate vertical leap, rocketing from the floor of the bottle, out the opening, and on to freedom. Later, Little Dude.

The Marines made friends with other local critters, too. During John's evening walks with Smoke small foxes frequently showed up. These tan-colored "sand foxes" are smaller than their red-fox cousins, roughly the size of a Chihuahua. Called Ruppell's foxes, they have huge ears, a feature that helps them cool off in the desert climate.

The foxes were fascinated with the donkey. As John and Smoke walked along their route at dusk, several foxes often slipped out of hiding and scampered along the tops of the walls and barricades, keeping the pair company. Later, after Smoke settled down for the night in his corral, several foxes curled up just a few feet away, keeping him company.

The Marines loved these foxes. Occasionally at breakfast they saved leftover sausages and held onto them until evening. They broke the sausages into small pieces, tossing them onto the ground. The foxes ran up and snatched the food, carried it off to bury in the dirt, and then came back for more. The foxes repeated this ritual as long as the sausage held out.

Technically speaking, the foxes were not approved animals on the camp. Army veterinary policy called for euthanizing wild animals if a serious communicable disease was discovered. In fact, the Marines knew of a veterinarian who euthanized any stray animal she found. They nicknamed her Dr. Death.

The veterinary corps was obligated to look out for the health of the troops, and John understood that. But he found it heartless that a veterinarian, trained in animal health care, seemed intent on killing everything from the stray kittens and puppies that soldiers took in to the Ruppell's foxes that roamed the territory.

He thought it was particularly wrong-headed to kill the foxes. He exchanged emails with Col. Perry Chumley, the Army's veterinary medical consultant in the Iraqi theater, urging him to reconsider. No one was trying to make pets out of the foxes, so their interaction with humans was limited. Besides, they were part of the natural order of animals in the local ecosystem. The foxes served a useful purpose, ridding the camp of mice, rats, and other small rodents—which, left unchallenged, created their own health problems for humans. John also pointed out that when hyenas were captured on the base, they weren't euthanized but instead were released into the countryside. If hyenas, at the top of the food chain, weren't being killed, why were the foxes? He made his arguments and waited to hear back.

When Christmas rolled around, Smoke's celebrity status was still in force. A uso show visited Camp TQ, and Smoke attended, decked out in his "Kick Ass" blanket and a pair of goofy deer antlers made for dogs. Like the star he was, he strolled through the crowd, greeting one and all and graciously accepting pats on the back and head scratches. Among the vip visitors was the Marine Corps commandant, Gen. James T. Conway. There was Smoke, face to face with the top officer in the U.S. Marine Corps. And loving it.

Shortly after the holidays John began thinking seriously about Smoke's future. The First MLG was scheduled to head home in early February. It was time to explore the options. He contacted the commanding officer of the Mountain Warfare Training Center in Bridgeport, California. The center was training Marines in the use of pack animals, including donkeys, for work in areas such as the mountains of Afghanistan.

To: Cooling, Col Norman L
From: Folsom Col John D (TQ WST MLG BOS)
Date: Tuesday, January 13, 2009
Subject: Donkey

Greetings.

We have a young donkey that we adopted (or maybe he adopted us) after it wandered in looking for food. He wasn't in too bad of shape. He's a lot healthier now.

Can you use him? As you might expect, he's taken to Marines. I would hate to have to turn him back out and let him fend for himself.

Thanks
Semper Fidelis!

John D. Folsom, Colonel, usmcr

The reply John received the next day gave him cause for hope. Cooling told him he would love to add a donkey "with an Iraqi Campaign Medal" to the training center's horses, mules, and five other donkeys. That is, if John could get Smoke there. John was optimistic. With a fleet of KC-130 cargo planes making regular supply runs between Iraq and the States, he figured all they needed to do was make a special crate for Smoke, load him up, and wait for "Space A," when cargo space was available for a tagalong donkey. He checked the plan with the military veterinarians, who not only assured him Smoke could make the trip safely but also volunteered to escort him home.

So far, so good. He fired off another email, this one to the office of Mike Johanns, the senator from Nebraska, asking for information about the requirements to import a donkey from Iraq. "'Smoke' is about 18 months and in good health. He has been examined by a U.S. Army veterinarian who administered a rabies vaccine," he wrote to a Johanns aide. "We would bring him back in a U.S. military aircraft. Please get an answer as soon as you are able. This is not a joke." Within hours John received a response:

> To: Folsom Col John D (TQ 1ST MLG BOS)
> From: Lempke, Roger
> Date: Wednesday, January 14, 2009
> Subject: The Donkey
>
> John—
>
> Let me introduce myself first. I am Roger Lempke, retired National Guard Major General and former Adjutant General for Nebraska. I now work as the Military Affairs Director for Senator Johanns. Someone in our Omaha office is working the import question. Let me ask you a few questions about getting the donkey out of Iraq.
>
> Since you mentioned military airlift for transporting the donkey can I assume you are making arrangements through USTRANSCOM for the Air Force to haul the donkey back to the US?

I'm remotely familiar with cases of Army personnel wanting to bring animals home. Getting chain of command approval was usually quite difficult. Is a process now in place for requests like yours?

Since the donkey will be moved from a military unit in Iraq to the warfare training center will import rules even apply?

All the best to you for the rest of your tour. I had a National Guard unit that served at TQ a couple of years. It was an exciting place then. Hopefully, things are much calmer now.

Roger

John was confident he could get clearance. Surely the U.S. Marine Corps would see the public relations benefit to this unusual—yet to him simple—request. Back home the military reporter for the *Omaha World-Herald* heard about John's plan and decided it was worth a story. He contacted John and conducted a lengthy interview.

"His name is Smoke, he likes hay and long walks in the desert, and he'll soon be married to the Marine Corps if an Omaha Marine stationed in Iraq gets his way," reporter Matthew Hansen wrote in his January 17 article. Hansen described the effort to bring Smoke back—which John had dubbed Operation Donkey Drop. He included comments from Lempke. "The best thing about it from my perspective was that it was my first day in (Johanns's) office," Lempke told Hansen. "So I got to go home and tell my wife that I worked on a donkey problem."

The article circulated widely. Soon afterward John was contacted by a reporter for Radio Netherlands Worldwide. They talked about the donkey and John and his time in Iraq. He thought the interview was going well until the reporter asked him with a sneer, "Well, do you '*love*' the donkey?"

"Let's define our terms," John replied sternly. "You asked, 'Do I love Smoke?' I love the donkey in the same way any human loves a pet."

John decided he was dealing with two asses: Smoke and this Dutch reporter.

Next on John's list: obtain permission to transport the donkey on a military flight. He called Plans, Policies & Operations at Headquarters Marine Corps.

"This would be a great story for the Marine Corps," John told a colonel in the office. "And we could use a 'good news' story. You remember what happened last year, don't you?"

John reminded him of the scandal: A lance corporal deployed to Iraq with the Marine Corps had thrown a puppy off a cliff while a sergeant captured it on video. They posted the video on YouTube, and it went viral. In the wake of outrage from animal advocacy groups, both were punished, and the lance corporal was discharged.

"That made the Marine Corps look really bad," John reminded the colonel. "So if throwing a puppy off a cliff makes news for the Marine Corps, then showing a humanitarian effort toward a donkey, by bringing him back and putting him to work at the Mountain Warfare Training Center, would make news in a very positive way. Think about it. The donkey doesn't weigh more than two hundred pounds. And we're continually flying c-130s back and forth, so it wouldn't cost a dime. We just need a relatively small space for his travel crate. We already have a couple of vets who are willing to travel with him. They're all over it. So it wouldn't inconvenience the flight crew."

But the colonel at PP&O wasn't as visionary as John. He didn't recognize the public relations value of getting Smoke the Donkey to the Mountain Warfare Training Center. And he certainly wasn't about to sign his name to shipping a donkey across the ocean on the military dime.

Little did they know it, but the two colonels were replaying a bit of Marine Corps history. During the Korean War another Marine unit had adopted an equine: the famous Sgt. Reckless.

This small Mongolian mare was no stray, though. She was actually recruited by the Fifth Marine Regiment in 1952. First

Lt. Eric Pedersen, platoon commander of the Recoilless Rifle Platoon, Antitank Company, was looking for ways to ease his Marines' workload. The recoilless rifle took three or four men to carry. It fired twenty-four-pound, 75-mm shells. One Marine could carry only two to three shells. During a sustained battle the gun used plenty of shells, and Pedersen figured a packhorse could come in handy.

He persuaded his colonel to let him procure a horse. Pedersen and a couple other Marines drove to Seoul and talked a needy young Korean into selling his racehorse, "Flame." Pedersen paid the man $250 out of his own pocket for the mare. The Marines renamed her Reckless—the nickname for the recoilless rifle— and she quickly became a beloved comrade, showing courage and determination time after time on the battlefield. Her bravery became the stuff of magazine stories and eventually books— some of which are still being published today.

When the fighting in Korea ended and the Marines went home, many wanted Reckless to follow. Lt. Col. Andrew Geer took particular interest in Reckless and vowed to get her to the United States. He wrote a letter to Headquarters Marine Corps seeking permission to ship the horse to California. The response: Because Pedersen had used his own money to buy Reckless, she was not government property. Therefore, despite her bravery in action and her promotion to sergeant in the Marine Corps in April 1954, no federal funds could be used to transport her. Reckless eventually made it to California—but not through the aid of Headquarters Marine Corps.

Fast-forward fifty-odd years to Colonel Folsom and Smoke. Just like the Fifth Marines he didn't want to leave his comrade behind. And he had found a useful purpose for Smoke, training Marines at the Mountain Warfare Training Center. But like Lieutenant Colonel Geer before him he couldn't get headquarters to see his vision and bend the rules.

With PP&O issuing a flat rejection to transport Smoke, John was back to square one. And the clock was ticking. By now he was shouldering most of Smoke's care as the First MLG staff began to focus on handing off duties to the Second MLG, packing up, and getting home. The pressure was building on John to resolve Smoke's future.

He and Smoke set out one day on their regular hunt for a grazing area. They headed toward the northern edge of the base, near Entry Control Point 1, which faced north toward a wide plateau and the Euphrates River. Suddenly, all the responsibility John felt overwhelmed him. John stared at Smoke.

What am I doing? he wondered. Everywhere he looked as he tried to get Smoke out of the country, he ran into bureaucratic roadblocks. What if he couldn't get the job done? And if Smoke couldn't leave, what were the odds that the Second MLG would want to deal with the time-consuming little donkey? Wasn't it much more likely they would consider the donkey a nuisance?

John and Smoke had reached a low-lying area, a former sewage lagoon. It had largely dried up but retained enough moisture and nutrients to support a few reeds. He stood there watching as Smoke grazed on the reeds. For the first time since he had taken in the donkey, John felt powerless, unable to control the situation.

The Second MLG Marines might not want to put up with him. Why don't I just leave him here? he thought. *Maybe he'll wander off to the north. He'll go out the camp gate and wander down by Habbaniyah. Maybe he'll find some other donkeys to hang out with. After all, that's just the way of life for donkeys in Iraq.*

He took off Smoke's little red halter. He looked at him one last time, and then he turned and walked away. Away from the daily searches for donkey food. Away from the daily donkey grooming. Away from the daily donkey headaches.

The colonel didn't get far. After walking for a few yards, he stopped and turned around. There was Smoke, standing there amid the reeds, watching the man he had come to depend on for food, for shelter, for companionship and affection. John looked at the donkey a full minute or more. By now his mood had changed from frustration to anger. Anger with himself. He was angry because he had shown weakness and a lack of resolve.

What am I doing? he asked himself for the second time that day. *Turning Smoke loose just isn't right. I can't do this. He trusts me. I accepted responsibility for Smoke when I took him in. And a lot of other folks have enjoyed him, too. We cared for him and showed him affection and respect, and he repaid us with loyalty and affection.*

He walked back and strapped on Smoke's little red halter. Off they walked, back to the BOS. Together.

John continued to hunt around for someone who could help him with Smoke. He reached out to the donkey lovers he knew, including Crystal Ward. She had guided him when he first found Smoke, teaching him about feeding and disciplining the little donkey. Crystal and a couple of others went so far as to offer Smoke a home if he needed one—if John could get him to the States.

About the same time John also came across a website for SPCA International, a nonprofit group based in New York that conducted animal rescues. He contacted the organization and soon heard back.

> To: Folsom Col John D (TQ IST MLG BOS)
> From: Terri Crisp
> Date: Friday, January 23, 2009
> Subject: Smoke
> Importance: High
>
> Hi John:
>
> I am the Program Manager for Operation Baghdad Pups, a program designed to help our troops serving in Iraq get dogs and cats they have befriended to the U.S. The program is just about a year old and since we started last February we have successfully gotten 67 dogs and 8 cats out of Iraq. . . . SPCA International would still be very happy to help in any way we can with Smoke.
>
> I have several contacts that I think would be very helpful. The first one is an animal organization in Kuwait that we have worked with called PAWS Kuwait.

They have a shelter in Kuwait and there is room for equine. The last time I was there they had a donkey in their care. The PAWS volunteers are very experienced in getting animals flown from the Middle East to all parts of the world. . . .

The other animal group that we have worked with is in Israel and they specialize in the rescue of just donkeys. They could certainly advise us on how to safely transport Smoke and they may have some other Middle East contacts that could come in handy.

Here in the states, because of bringing in the number of cats and dogs that we have from Iraq, we have a very good relationship with the Centers for Disease Control. . . . We would also have to be in contact with the U.S. Department of Agriculture and the state health department where Smoke will be living permanently. . . . Once Smoke got to Kuwait he would fly from there to Amsterdam and then on to the U.S. . . . The port of entry would be Dulles near Washington, D.C. . . .

So the bottom line is, this is definitely doable. We just have to come up with the best plan possible and then put it in motion. . . .

It would be an honor to work in getting Smoke home. He is indeed one very fortunate guy to have crossed paths with all of you. Without a doubt he deserves the kind of life he would have here in the states. I will do all that I can to help make this possible.

Humanely,

Terri Crisp
SPCA International
Operation Baghdad Pups Program

John's hopes rose. He tracked down the donkey sanctuary in Israel, Safe Haven for Donkeys in the Holy Land. A British woman named Lucy Fensom had established the nonprofit sanctuary in 2001 to take in aging, abandoned, and injured donkeys. John talked to staff member Wendy Ahl, who assured him Smoke would be welcome at the sanctuary if John could make travel arrangements for him.

In the meantime he had forwarded the email from Operation Baghdad Pups to Colonel Chumley, the top Army vet in Iraq. Chumley was the same officer John had been petitioning to stop killing Ruppell's foxes. His reply was disquieting.

> To: Folsom Col John D (TQ IST MLG BOS)
> From: Chumley, Perry R COL VC 44 MEDCOM Staff
> Veterinarian
> Date: Saturday, January 24, 2009
> Subject: RE: Smoke
>
> John,
>
> This organization's heart is in the right place and
> they mean well. Unfortunately, they also "assisted" in
> getting a rabid dog to the states a few months ago that
> cost the US Government a lot of resources in tracking
> down potential rabies contacts and getting people the
> prophylaxis required. Bottom line—they may help
> with the logistics and cost, but they need to know the
> required ports of entry (in New York and Miami) and
> other precautions required to keep the US safe from
> foreign animal diseases. . . . Proceed with caution.
>
> *Perry*

John appreciated Chumley's concern, but he had already taken steps to ensure that Smoke was healthy. He had sent blood samples to the National Veterinary Services Laboratories in Ames, Iowa, for testing. If he used the services of Operation Baghdad Pups, it would be only for logistics, as Chumley recommended.

But for the first leg of the journey he decided it was time to talk to Mr. Gene, a Lebanese businessman who worked as a contractor at Camp al Taqaddum. Mr. Gene handled transportation work and anything else the military needed help with—he was quite entrepreneurial and spoke excellent English. And he never said no. John queried him about shipping Smoke to Jordan. From there, John thought, the donkey could be taken to one of the sanctuaries Terri had mentioned.

> To: john.folsom
> From: mrgene
> Date: Sun, 25 Jan 2009
> Subject: RE: Smoke the Donkey
>
> Hi My Friend,
>
> I should be in TQ soon even before you leave for home.
> As for Smoke, I can send him to Jordan but I need some one to take from the driver over there also I need letter for the border.
> The Coalition forces won't allow to take any thing out of Iraq without letter.
> I will see you soon and we will talk about.
>
> > Regards,
> >
> > *Gebran*

John was puzzled. "Why would you need permission from the coalition to take Smoke into Jordan?" he wrote back. "If it is too difficult, then we would have to take him to Basra and give him to the SPCA International people who will then take him to Kuwait."

Mr. Gene replied that, in his experience, "the U.S. government doesn't allow for any thing to go out of Iraq without letter from Coalition Forces."

As John worked to arrange Smoke's future, the advance contingent with the Second MLG had arrived, led by Brig. Gen. Juan Ayala and his staff, to begin the transition work. Among them was Maj. Steve Castora, who would take over the role of camp commandant from John. And with that came the big question: Did Castora want to inherit a donkey?

Castora warmed up to Smoke quickly, easing John's anxiety—

although not completely. After his experience with the combat stress office he knew that an initial interest in the donkey could fade. The next day he laid out his plan for Smoke in an email to Terri Crisp with SPCA International, Mr. Gene, Castora, and Lt. Col. Louis Bainbridge, an Army officer stationed near Basra.

"The easiest course of action is to send Smoke to either Kuwait or Basra. The other option involves more paperwork. Blood work is being sent to Ames and I should have information within two weeks. Once I have that I will send it to Terri," John told them. "I am leaving soon, so Gebran and the Marines here can get Smoke on his way. . . . Until then, the Marines will look after Smoke. As much as they would like to keep him, we won't be here forever. If we can get him to a good home now, that's what we need to do."

Three people had offered to take Smoke, including Bainbridge. His family ran a farm in New Jersey called Long Ears Acres, where they kept donkeys—both miniatures and mammoths. John would leave it to Terri to sort out the best option for the donkey, once Smoke was transported to Operation Baghdad Pups.

John liked what he saw of Brigadier General Ayala. He exuded the confidence the colonel admired in a Marine leader. And there was something else likable about the general, in John's eyes. While Ayala was looking over the base one day, he passed Smoke's corral. When Smoke saw the brigadier general, he let out a heehaw. Ayala promptly walked over and introduced himself by scratching Smoke on the head. Smoke shoved his head through the rails to get better acquainted with the new brass.

A new friendship began, which boded well for Smoke. February 4—four days before John was scheduled to leave Iraq—brought two pieces of news about the animals of Camp al Taqaddum. The first involved the Ruppell's foxes.

> To: Folsom Col John D
> From: Smith CPT Brian W (64th MED DET Vet Services OIC)
> Date: Wednesday, February 04, 2009
> Subject: Fox policy

Sir, I have just returned from the Mayor meeting here at Al Asad, and proposed with approval a new policy for foxes and other wildlife. I will now sedate, vaccinate for rabies, microchip, deworm, draw a blood sample for various testing, and keep records on any healthy foxes that Vector Control brings to us, and then we will release them back onto the perimeter. It is a more scientifically sound practice, as now we will create a buffer of healthy and vaccinated animals who will in turn pass that immunity to their pups, as opposed to continually killing the wildlife, which will no doubt be replaced by new animals ad infinitum. This will also help with the ecosystem and the foxes will help to keep the rodent population down.

My command is working to change the MNC-I policy of "kill everything," but until that happens, I have been authorized to implement the above practice on wildlife in my local areas upon the approval of all interested parties at the local level. We will still humanely euthanize feral dogs and cats, because they are more likely to interact with humans, and they also disturb the ecosystem. My command is working on a capture/vaccinate/neuter/release program for them as well, to be implemented where feasible. . . .

Regards,

Brian Smith, DVM
Captain, Veterinary Corps

"Great news!" John replied. "Truly. Our Ruppell's foxes are a joy to watch as they watch us. . . . I spoke with Brig. Gen. Ayala the other evening when he told me that he loves animals. I am sure that he would approve of the new program."

The second piece of news: the Second MLG Marines told John they would continue to take care of Smoke. John was relieved to hear it.

"If anything changes and it turns out you can't keep Smoke, let me know, and I'll do my best to make other arrangements," he told Castora.

He gave Castora his civilian email address. If the Second MLG decided later that Smoke was too much work, John figured he could exercise one of his other options, with either a donkey sanctuary or one of the kind offers from donkey fans back home. When Wendy Ahl, with the donkey haven in Israel, asked for an update, John told her the Second MLG would look after Smoke.

"I will stay in contact with them (and you) about Smoke and his future home when we leave Iraq," he told Wendy. "He will not be left behind."

1. Col. John Folsom in Iraq.

COURTESY OF LT. COL. NEIL MURPHY
FOR THE U.S. MARINE CORPS.

2. Smoke gets a checkup from Navy Cmdr. Joseph Penta.
COURTESY OF JOHN FOLSOM.

3. Smoke dines in style on leftover hamburger and hotdog buns.
COURTESY OF JOHN FOLSOM.

4. Smoke with Army Lt. Col. Anthony Bostick, commander of the Forty-third Medical Detachment Veterinary Service.
COURTESY OF JOHN FOLSOM.

5. With Smoke at the 2008 Freedom Walk are (*front row from left*) Command Sgt. Maj. Delbert Hoskins, Lt. Col. Doyle Lassiter, Sgt. Lonnie Forrest, and Brig. Gen. Robert Ruark.
COURTESY OF FIRST MARINE LOGISTICS GROUP, COMBAT CAMERA.

6. Smoke gets a smooch at the Freedom Walk.
COURTESY OF FIRST MARINE LOGISTICS GROUP, COMBAT CAMERA.

7. Smoke visits Sgt. Lonnie Forrest.
COURTESY OF JOHN FOLSOM.

8. Marines build a shelter for Smoke.

9. Smoke and members of the Base Operations Section at Camp al Taqaddum. COURTESY OF JOHN FOLSOM.

10. Civilian contractor Lance Robinson, a gunnery sergeant in the Marine Corps Reserve, visits Smoke. COURTESY OF JOHN FOLSOM.

11. Staff Sgt. Matthew Shelato and Smoke take a walk.

12. Smoke with Brig. Gen. Juan Ayala and Sgt. James McGarr.
COURTESY OF BRIG. GEN. JUAN AYALA.

13. Smoke gets his blood drawn by Capt. Brian Smith.
COURTESY OF JOHN FOLSOM.

5.

Reflections and Resolve

The colonel said farewell to Smoke and headed home. He was ready to get back, and he was confident Smoke was in good hands. Partings come with the territory in the military—people work and live together for months at a stretch and then move on to the next assignment or return to civilian life, if they are reservists or National Guard members. Saying goodbye to Smoke was just part of the drill. Now it was time to think of home, family, friends, and future.

Back at Camp al Taqaddum Smoke continued to give the Marines something to write home about. Ayala's daily run took him past the compound where Smoke stayed, and the donkey always greeted him with a "heehaw!" The general sent a photo to his wife and children showing him with Smoke, wearing his "Kick Ass" blanket.

"The luckiest donkey in Iraq," he wrote. "His name is Smoke, he likes bagels and enjoys long walks. He has his own reflective vest/tape so vehicles will see him in the dark. Read his blanket. Things must be getting better here."

Not everyone liked dealing with Smoke. By that spring some of the Marines were trying to figure out a new home for him. Ayala mentioned that to friends back in Temecula, California. They responded, saying they knew folks with a ranch who had a "blonde" for Smoke—and sent along a photo of a tall cream donkey named Shirley. But Ayala knew that his animal-loving daughters would be furious if he got rid of the donkey, as would a lot of the Marines who enjoyed Smoke's company. One of the base doctors gave Ayala a T-shirt with the logo "Free the Donkey."

John fielded an email or two about the donkey that spring.

But he never saw a note from Castora. John was just getting back home, and somehow Castora's email got lost in the shuffle.

> To: johnfolsom
> From: Castora, Maj Stephen L
> Date: Wednesday, April 22, 2009
> CC: McGarr Sgt James
> Subject: Smoke
>
> Sir,
>
> Hope this message finds you. I need to know where you stand with regards to getting Smoke home. I am getting a lot of pressure to do something with him.
>
> Respectfully,
>
> *Maj Castora*

John set aside his thoughts about Iraq, Camp al Taqaddum, and Smoke and focused his attention on readjusting to life as a civilian, husband, and father. Memories of Smoke cropped up occasionally as he reflected on his service in Iraq or told yarns to friends and acquaintances, but he didn't dwell on the donkey. He was confident he had made provisions for Smoke.

Then came August 2010. John's thirty-year career with the Marine Corps would draw to an end in the coming month. And he began to reminisce. He reflected on how he had traveled the world with the Marine Corps. He had seen more than twenty countries in Asia, Europe, and Africa. His ports of call included Afghanistan, Cyprus, Egypt, Germany, Ghana, Hong Kong, Indonesia, Iraq, Israel, Italy, Kenya, Lebanon, Malaysia, Norway, Okinawa, Philippines, Republic of Georgia, Singapore, Somalia, South Korea, and Thailand.

He thought back to 1981, when he attended flight school in Pensacola, Florida. After being designated as a Marine aviator, John was transferred to HMT-204 at New River, North Carolina, where he trained in the CH-46E Sea Knight. In February 1983 he was assigned to a fleet medium helicopter squadron, HMM-

165. In September the squadron was sent to Beirut. The well-intentioned "peacekeeping mission" erupted in violence, caught up in the Lebanese Civil War. John escaped injury, but two of his friends were killed that October in the infamous Beirut barracks bombing.

John's leadership skills and resolve were tested any number of times during his career. An early opportunity came in July 1984. He was a forward air controller to Third Battalion, Third Marines. FACS, as they're called, serve on the front lines, communicating with aviators to coordinate tactical air operations with ground troops. The Marines had flown to Iwo Jima from the USS *New Orleans* for an exercise. They were hiking to the top of Mount Suribachi. It was brutally hot, and several Marines collapsed with heat stroke. Confusion and alarm set in. First Lieutenant Folsom ended up ordering a helicopter from the ship to land for an urgent medevac. It wasn't his job, but no one else had taken charge, so he did. Then he ordered the helicopter to return after delivering its first patient to the ship.

Seconds before the helicopter landed again, a corpsman collapsed. The helicopter crew picked up the second set of casualties and headed for the ship. During the flight the corpsman went into cardiac arrest. Luckily, he was within two miles of the ship and was revived. Had there been any further delay, John was told afterward, the corpsman would have died. Lt. Col. C. C. Krulak, the battalion commander, wrote in John's fitness report that "his initiative and willingness to take action were noteworthy." Krulak, who eventually rose to be commandant of the Marine Corps, called John's action "typical of his dedication."

John left active duty in May 1986 and became a member of the Marine Corps Reserve, a "weekend warrior." Those weekends would convert to full-time duty again and again over the next two and a half decades. He was disappointed at missing the first Gulf War—he was called up, but by the time he arrived at Camp Pendleton, the "one-hundred-hour war" had essentially ended.

He had a chance to practice quick thinking in July 1991 as assistant operations officer with the First Armored Assault Battalion. Then-Captain Folsom was assigned as commanding officer of troops aboard the uss *Dubuque*. At the end of the deployment the *Dubuque* was moored at the pier at White Beach in Okinawa. Crewmembers were moving a companionway, or ramp, when it broke loose and fell into the water between the ship and the pier, pulling a staff sergeant overboard.

John, who was on the crowded pier, pulled off his boots and utility jacket and dove into the murky water, even though the ship's saltwater cooling suction pumps were still running. Both men could have been sucked against the ship's inlet screens and drowned. But John managed to swim twelve to fifteen feet down until he found the unconscious staff sergeant and pulled him to the surface. The man survived, and John received the Navy and Marine Corps Medal, the highest noncombat decoration for heroism awarded by the two service branches.

He returned home and settled into civilian life. Two children and ten years later the attacks of September 11, 2001, shattered Americans' sense of security with the devastating terrorist attacks on U.S. soil. During the next nine years John would take on four years of active duty assignments—to Hawaii, Afghanistan, Germany, North Carolina, and twice to Iraq—as the United States battled terrorism.

In March 2003 he was serving as a liaison officer to the European Command in Stuttgart, Germany, when the United States launched Operation Iraqi Freedom. While the first of the U.S. wounded were being transported to Landstuhl Regional Medical Center in Germany, John was monitoring the casualty reports and felt compelled to help. He passed the hat and collected fifteen hundred dollars in a day. Two days later he toured Landstuhl with Maj. Gen. Arnold Fields, deputy commander of Marine Forces Europe. The hospital was overrun with patients. John spent the donations on a big-screen television and a supply of dvds to give the wounded an entertainment outlet. As donations kept flooding in, he provided everything from clothing to magazines to laptop computers, so the wounded could communicate easily with their families.

John's labor of love eventually evolved into a nonprofit char-itable agency, Wounded Warriors Family Support, to benefit the families of killed, wounded, and injured service members.

Now here he was, back in Omaha in August 2010. His time as a commissioned officer was coming to an end, and that bothered him. Sure, he was fifty-seven, but he didn't feel ready to retire. It wasn't that he craved more adventures or relished spending more time away from family. But he believed that he had more to give his country—a wealth of knowledge built up over the decades, a proven ability to perform. The military machinery is built on rules, though, not personal wishes. His thirty years were up, and the Marine Corps no longer required his services.

John spent hours in his basement, sifting through the boxes of memorabilia he had gathered during three decades of Marine Corps service. He thumbed through old cruise books from his helicopter piloting days, dusted off his Basic School yearbook, and studied hundreds of old photos, reminiscing about the Marines and sailors he had known.

Some had died in service-related incidents, such as the two lieutenants killed in the Beirut bombing and a captain whose helicopter exploded in 1988. Others had died from other causes, such as the lieutenant who was shoved backward while trying to stop a fight in Kailua, Hawaii. He died when his head hit the curb. Another friend died of brain cancer. John flipped through stacks of snapshots and mused about the old days and began the inevitable whatever-ing. Whatever happened to Doug? Where did Joel end up? Wonder how Bill is doing these days? And just as he wondered about all the others, he began to wonder: What-ever happened to that little donkey back in Iraq?

But there was a big difference between the Marines and the donkey: his human comrades had returned to their families. They had ties back home. The donkey was just as much a part of the team as those other Marines. But he had no home and no future and no family except for the Marines. In the midst of these reflections about his past John began thinking about his future and what he would do next. But thoughts about this little donkey kept intruding. What ever happened to Smoke?

He decided to track down Castora, who had taken over as camp commandant when John left in early 2009. The Second MLG had wrapped up its Iraq rotation and returned to Camp Lejeune in North Carolina some time back. He tried to reach Castora there, only to be told he had deployed to Haiti after a devastating 7.0-magnitude earthquake leveled much of the island in January 2010.

Next John looked up Brig. Gen. Juan Ayala, commanding general of the Second MLG. By now Ayala was chief of staff at Southern Command in Miami. Ayala had gotten a great kick out of Smoke during his time at TQ. But he had left Iraq in July 2009, he told John, and didn't know the donkey's whereabouts, other than what he had heard through the grapevine: the donkey had been turned over to a local sheik.

A sheik?

John's sense of mission clicked on. He doubted that a sheik would tend to Smoke in the manner to which he had become accustomed at Camp al Taqaddum. He decided he must keep the vow he had made back in February 2009: Smoke must not be left behind.

It was early September when John heard back from Castora. "Hey, Steve, how are you doing?" John asked. "I thought I would just check in about Smoke. Whatever happened to him? General Ayala tells me he was turned over to a sheik."

That's right, Castora told him. Ayala had championed the donkey as long as he was in Iraq. Castora had turned over Smoke's day-to-day care to Sgt. James McGarr, who continued to feed Smoke bagels—and anything else he could find that the donkey liked, much as John had. Smoke still had the run of the camp: McGarr took him to every ceremony held on the base, and Smoke schmoozed with everyone from generals on down.

But as 2009 wore on and the Second MLG began preparations to end its deployment, Castora felt pressure from a colonel in his command to find a new home for Smoke. Castora was reluctant to turn the animal loose into the desert. But he remembered meeting a sheik during meetings with local officials. Castora approached him about taking on the donkey. And the sheik agreed to help.

"We tried to get hold of you, but we couldn't find you," Castora told John.

John was disappointed. He had missed the single email Castora had sent a year and a half earlier. He hadn't heard anything about Smoke until talking to Ayala.

"You don't happen to know how I can contact the sheik, do you?" he asked.

"Well, I might," Castora said. "Let me look around."

Sure enough, Castora dug up an email address for the sheik and passed it along.

Even with an accurate address emailing a sheik presented a challenge. John couldn't speak Arabic, and he had no idea how much English the sheik knew. But it was worth a try. He emailed the sheik, asking about the donkey. No reply. He tried again.

> To: Sheik
> From: John Folsom
> Date: Monday, September 13, 2010
> Subject: Greetings
>
> Greetings to you and your family.
>
> A few days ago I sent an email to you asking about a donkey that Major Castora gave to you before he left Iraq to return to the United States.
>
> As I have not heard from you, I now wonder if you received it.
>
> Please let me know.
>
> Thank you.
>
> *Colonel John Folsom*
> United States Marine Corps, Reserve (Retired)

Silence greeted this second attempt too. John realized he needed help. Searching around in Omaha, he discovered an Iraqi-Arabic–Middle Eastern market where Middle Eastern expatriates could find specialty foods. He dropped by and explained his predicament. The market owners looked at him as though he was crazy. No help there. Then he came across an *Omaha World-Herald* article about Iraqi expatriates who had moved to the United States. He called reporter Cindy Gonzalez and explained that he needed an Iraqi interpreter.

Gonzalez put him in touch with an Iraqi woman, who referred John to her husband, Isaam. The family had been given U.S. political asylum and settled in Omaha. John told Isaam about Smoke and asked if he could help by being his interpreter, if John was eventually able to contact the sheik. Isaam agreed.

Based on the legwork John had done before leaving Iraq, he thought he knew how to get the donkey to the United States—he assumed that the offer by Terri Crisp with SPCA International was still open. But once Smoke was in Omaha, would he have any job prospects? John contacted his friend Lisa Roskens, a businesswoman and horse lover who headed an equine therapy program in Omaha called Take Flight Farms.

"Lisa," he emailed on September 27. "I want to talk to you about Smoke. If we get him back, is there any reason that he could not be a therapy animal at Take Flight?"

"He sounds so cool," Lisa replied. "I forgot the back story, but love the concept."

"I know who has Smoke," John told her. "What I need is for someone from the State Department to help us get to the sheik through our embassy in Baghdad."

Lisa was all for helping Smoke. She loved a good rescue story, and it seemed to her like the most natural thing in the world to transport a donkey from a war zone in Iraq to the middle of America to give him a better life. She told John that Take Flight Farms would be happy to hire Smoke.

John turned his attention back to finding the sheik. Ever the optimist, he figured this would be easy. At least it seemed as if it should be easy. If only he could get help from someone on the Provincial Reconstruction Team (PRT). These groups of military, diplomatic, and reconstruction experts were established to aid local governments in Iraq and Afghanistan during the war years. He searched the Internet for a point of contact and found nothing of any consequence. But he did find an address for the local webmaster and gave it a shot, for what it was worth.

To: Baghdad webmaster
From: John Folsom
Date: Tuesday, September 28, 2010
Subject: PRT Anbar Contact

Greetings . . .

I am writing to you in order to get an email/phone contact with the PRT that is responsible for the Anbar Province, specifically Fallujah.

I would like to get in touch with [the sheik].

When I was camp commandant of Camp Taqaddum in 2008–9, we adopted a young donkey. When our unit (1st Marine Logistics Group) redeployed, 2nd Marine Logistics Group took over the care and feeding of "Smoke." When they redeployed to the States they gave "Smoke" to [the sheik].

If [the sheik] will make a gift (or we will purchase him) of "Smoke" to us we will arrange for him to be transported to Basra and then Kuwait. From there, SPCA International will care for him and get him to the States.

Once "Smoke" is back in the States, he will be transported to Omaha where he will work once again as a therapy animal at Take Flight Farms where they assist my group with military families with children.

What I need is for a PRT to contact [the sheik] on my behalf.
Thanks.

John D. Folsom,
Colonel, USMCR (Retired)

John never heard back. Nothing. Zilch. He wasn't all that surprised. It was a long shot, and he knew it. After all, "Baghdad webmaster" was probably some overpaid civilian who would ignore such a strange request. Working only with nonsecure websites was going to make this more difficult. But he figured all he needed was one lucky break.

Lisa, with Take Flight Farms, made her own inquiries, which were more focused than John's shot-in-the-Internet-dark. Her day job was as chairwoman and CEO of the Burlington Capital Group, an investment company. Several years earlier she had attended JCOC 66, a Joint Civilian Orientation Conference. Organized by the Pentagon, this program educates civilians about the military. In return the civilians offer business-oriented suggestions to improve government operations.

Lisa still kept in touch with Joe Yoswa, a retired Army lieutenant colonel who had led JCOC 66. Yoswa now worked in public relations with Fluor, a global engineering construction corporation. She knew he had contacts with the Afghan government, as well as with the U.S. military, and wondered if he would be able to help John.

> To: Joe Yoswa
> From: Roskens, Lisa
> Date: Tuesday, September 28, 2010
> Subject: FW: PRT Anbar Contact
>
> Joe,
>
> How are you??? It is funny to me that I'd been meaning to email you and catch up and then got this email from a very good friend of mine. He is trying to get a donkey back from Iraq in order to have him work with the returning veterans. I've agreed to take care of the donkey as the therapy program is run out of my farm. Anyway, all of the logistics are covered, but we can't get the Sheik who is caring for the donkey to release him. Part of the problem is we don't have anyone on the ground in

Anbar Province to handle the details. We'd happily pay someone to get the job done. Any ideas?

Thanks!

LYR

To: Roskens, Lisa
From: Joe Yoswa
Date: Tuesday, September 28, 2010
Subject: RE: PRT Anbar Contact

OK, so you have a friend stuck in Anbar cause he can't cover his Donkey bill. Is that about right? :)

Who is your friend and who is the sheik, where in Anbar and what time frame are we looking at. . . . I have friends in business, state and the military, but need more details. . . .

Joe

After John passed along more details Yoswa reached out to some friends to explain the situation and ask for advice about a facilitator who could work with the sheik. U.S. Army Col. Barry Johnson, assigned to United States Forces–Iraq at the U.S. embassy in Baghdad, was intrigued. A string of emails followed as Yoswa's inquiry was handed around the public affairs community.

To: Aaron Snipe (state.gov); Bloom, Eric LTC USD-C PAO
From: Johnson, Barry A COL USA USF-I OCG/PAO
Date: Thursday, October 07, 2010
Subject: FW: Need a facilitator in Iraq

One of the more entertaining requests I've seen in a while.

Either of you know somebody out West (PRT or unit) that may be willing to help our Marine allies with this?

Probably a good human interest story, if nothing else. Better than the usual rescued dog.

Thanks, B

To: Bloom, Eric LTC USD-C PAO
From: Burrell, Matthew A. CIV USD-C West PAO
Date: Thursday, October 07, 2010
Subject: RE: FW: Need a facilitator in Iraq

Yes, sir, we will be able to get in touch with [the sheik] but not sure about the donkey. A strange request indeed, but I will do my best to support it. I forwarded it along to MAJ Ceralde and will get back to you when he gets a response from [the sheik]. Shouldn't be too long, as he's a prominent figure here in Anbar.

LTC Bloom

To: John Folsom
From: Joe Yoswa
Date: Fri, 8 Oct 2010
Subject: RE: [U] FW: RE: FW: Need a facilitator in Iraq

John,

I have had many conversations about GO 1 and "pets"– lots of issues there. FYI: The Army is experimenting with having therapy animals on the ground. There is a CPT that walks around a yellow lab here on Bagram Air Field. Her job is to count how many people come up to start petting him and how long they stay and how it appears to change their attitudes. Maybe the Army is shifting its view.

Hope you can make this happen. In my request for help I asked a couple of reporters. Jane Arraf, Christian Science Monitor, said she would help, but her contact would be out for another week before he got back to Anbar. If this works out, she may want to cover it. Not sure, let's see what happens.

Joe

With all these lines cast into the water, perhaps what happened next wasn't surprising. But no email was more exciting to John than the one that arrived the next day.

To: John Folsom
From: Ryan Mannina
Date: Sat. 9 Oct 2010
Subject: Sheik

COL Folsom,

Sir, I am 2LT Ryan Mannina PL, 2/A/3–7 IN. We
are currently posted here at Camp Taqaddum, near
Habbaniyah, Iraq.

Today we had a Sheik . . . come by, asking us if we
could get in contact with you.

He wouldn't say what it was he needed to speak to
you about; he mentioned it was some kind of a personal
issue and that you would know what it was about. He
left his business card with contact information, which
follows. . . .

Respectfully,

Ryan Mannina

2LT IN

There was the sheik's name. There was his email. And there
was his cell phone number. Bingo.

6.

The Thirty-Thousand-Dollar Donkey

Now that John had contact information for the sheik, everything seemed to be falling into place. Maybe Smoke could be home by Christmas. He quickly put in a call to Isaam, the Iraqi expatriate living in Omaha. They arranged to meet at a Borders bookstore later that day to get acquainted. He was curious about Isaam. What was his background? Why would he want to help with this strange request?

John was cautious by nature, and he knew nothing about Isaam other than that he was a foreign national from a country the United States was at war with. Not all Iraqis like Americans, and it's uncommon that anyone would want to be helpful without wanting something in return. John wanted to learn more about Isaam's motives.

Over coffee at the bookstore Isaam told John about his life in Iraq. He was an engineer by training, and his wife was from a prominent family. Isaam had visited Omaha once before the war, at the invitation of a friend at one of the city's medical centers. When violence and persecution grew worse in Iraq, Isaam sought political asylum. Eventually, he succeeded and moved his family to Omaha. In the course of their talk the two men discovered they had more in common than their connection to Iraq: it turned out that John's son and one of Isaam's daughters attended the same high school. As the conversation progressed, John decided he could trust Isaam. He told him all about Smoke and his current situation.

"Would you be willing to help me get Smoke back?" John asked.

"Yes, of course, I will help you," Isaam told him.

America had been good to Isaam. Not only were Americans

fighting and dying to bring peace to his homeland, but the United States was sheltering his own family. It had become his home. "My daughters and my son, they are doing great. It is a wonderful country," he told John.

He also felt he understood the reasons behind John's quest. The colonel's story reminded him of a book he had read once, about passengers stranded on a sinking ship. "There were people in the ocean, and the ship started to sink. One guy, he promised his daughter to bring her home a toy. Because of this promise he struggled to stay alive—so he could take this gift to his daughter," he explained. "I understand what the American soldiers suffered when they were in Iraq. So when they found this donkey, they took him as a mascot. I know how their kids suffered because their parents were taken away from them and how they liked hearing about this donkey. So I will try to help as much as I can to make this true, that they can meet this donkey."

He invited John to his home, where they placed a call to the sheik. John listened as the two countrymen spoke in Arabic. What the sheik told Isaam caught both him and John by surprise. Isaam had gone into the conversation thinking that the sheik had already agreed to turn over Smoke and that his role would be to arrange the details. Instead the sheik told Isaam that while it was true the Marine Corps had given him Smoke, he unfortunately no longer had the donkey. He said he had given Smoke to a family that farmed. After that, he claimed, word had spread about this special donkey who would eat cigarettes and do tricks. Children loved him, the sheik said, and people had flocked to see him. So obviously the family was reluctant, he told Isaam, to give up the donkey without compensation. Specifically: they wanted thirty thousand dollars.

John and Isaam were shocked, not to mention dubious. "There's no way some Iraqi family is keeping that donkey as a tourist attraction," John told Isaam. "He's probably wandering around the desert near Fallujah like all the other donkeys." Feeling frustrated, he made an impulsive suggestion. "Maybe I should just go to Iraq myself and get Smoke back," he told Isaam.

He began thinking out loud. He could fly to Baghdad, he told Isaam. But an American would be easily spotted in that busy international airport. What if he were noticed going through customs? What if he were detained on some pretext? It might be safer to travel to Irbil, a smaller city in northern Iraq where other Americans were already based. From there he could get a private car and drive south to Fallujah.

He kept brainstorming. Perhaps he could fly to Kuwait and then make his way to Basra in southeastern Iraq, which was still controlled by British military units. From there he could make his way to Fallujah. Isaam could help him arrange for a guide and interpreter, and together they could find out where Smoke was, hijack him, and disappear into the Iraqi night. John stopped talking and looked at Isaam, who had been listening patiently.

"You know," Isaam told John, "this is quite a dangerous idea."

"I know, I know," John replied. "That's why I'm not seriously considering it."

Whatever route John chose, he would stand out like a sore thumb in the volatile nation. And he certainly couldn't count on support from the U.S. government for flying into the country on a solitary donkey rescue mission. It would be dangerous and, frankly, idiotic for a lone American to wander around al-Anbar Province looking for a donkey, even with a local translator and guide. He would be an easy target for kidnapping or worse. Isaam quickly agreed.

The two men moved on, discussing other options. John thought an "operational pause" would be the best course of action for the time being.

"Yes," Isaam agreed. "I think it is better to wait."

John prepared to leave, but Isaam asked him to wait a moment. He left the room and returned with a bottle of Gucci cologne, which he presented to John as a gift. At first John refused—not because he was more of an Old Spice kind of guy but because it was John who should have a gift for Isaam, who was doing him great favor. But, having learned a little about Arabic culture and honor from his deployments, John accepted the gift. He never used the Gucci cologne—not because he was an Old Spice kind of guy but because he wanted to keep it as a reminder of a man who had shown him a great kindness in his quest to reunite with Smoke.

John quickly spread the news about the sheik's demand to friends, including his horse-set friend Lisa Roskens, her Mideast contact Joe Yoswa, and Terri Crisp, who had reaffirmed SPCA International's commitment to transport Smoke to the United States.

> To: John Folsom
> From: Joe Yoswa
> Date: Sunday, October 10, 2010"
> CC: Johnson, Barry A COL USA USF-I OCG/PAO; Bloom, Eric LTC USD-C PAO; Roskens, Lisa; Terri Crisp
> Subject: RE: Smoke
>
> John,
>
> Glad you found him. Let the bidding begin.
>
> As everything happens in the market, with time things will change.
>
> *Joe*

> To: Joe Yoswa
> From: John Folsom
> Date: Sunday, October 10, 2010
> CC: Johnson, Barry A COL USA USF-I OCG/PAO; Bloom, Eric LTC USD-C PAO; Roskens, Lisa; Terri Crisp
> Subject: RE: Smoke
>
> You know, I'm having a great time with this. $30,000. I laughed when I heard that. . . . I know that the Iraqis think that we're extraordinarily wealthy since they've seen money thrown around their country like confetti. . . .
>
> I've waited this long, I can wait longer.

To: John Folsom
From: Roskens, Lisa
Date: Sunday, October 10, 2010
Subject: RE: Smoke

John,

I'm an arab and know how we negotiate. Don't respond for a while—ice 'em. When you do respond, respond low and explain that you're exploring other donkeys. After all, a donkey is a donkey is a donkey. :-s

LYR

John agreed it was wise to "ice 'em." He reinforced that idea the next day with Isaam. While John didn't believe for a minute that some Iraqi family was dependent on Smoke for its livelihood, he knew it was important not to confront the sheik openly.

To: Isaam
From: John Folsom
Date: Monday, October 11, 2010
Subject: Donkey

Thank you for your help in this.

We will need to wait for a while, perhaps a long time. I would like to get Smoke back to the States, but I must be realistic.

Please tell the sheik that I appreciate and thank him for his help. He is an honorable man and did his best to help us.

The family who has Smoke is very happy with him. It seems that he has a good home and that is important. I wish you the best!!

John D. Folsom

A few days later Joe passed along a request to John and Lisa from the *Christian Science Monitor*, which has a stable of foreign correspondents.

"Jane Arraf, formerly of NBC and CNN and now with *Christian Science Monitor*, would like to talk with the two of you about Smoke and your program. Would it be ok for me to provide introductions via email?" Joe wrote. "I believe Jane is in Iraq and might also be able to contact the sheik and ask about Smoke after she's talked with you. Nothing like the media asking why the sheik's friend is asking the price of a new automobile for a donkey."

Weeks went by before Isaam decided it was time to contact the sheik again. By now it was Eid al-Adha, an important Muslim religious holiday. Also known as the Festival of Sacrifice, Eid al-Adha honors the prophet Abraham, who was willing to sacrifice his first-born son at God's command.

This is a significant story not only for Muslims but also for Jews and Christians. While the three dominant religions are unified in revering the story of Abraham's sacrifice, they split on a key point: which of Abraham's sons was to be sacrificed. As told in the Bible, it was Isaac, son of Abraham's wife, Sarah. According to the Koran, it was Ishmael, son of Sarah's handmaiden, Hagar. Abraham later sent Hagar and Ishmael into the desert, and Ishmael became the father of Islam.

Isaam took the occasion of Eid al-Adha to call the sheik and wish him well. In the course of their chat Isaam brought up Smoke. He suggested that thirty thousand dollars was a huge amount of money to ask for the donkey. The American who wanted Smoke back would never agree to pay it, Isaam told him. He suggested that the sheik might benefit more if he helped get the donkey to the Americans for free.

Perhaps the strategy of waiting had paid off. Or perhaps the holiday spirit of sacrifice and mercy was influential. Whatever the reason, this conversation ended on a different note, as John soon found out when Isaam called. He described his conversation with the sheik.

"He has agreed to help," Isaam told John. "He will buy the donkey and will give it to you for free, but he said he can't take it out of Ramadi."

John was surprised that the sheik had agreed to return Smoke without compensation, but Isaam assured him, as he had from the beginning, that the sheik ought to give him back free of charge. Isaam asked whether John had lined up someone to pick up the donkey or if he needed help.

John returned to Isaam's house, and they called the sheik together. Through Isaam the colonel wished the sheik well and thanked him for taking care of Smoke. As the conversation went on, John felt reassured that the sheik did really intend to turn the donkey over without compensation. Then the sheik posed a question. He was interested in obtaining a contract with the U.S. Army. Did John think that would be possible?

The U.S. government had been hiring Iraqis to do various jobs as part of an initiative to turn over some services, especially construction, to local residents. Such contracts could be quite lucrative. John replied that he was in no position to make any guarantees about contracts with the U.S. Army. However, he told the sheik through Isaam, many Americans knew about Smoke. If the sheik helped return the donkey, that would become known, and the Americans would be sure to see the sheik in a good light.

But the sheik made it very clear: he could not be openly involved in such a transaction. He wasn't about to be known among his people as "the donkey sheik." John understood. Back when he was serving in Iraq, the colonel had told Iraqi Brig. Gen. Ali Haider Abdul Hameed that he was thinking of taking Smoke to the States. The general had been incredulous. "Why would you want to bring a donkey?" he asked John. "Donkeys are unclean animals. They have no honor."

It's true that donkeys lack the beauty and grandeur of a horse. As Isaam's wife put it, "A horse is a symbol of greatness. A donkey is a symbol of stupidity."

Donkeys have had diminishing value in the Middle East since the proliferation of automobiles over the last forty or fifty years. Though still used to haul goods in the oldest parts of major cities like Baghdad, where the streets are too narrow to accommodate cars and trucks, in general they have little value—so little that live donkeys are fed to the lions at the Baghdad zoo.

Isaam didn't think any but the poorest farmers still made use of them—the humble animals mostly wander the countryside, fending for themselves.

That's how Smoke wound up at Camp al Taqaddum in the first place. It wasn't as if the Marine Corps had stolen someone's valued property, Isaam told John, laughing at the idea. Knowing the Arab mentality toward donkeys, John wasn't surprised by the sheik's attitude. He assured the sheik he would send someone to collect the donkey. Then the donkey would be transported to the SPCA International program in Irbil. Once the donkey was turned over, the sheik needn't be involved further.

Isaam called a friend back home. Would you go catch this donkey? The friend called a nephew to help him, and they recruited a man with a pickup truck.

The friend and his nephew and their driver set out to look for Smoke, guided by directions from the sheik. Sure enough, they found the donkey. Far from living under the protection of a family, Smoke was roaming around—and he wasn't about to be caught by some strangers. While well intentioned, these donkey hunters were unable to capture the suspicious animal.

By the end of November the donkey had roamed onto private property, and John was again looking for help in rounding him up. He touched base with Jane Arraf, explaining that Smoke had become wary and aggressive without the social contact he had at Camp al Taqaddum. What Smoke needed was someone who had experience with donkeys and horses, someone who knew how to coax him with treats and sweet-talk him into an enclosure—or who at least knew how to get close enough to slip a rope around Smoke's neck. He also needed someone with a suitable truck, not a pickup truck with low sides that would allow Smoke to jump from the back onto the highway at the slightest provocation should he get spooked.

By early December John was getting impatient enough to wonder once again if he should take charge personally. He brainstormed with Craig Pirtle, a U.S. Army veteran and polo player in Virginia who worked with John's nonprofit group. John suggested that Craig could accompany him to Iraq. They would have to keep their travel dates quiet for security reasons. But John thought perhaps they could slip in, meet the sheik, find Smoke, and round him up in one day. Smoke knew him, after all, and his presence might make the difference in accomplishing the task.

While John sat in Omaha, plotting a dangerous trip to Iraq, Isaam was half a world away, doing the same thing. Isaam was visiting family in Jordan and Syria, next-door neighbors to Iraq. And he couldn't get his mind off the donkey. "I could slip into Iraq by myself and just pick up Smoke," he thought to himself.

In a way, though, such a trip would be riskier for Isaam than it would be for John: not only would Isaam run the physical risk of traveling to this still-volatile nation, but he would also risk losing the U.S. political asylum he had worked so hard to get.

Fortunately, a third option surfaced: Jane talked to Khalil, a newspaper stringer in Fallujah. She notified John on December 11 that the stringer was willing to help. So John and Isaam set aside their plans and concentrated instead on making arrangements from afar. Emails soon were flying back and forth between Omaha and the Middle East.

John sent photos of Smoke to Khalil to make sure he found the right donkey. Smoke's characteristic markings on his back would prove useful, if Khalil could download the high-resolution photos using his slow Iraq Internet connections.

"Khalil has worked for our sister organization for years and we've found him to be entirely trustworthy as well as a really nice guy," Jane told John. "He does however need to be given clear guidance about what you are authorizing him to do. The Kurdish checkpoints closer to Irbil will be wary of a truck from Fallujah so it would be helpful if whoever you have in Irbil can look into what documentation would be needed to get across the green line."

John volunteered to meet the truck at the Kurdish checkpoint and even travel to Irbil to help, if needed. But he wouldn't venture to al-Anbar under any circumstances. He had spent enough time there over the years to know there would likely be people around who would love to capture or kill an American, especially a former Marine Corps officer. No thanks.

He asked Isaam for advice on a fair payment for Khalil, considering that he would need to rent a truck and hire help to collect the donkey. Would two hundred dollars be enough? He also asked Isaam to contact the sheik. "Please tell the sheik that I consider him my friend and that I will tell my contacts in Baghdad, Ramadi, and al Taqaddum that he helped us in an important matter. As a token of my respect for him I would like to send him a watch."

Khalil collected a couple of friends and a truck and set out to find the donkey, armed with directions from the sheik about where to look and with the high-resolution photos of Smoke from John. A few days later he sent word to Isaam: We found the donkey!

John was thrilled—this was moving quickly. But as it turned out, finding a donkey and catching a donkey were two very different things. Khalil and his friends, far from being donkey experts, had no experience with livestock. They had no idea how to round up Smoke. They described in detail how they chased the donkey around and around, with no end in sight. John had visions of the Iraqi version of the donkey chase, with "Yakety Sax" playing in the background.

But Khalil was nothing if not persistent. Day after day he and his crew tracked down the donkey again and followed him around. Day after day he sent Isaam his reports, which became painfully repetitive: We will catch the donkey—*tomorrow*.

Christmas was drawing near, and Smoke the Donkey was no closer to America.

7.

Donkey Roundup

The colonel wasn't destined to spend the holidays with Smoke. But he did get a nice Christmas present from Jane. Her article about Smoke appeared on December 21 in the *Christian Science Monitor* under the headline, "Pop Smoke? A Marine and his fight for Iraq's $30,000 donkey." "It's probably safe to say that Smoke is the most sought-after donkey in Iraq," Jane wrote.

Having Jane tell the world about Smoke was quite a coup. A longtime foreign correspondent, she had become famous covering the war in Iraq for cnn. Jane's byline on the story meant instant credibility and international attention for Smoke.

Various news organizations republished her story, and other reporters—from radio, television, and print—reached out to John, asking for interviews. Media outlets across the United States, Europe, and beyond spread the donkey tale.

John began hearing from old acquaintances, from retired Marines he had never met, and from donkey fans of all kinds. People passed along the article to their email chains, sent copies to their congressional members to urge support, or simply passed along an "Attaboy!" to John. One correspondent was John's commanding general at Camp al Taqaddum, the man who had inspired the donkey quest.

> To: John Folsom
> From: Ruark BGen Robert R
> Date: January 03, 2011
> Subject: RE: The Donkey Resurfaces!

John,

Greetings and I had to ensure you saw the below article printed recently. Of course, I didn't realize you were still working the Smoke project! . . .

Good luck with the great work you and your organization do! Next time you're in the Pentagon, do stop by!

Semper Fi!

Brigadier General Robert R. Ruark
Headquarters, U.S. Marine Corps
Assistant Deputy Commandant for Installations and
Logistics

In the meantime the donkey roundup continued, somewhere near Fallujah. Khalil and his friends sent daily reports that were monotonously apologetic yet tirelessly hopeful. "Tomorrow" was fast becoming a dirty word to John.

By now Khalil and his friends sounded desperate. One day Khalil had a brilliant idea—or so he thought. He excitedly floated it past Isaam and John during one of their Saturday phone calls to Iraq. "The University of Anbar has tranquilizer guns," he told Isaam. "We can borrow one and shoot the donkey with it!"

Right, thought John. That was just what they needed—two hundred pounds of doped-up donkey, passed out in the Iraqi desert. John and Isaam looked at each other in shock.

"Absolutely not!" John told Isaam.

"Absolutely not!" Isaam relayed to Khalil. "How would you lift him into the truck?"

Khalil hadn't considered that. Scratch the tranquilizer gun.

Once again John explained how to catch Smoke. "You've got to coax the donkey. Show him a treat. You've got to get him to come to you," John said. "You can't chase after him—that will never work."

Nearly two weeks went by. During a business trip John was checking his email as he ate breakfast at a diner in Illinois. Up popped a note from conservative talk-show host Mark Levin, asking for his phone number. Levin thought the story of Smoke was wonderful and wanted to know how it would turn out. John, a lifelong conservative, was thrilled that Levin had taken notice and assured him he would inform him when the donkey was caught.

"It's only a matter of finding the right people," John told Levin. "If my going to al-Anbar wasn't tantamount to a death sentence, I would go."

That was on Friday, January 14. Within a day "the right people" showed up: one of Isaam's friends in Iraq offered help from a family member who had experience in handling donkeys. Isaam arranged for the man to rendezvous with Khalil. John didn't hear any more until Monday night. He was in Washington DC when his cell phone rang.

It was Isaam: Smoke had been captured at last! Isaam had gotten an email from Khalil, who said the donkey wranglers had driven to the area described by the sheik and found four donkeys grazing together. One of the four matched the photos John had sent of Smoke—with the distinctive dark line across his back and a mark on his leg. Khalil sent Isaam new photos of the captured donkey, and when John saw them, he was confident Khalil had the right donkey.

A wave of relief washed over him, followed by a surge of adrenaline. He had never doubted that the donkey would be caught, once he had reached an agreement with the sheik. It had simply been a question of when. But for a man of action it had been downright painful to wait, day after day, from half a world away, while strangers who didn't even speak his language struggled to carry out his instructions. Now John could do something again.

He spread the good news to friends and fired off an email to the folks at spca International.

> To: Terri Crisp
> From: John Folsom
> Date: Tuesday, January 18, 2011
> Subject: Smoke

Terri . . .

See the attached photos. The donkey with the Eeyore
"woe-is-me" look is Smoke.

   We will start moving him to Irbil and will coordinate
a hand off at the checkpoint.

   I will wire funds to you so the driver and others can
be compensated. Please send wire instructions and I'll
get this done right away.

All the best!

John

To: John Folsom
From: Terri Crisp
Date: Tuesday January 18, 2011
Subject: RE: Smoke

Hi John:

This is great news! I cannot wait to meet your friend.
Who captured him? . . . Ameer is contacting our vet
right now to confirm what it will cost to get Smoke
vaccinated and a blood test done. The cost for the driver
to bring Smoke from the checkpoint to the Reed kennel
will be approximately $100. I will keep track of all the
costs and send them to you. I assume you want us to pay
the driver once he delivers Smoke to us. How much are
you paying him? I will wait to hear from you.

Humanely,

Terri Crisp

   Meanwhile Isaam, always cautious, began worrying about
Khalil making the 250-mile trip to Irbil. "It is not safe for those
people who live in al-Anbar to travel to Baghdad," he told John.
"So is he going to take that risk?"

   Operation Iraqi Freedom had converted to Operation New

Dawn in 2010, and U.S. forces still in Iraq were being steadily reduced in numbers. The road north from al-Anbar Province to Irbil would be rough. John wasn't worried about an IED attack on a civilian truck hauling a donkey. He did, however, wonder whether the Kurds would allow someone from the Sunni south to enter their region. While the city of Irbil is in Iraq, it is also the capital of Iraqi Kurdistan, an autonomous area with its own regional government. And there had long been tensions between the Iraqis and the Kurds.

Driving from al-Anbar was a precarious and involved affair. Travelers must pass through military checkpoints when crossing into the Kurdistan region. But by now other nationalities were living in Irbil safely. Terri spent significant blocks of time in the city without incident. And when Isaam questioned the wisdom of making the trip, Khalil shrugged off any risks. Now that the donkey had been captured, he was back on more familiar turf. "I am a reporter," he assured Isaam. "I can handle it."

Khalil rented a truck with an enclosed bed and hired a driver. They loaded up Smoke and drove to Irbil. John wired three thousand dollars to Terri to pay them for their work, and Khalil's job was finished.

The thirty-thousand-dollar donkey was now the three-thousand-dollar donkey. No more schmoozing with sheiks. Now Smoke was palling around with pooches at Operation Baghdad Pups.

While Smoke was experiencing new parts of his native country, John was exploring his own nation's capital. That Wednesday was overcast but warm in Washington when he set out from the Army Navy Club, a few blocks from the White House. He walked north to Dupont Circle and then turned onto Massachusetts Avenue, which angles northwest from the heart of the city.

He was on something of a diplomatic mission. While the donkey roundup was under way, he had been plotting the next step: establishing a safe route to transport Smoke through the Middle East to Europe and beyond. Originally, he had thought the donkey could be taken by truck to Kuwait, a U.S. ally bordering Iraq on the southeast. The plan hit a snag when he discovered that Kuwait would no longer let foreign donkeys cross its borders.

John weighed some of his other options. One possibility was to plot a route through Israel. As a key U.S. ally Israel surely would be friendly to the idea. And he had made contacts with the donkey sanctuary Safe Haven for Donkeys in the Holy Land in 2009, while he was still deployed to Iraq. He knew Smoke would be welcome there.

He studied the possible routes. The most direct path from northern Iraq would require a trip of more than 720 miles through Syria and Jordan and on to Israel. While the logistics would work, John resisted any association with Syria, a nation that harbored and trained terrorists.

Or he could trek 750 miles west across Iraq to ar Rutbah and then through Jordan, a relatively stable nation that had been cordial to the United States. John knew that part of Iraq—he had been deployed near ar Rutbah in 2005, working as the air boss at the isolated base of Camp Korean Village. John's old friend Mr. Gene had connections that would help, and in 2009 he had been willing to take the donkey to Jordan. From there to Tel Aviv would be a short hop.

But by the winter of 2010–11, a route through Turkey seemed much safer. Even though Istanbul was more than eleven hundred road miles from Irbil, it was eleven hundred miles that didn't cross volatile Sunni and Shia regions of Iraq or a harsh desert. The Islamic nation borders Iraq on the north, relatively close to Irbil. Terri and Smoke could cross the border and travel to the city of Istanbul in western Turkey. And international cargo flights regularly transported horses from Istanbul to Europe.

While the Turks and the Kurds had centuries-old tension and mistrust, John figured no one would interfere with an American woman transporting a donkey to Turkey. Terri's mission might be unusual, but it was not provocative.

Now that he had settled on a route, it was important to get government approval for the donkey to enter Turkey. Every country has rules and regulations involving the importation of animals, even if they are simply passing through. Since John happened to be in Washington when Smoke was captured, he decided to make a personal call on the Turkish embassy.

He walked up Massachusetts Avenue along Embassy Row, past block after block of stately mansions that had been repurposed as diplomatic missions. His path took him on a disjointed world tour of embassies: past Portugal, Indonesia, and India, followed by Georgia, Luxembourg, Turkmenistan, Togo, the Sudan, Greece, the Bahamas, Ireland, and then Haiti, Burkina Faso, Croatia, the Kyrgyz Republic, and Madagascar, not to mention Paraguay, Malawi, Côte d'Ivoire, Chad, the Marshall Islands, South Korea, Lesotho, Japan, and finally Turkey.

He stood on the sidewalk, looking at the diplomatic complex behind the wrought-iron gates, with its carefully coiffed landscaping and dignified brick buildings. How hard could it be to enlist the aid of the diplomatic mission of the Republic of Turkey to help a single donkey pass through its borders?

Surely this would be easier than it had been to find Smoke again after a long separation. Easier than tracking down the sheik who had acquired him. Easier than persuading the sheik to give up the donkey. Easier than waiting for amateur Iraqi cowboys to capture Smoke. Or so John thought that afternoon as he stood outside the embassy.

The gate was open, and the distinctive red Turkish flag, with its single star and crescent, flapped gently in the breeze. He stepped into a lobby filled with Turkish expatriates who were there to discuss visas or other issues. Chances were good he was the only one there to discuss a donkey.

The Turkish embassy houses the offices of the Armed Forces Attaché, the Education Counselor, the Social and Religious Counselor, the Press Counselor, the Commercial Counselor, the Customs Counselor, the Economic Counselor, the Agricultural Counselor, the Planning Counselor, and the Culture and Tourism Counselor.

John, the only American in sight, approached the woman at

the counter behind the bulletproof glass. He knew just who he wanted to see. His Marine Corps career had given him some familiarity with how embassies operate. In July 2003 he had been dispatched to Ghana in support of a Liberian humanitarian crisis. He had worked with the U.S. embassy staff there to assess the peacekeeping abilities of the West African nations.

"I'd like to meet with someone from 'Cultural,'" he told the woman.

A few minutes later Vice Counsel Tülay Bağ stepped into the lobby. She introduced herself and escorted John to her neatly appointed office, with tourist posters on display. Tülay's office was not upstairs but in the basement. John wondered fleetingly whether her level of influence matched her office location, but he dismissed the thought. He gave his spiel about Smoke and what a heartwarming story it was and how he hoped to transport him across Turkey to Istanbul and then to the United States. Could her government help facilitate this journey?

The petite, unassuming-looking woman looked at him incredulously. A donkey? Cultural diplomacy? Come again? She politely explained that he was in the wrong place. He should talk to her colleagues in the Commercial Counselor's Office. John acknowledged that was one way of approaching things but tried to explain his point of view. This really was a cultural issue, from his perspective—it was a people story, a feel-good mission. Think of the nice publicity it would give the people of Turkey and their government, he urged her, if they would lend their help to reuniting an American war veteran with the little donkey he had befriended. He left the office without a commitment—but filled with confidence that Tülay had bought into his vision. He hadn't heard the word "no." So to John the optimist that meant "yes."

Operation Baghdad Pups was just over a year old back when John and Terri had first communicated in January 2009. It was a major initiative of spca International, which had been established in 2006 by three Canadian animal activists. spcai had a lean staff—five full-time employees—and lofty goals, as spelled out on its website: "SPCA International strives to assist the growth and impact of independent shelters through alliance building, information networking, national and international programs." With offices in New York City the group operated under the direction of a four-member board based in Montreal, Quebec.

The organization embraced John's quest to bring Smoke to the United States, but not before overcoming some reservations. After all, none of them had much experience with donkeys, and some wondered what kind of a bond the Marines could have possibly formed with Smoke. Then they read news articles about how John had befriended the donkey and saw photographs from Camp al Taqaddum of Smoke ambling around, wearing his "Kick Ass" blanket.

They recognized John's affection for Smoke and his determination to get the little donkey to the United States. His request fit in perfectly with the goals of Operation Baghdad Pups: to reunite members of the military with the animals they had befriended during the war. The organization was well aware that donkeys weren't typically valued in the Middle East and recognized the potential for abuse or neglect if Smoke remained in Iraq. John's plan to train Smoke as a therapy animal once he was in the United States also appealed to the group.

The other hurdle for SPCAI was whether it could overcome its lack of experience with livestock. This wasn't Operation Baghdad Ponies, after all. They would be starting from scratch navigating the importation and transportation issues involved. Dogs can travel on regular domestic flights, for example, but not so for donkeys. Some of those involved worried about whether the staff could sort out the logistics. But Terri was confident, and John's love for Smoke was obvious, and his commitment to getting him back was absolute. SPCAI decided to go for it.

Despite being the program manager of Operation Baghdad Pups, Terri wasn't based permanently in Iraq. She worked primarily out of her home in northern California. From there she arranged missions for Operation Baghdad Pups and then traveled to Iraq to pick up the animals—mostly dogs and a sprinkling of cats—and accompany them back to the United States.

Home base in Irbil for Operation Baghdad Pups was a villa owned by Reed Inc. This international contractor handles a variety of services, including security and risk management, logistics, construction management, environmental services, and demining work. The company had a small footprint in Irbil. The city is built around an ancient citadel, which is surrounded by an equally ancient walled town. The citadel has a historic claim as the world's oldest continually inhabited settlement. Its imposing, ochre-colored walls made it impervious to enemy attack in ancient times, and it remained an impressive sight centuries later, looming over the modern city of Irbil. The city at its feet had developed in an elliptical pattern around the citadel. Its narrow streets were restricted to one-way traffic, making navigation a challenge for drivers.

The Reed villa was in the Ankawa neighborhood, an area originally settled by Assyrians. The villa was a typical Middle Eastern residence, a two-story structure with a wall running along the street and a small courtyard inside. Reed maintained a couple of employees at the villa and rented out rooms to Operation Baghdad Pups and other contractors. A Reed driver was always available to take Terri where she needed to go since women don't travel unaccompanied in this part of the world.

In addition to the villa, Reed maintained a farm on the outskirts of the city, near the airport. The farm had about twenty dog kennels. During the war the company employed working dogs for some of its demining work. Reed let Operation Baghdad Pups board animals at the kennels until they could be shipped out. The landscape was typical of Iraq—flat and arid, with little vegetation. The view extended for miles, with low mountains along the eastern horizon.

Smoke quickly learned his way around the farm. The lessons he had learned back at Camp al Taqaddum came in handy here. The lock on the door to the building was just as easy for him to master as those at the military base. He spent his days roaming around the fields and annoying the dogs. It didn't take him long to figure out that twice a day a man drove up in an suv with food for the dogs. As soon as he heard the car, he headed for the gate, heehawing all the way. He waited impatiently—often poking his head into the back seat—for a treat, especially carrots and apples.

Like any self-respecting donkey he wasn't particularly friendly to the dogs. After all, along with wolves and coyotes, dogs are a donkey's natural predators. He lorded his freedom over the dogs, who were confined to their quarters much of the time. They voiced their indignation loudly as Smoke stood outside their kennels and smirked at them. If donkeys can smirk.

Terri and the farm's caretaker had to improvise as they tried to care for a donkey without the proper supplies. On some particularly cold winter nights they tried to keep Smoke warm with a blanket. But by morning the blanket always worked its way off his back. Then Smoke pulled it outside his shelter by his teeth and tossed it into the air. He was either making up a new game or trying to land the blanket on his back again. Whatever his goal was, he succeeded in entertaining anyone who happened to be watching.

John was glad to have spcai on board to fund his project and help deliver the donkey. But he, like the organization itself, worried about its lack of expertise in transporting an equine. And he worried that Terri wasn't seeking the professional assistance she should. He put her in touch with Dr. Ellen Buck, a veterinarian in Maryland with the U.S. Department of Agriculture. John had communicated with Buck in 2009, before he left Iraq, and he knew she was knowledgeable about the U.S. regulations that he would need to comply with in order for Smoke to enter the country.

> To: Terri Crisp
> From: Ellen Buck
> Date: Monday, January 24, 2011
> Subject: Donkey from Iraq

Hello Terri,

I remember Smoke—he's become pretty famous! Quite
some time ago—maybe more than a year ago?—the
officer who was in charge of the unit was in touch with
us regarding bringing Smoke to the U.S. We emailed
back and forth for a while, then I never heard anything
more about the donkey.

We do not prohibit import of horses from any
country. Our import quarantine requirements differ
depending on the country of origin of the horse/donkey.
We do strictly prohibit entry of horses that test positive
for the following diseases: dourine, glanders, equine
infectious anemia, and piroplasmosis (*Babesia equi* and
B. caballi). Piroplasmosis is the most frequent problem
for equine imports. We recommend having the blood
samples tested at the USDA National Veterinary Services
Laboratories in Ames, Iowa. Blood samples must be
accompanied by an import permit. NVSL can issue the
permit.

Horses/donkeys must be quarantined at an
APHIS [Animal and Plant Health Inspection Service]
import center while official blood tests and physical
examinations are conducted. Horses from Iraq must be
quarantined for a minimum of 7 days. . . .

Smoke cannot arrive at any of the DC area airports
initially. He needs to arrive at one of the airports near an
import quarantine center—usually Miami, JFK, or LAX.

Please feel free to contact me directly if you need
additional information.

Sincerely,

Ellen Buck D.V.M.

At Terri's suggestion John emailed an SPCAI supporter in Philadelphia, a marketing consultant who had contacts in Dubai.
John asked the consultant what the shipping options were and

told him the Turkish consular section had agreed to help. The consultant thought his Dubai contact could advise John since he knew people in Turkey, as well. But nothing ever came of the discussion.

John thought Terri needed a consultant who knew the ropes of equine transportation. Dr. Buck had recommended Paul Weygand of Mersant International, an equine transportation company, as a competent customs broker and a knowledgeable source. His company had transported thoroughbreds for the Olympics, the Breeders' Cup, and other prestigious events. Surely the company could handle a stray donkey. Paul told John he would be happy to help but warned it wouldn't be easy. Iraq didn't have much in the way of regular cargo service, and the logistics would be a challenge.

John forwarded Paul's contact information to Terri and passed along his initial suggestion that Smoke be taken overland to Frankfurt, Germany, and flown to New York from there. John and Terri talked over the option by email. Terri objected to the idea of overland transportation.

"Why are we trucking Smoke to Frankfurt? That would be a nightmare taking him into so many different countries because of paperwork and really hard on him," she told him. "There is also the issue of finding a truck that could cross into so many different countries. There are no rental car companies here that would allow a one way rental, if they even had trucks suitable to transport a donkey available."

John told her that according to Paul, if they went overland, the paperwork would be simplified since all the countries involved were part of the European Union or had agreements with the EU. He encouraged her to tap Paul's expertise. "Mersant can help us with this. They come highly recommended," John said.

Paul checked in later, after doing some research. He told John that Iraq had a problem with screwworm, which would increase Smoke's time in quarantine if he flew directly to New York from Iraq. And he had stumbled on a problem with the European route. "It seems that horses from Iraq can NOT transit the EU, so driving or flying to Frankfurt may not be an option," Paul wrote.

Terri continued talking to her own contacts. Information wasn't consistent or easy to come by. She was hoping for help from a donkey organization in Syria. But John was still pushing to travel through Turkey.

While the route discussion continued, Terri decided to collect blood samples from Smoke to have him tested for disease in Irbil so she could get a health certificate from the Iraqi government. But the veterinary staff struggled with the task—perhaps one more sign that Iraqis don't routinely tend to their donkeys.

> To: John Folsom
> From: Terri Crisp
> Date: Mon, 7 Feb 2011
> Subject: Update
>
> Hi John:
>
> Attached are some new photos of Smoke. These were taken yesterday when the vet came out to draw blood. Unfortunately, he could not find a vein. I don't know if it is just difficult to draw blood from donkeys or that the vet doesn't have enough experience. I would suspect the second. The blood test is not required to get him into the U.S. so after he continued to attempt to draw blood and failed I finally asked him to stop because Smoke was getting stressed. We might try again with another vet after I get Smoke's halter and lead rope on Saturday. Then we can restrain him better. . . .
>
> Meanwhile, Smoke is doing great. He loves to tease the dogs, eat the pet rabbit's food and run to the gate to greet anyone that arrives. He is quite the character.
>
> Will be back in touch soon.
>
> Humanely,
>
> *Terri Crisp*

John was appalled that Smoke was being subjected to repeated pokes by incompetent veterinarians. He let Terri know, in no uncertain terms, that she needed to get competent doctors. Eventually, the blood was drawn, and preparations began for Smoke to head for the Turkish border—and eventually to Nebraska, which, as its unofficial motto boasts to travelers, is "the Good Life."

While John waited for developments, he kept occupied by reading and responding to inquiries. There were supporters who wanted to trade donkey stories or who were so taken by the story of Smoke that they wanted to offer him a home. One woman in Texas had read about Smoke in *usa Today* in late January and loved the tale. She was hoping John could help her with her own cause: finding homes for animal amputees. Another woman wrote from Atlanta, wanting to send a donation. She liked Smoke's story on several levels. She ran her own nonprofit organization, which rescued critically ill horses and donkeys. And she had heard about Smoke from her father, a retired Marine.

A note arrived one day from a petty officer John had known from the First Marine Logistics Group. James F. L. Bowes had read about Smoke in the *Navy Times* and wrote to recall that he had met Smoke when the donkey first arrived at Camp al Taqaddum.

"Attached are a few pictures I took with him," wrote Bowes, a hospital corpsman who had helped the surgeon examine Smoke when he first arrived. "Forgive the Go Navy blanket he has on."

Reporters and bloggers made inquiries, as well.

"I write a popular daily equine blog called Horse and Man," wrote Dawn Diovera. "Today, I wrote about Smoke (and you . . .). I'm sure you never thought you'd be on an equine blog but today is your day!"

An editor at the *Christian Science Monitor* asked for an update on Smoke, after Jane's article in December. And a Baghdad correspondent with *Agence France-Press* was hoping for a progress report, as well.

Not everyone was sympathetic to John's cause. One writer questioned his plan to take the donkey out of Iraq. John responded, trying to explain his viewpoint, interspersing his comments with Belen's criticisms.

To: Belen
From: John Folsom
Date: Friday January 21, 2011
Subject: Smoke the Donkey

Belen . . .

To help you understand the Smoke situation:

"No matter that there are presumably already a sufficient number of donkeys in America to go around, and that Smoke is presumably serving some sort of function in the familial context in which he is currently located in Iraq."

Smoke was found near Fallujah with other feral donkeys. Donkeys are not kept in a corral or fenced enclosure that you must imagine exist in Iraq. They are allowed to roam freely and fend for themselves. In other words, they are neglected.

"The fact that such feel-good mobilization can occur on behalf of a donkey while the devastating effects of war on the human population of Iraq are ignored meanwhile suggests that ours is not a humane society at all."

Smoke did a great deal of good for us while he was with us. He helped fathers connect with their children while they were deployed to a combat zone. As a father who spent four years out of eight away from his family, I understood the value of maintaining relationships. You may not believe or understand it, but he did.

You have to have experienced it first hand to understand it.

Donkeys are intelligent animals. We found him when he was about a year old and malnourished. He came to trust us.

To not have brought him back would have been inhumane.

John D. Folsom

One day John opened an email from a retired senior chief petty officer in New Castle, Delaware, and began to laugh. Military guys love to trade war stories. This writer had a war-horse story.

To: John Folsom
From: Lawrence Riccio
Date: Fri, 11 Mar 2011
Subject: Sr. Chief Riccio USN Retired

Sir,

Enclosed please find a photo of Smoke's "Big Brother" who is waiting here for Smoke in the USA!

Thought you would enjoy this.

In 1958 got this little fellow safely in and out of a cockpit of a heavy attack bomber while I was stationed on the USS Essex CVA 9 in Port Leodi [Lyautey] Africa: then a Naval Base. We went on plane every few months for R&R and major repairs on the plane.

Hope you enjoyed this as much as I did!!! (Vivian told me I had to send it to you!)

Semper Fidelis

Sr. Chief Lawrence J. Riccio USN Retired (31 years)
& Vivian C. Vischetti

Riccio sent along a newsletter dated September 1, 1958, published by the VAH-7 detachment based at Naval Air Station Sanford (Florida). The cover photo was of an AJ-2. These twin-engine bombers, designed to carry atomic bombs, were based on aircraft carriers during and after the Korean War. Smaller detachments from their parent squadrons would deploy to Port Lyautey, Morocco. Typically they sailed the Mediterranean Sea as part of the U.S. Sixth Fleet. It was the detachment's task to be prepared to drop nuclear weapons on the Soviet Union in the event of war.

Peering out of the cockpit of the AJ-2, and looking quite at home, was a donkey. Shades of Francis the Talking Mule—Hollywood's "talking" Army mule who starred in several World War II–era comedies. Now here was his Navy cousin. Even during the Cold War sailors liked to have fun.

8.

On the Road Again

Until late February Terri still harbored hopes of routing Smoke through Dubai. She wrote to her boss on February 23, telling him that an equine flight would be arriving there in early March. "I am praying I can get Smoke on this return flight to Dubai, where he would transfer to U.S. bound flight," she told him in an email.

Ultimately, though, the Dubai plan didn't pan out. It would have involved a flight out of Baghdad, which was highly unlikely, or a fourteen-hundred-mile road trip across much of war-torn Iraq, in addition to crossing Kuwait and Saudi Arabia. The logistics were simply unworkable.

Eventually, John and Terri agreed the donkey should be taken overland from Irbil to Turkey, the closest friendly nation. The staff back home worried about this cross-country trip: Would this put Terri at personal risk? Was the trip really worth such a risk? The organization was very conscious of employee safety. In fact, when it first began Operation Baghdad Pups, the employees and volunteers spent almost no time in Iraq. The program's regional base was in Kuwait. From there SPCAI booked flights with a charter airline that flew into Baghdad International Airport.

When dogs were ready to transport, Terri made arrangements with a security company to take them to the Baghdad airport, using armored vehicles for safety. The dogs were staged on the tarmac in their travel kennels. Then Terri or another SPCAI staffer or volunteer would fly in, touch down, get the dogs loaded into the passenger compartment, and fly out, never setting foot outside the airport. Each person was authorized to travel with up to two dogs and one cat. The charter airline flew the animals to

Kuwait, where they and their escorts caught a commercial flight to Europe and then to the United States.

Eventually, however, the airline lost its contract to fly into Baghdad. After that SPCAI shifted its Iraqi base to Irbil, a far less volatile area to the north. Irbil was safe enough, in fact, that Terri could spend some time there. Beginning in 2008 she was traveling to Irbil four times a year. She remained long enough to make arrangements for waiting pets, then returned with them to the United States, flying into Dulles International Airport in suburban Washington DC. In January 2011, when Smoke was finally corralled, Terri was in Irbil, coordinating the transportation of several dogs and cats.

The road trip would add to the length of this rescue operation. But Terri thought she would be safe if she took the proper precautions, and John agreed. While travel in Iraq always involves some risk, he couldn't envision anyone bothering a woman traveling with a donkey.

Terri had a busy February and March, coordinating the transportation of twenty-eight dogs and cats from Iraq to the United States and their new homes. She escorted one batch of animals to Virginia herself in early March.

She left the United States on March 23 to return to Irbil and plunged into work on her travel plans for Smoke. She made arrangements to be escorted by Ameer, an employee of Reed Inc. who also volunteered for Operation Baghdad Pups. She and Ameer obtained their Turkish visas. She rented a truck and hired a driver who would take them from Irbil to the Turkish border, about three and a half hours north. She arranged for a Turkish transport service to take over at the border crossing and then travel with the donkey on to Istanbul. That would be a fourteen-hour journey. She hired two drivers for that leg of the trip so they wouldn't have to stop overnight. Terri bought airline tickets so she and Ameer could fly from the Turkish border to Istanbul and rendezvous with the donkey there.

Her checklist went on, with points large and small: She bought rubber matting for the truck bed, along with buckets and rope.

She found a place to board the donkey in Istanbul. A newspaper reporter from Istanbul was planning to meet her at the border and write about the Istanbul portion of the adventure. She told John that SPCAI would hire Paul Weygand, the equine transportation expert in New York. She emailed Paul, putting him in touch with Safak Asparuk, who worked for MNG Cargo Airlines in Istanbul. Safak had told Terri that MNG would fly Smoke from Istanbul to Paris and that Air France would fly him to New York, all free of charge and in an equine stall rather than a wooden crate.

Terri decided to do a dry run to the border, without Smoke. If that went well, the travelers would pick up Smoke and leave Irbil on April 5. According to her tentative schedule, they would arrive in Istanbul on April 6. After a seven-day minimum stay in quarantine Smoke could be ready to head to the United States as early as April 14. She felt well prepared, but on the off chance something went wrong at the border, she planned to retreat to Ameer's village, an hour and a half away from the border. They could keep Smoke there while ironing out any needed arrangements. She emailed John on March 29, laying out all her plans. "Let me know if you have any questions," Terri told him. "Thanks and we are definitely getting closer to reuniting you with Smoke."

John began making tentative plans to pick up Smoke in New York on or about April 18. Terri asked Paul whether he knew anyone in Paris who could look after Smoke in between flights. Otherwise she might need to ask John to fly to Paris. Meanwhile the veterinary lab in Irbil sent staff to the farm once again to draw blood from Smoke. When the results were back, Terri would be able to get the health certificate and the official paperwork needed from the Kurdistan Ministry of Agriculture. John sent her a formal memo she could present to Turkish officials, explaining the reason behind shipping a donkey across their country.

> From: John D. Folsom, Colonel, United States Marine Corps, Reserve (Retired)
> To: Terri Crisp, Regional Director, SPCA International
> Subj: Transportation of therapy donkey

Date: 3 APR II

1. Transportation of the therapy donkey from Erbil, Iraq to the United States is critical and time sensitive. It is imperative that we get the therapy donkey to the United States as we have people in place and ready to receive him.

2. I have personally met with Ms. Tülay Bağ, Vice Counsel, Embassy of the Republic of Turkey in Washington, D.C., U.S.A. Ms. Bağ has assured me that because of the international interest in bringing the donkey to the United States, the Republic of Turkey will cooperate to the greatest extent possible in expediting entry into Turkey. If you have any problems she is to be contacted at [contact information included].

3. All health papers should be in order and ready for inspection.

4. Please advise me soonest if any problems are encountered. If so, I will immediately contact Ms. Bağ who will then advise the Ministry of Foreign Affairs principal, Dr. Ahmet Davutoğlu that his assistance is required.

5. The safe and expedited movement of our therapy donkey is of the utmost importance.

6. Please advise me once you are in Istanbul as we will issue press releases to the Associated Press, CNN and other news organizations. A press release will also be sent from the MFA in Washington, D.C. to news organizations in Turkey.

7. I appreciate your cooperation.

John D. Folsom
Colonel,
United States Marine Corps, Reserve (Retired)

At Terri's request he also alerted Tülay Bağ that Smoke was heading for Turkey. He asked her to inform the appropriate government agencies in Turkey so they would be prepared. Tülay advised him that they should double-check their arrangements since the regulations on transferring live animals through Turkey were changing rapidly.

When John asked Tülay if she could alert customs officials at Habur Sinir Kapisi, at the border crossing with Iraq, she suggested that he contact the U.S. embassy in Ankara himself to ask for assistance because the Turkish consulate would need at least three days for such arrangements. John forwarded the information to Terri, assuming that if she were worried about changing regulations, she would make inquiries. But Terri was confident she had done her research and could resolve any problems that bubbled up along the way.

After an overnight downpour in Irbil the morning of April 5 dawned clear, and the small entourage headed to the farm where Smoke was being boarded. Terri was relieved to find that while the roads were muddy, they were passable. As they drove toward the border, she spent her time keeping her Smoke fans updated about her progress in an SPCAI blog.

"As far as we can tell we have all the documents in order to satisfy the Turkey agriculture officials," she wrote. "This morning we got the Kurdistan Ministry of Agriculture to sign off on all the necessary documents too, so I think we are good to go—hopefully!"

The route from Irbil to the border was over rough roads. It took the travelers through a mix of farm fields and rugged hills. The main road from Irbil to the border runs past Mosul Dam, which holds back the Tigris River to form Mosul Dam Lake. It's the country's largest dam, with about one-third the capacity of America's Hoover Dam. Its water irrigates thousands of acres in the region and provides hydroelectric power to the area, including the 1.7 million residents of Mosul downstream. Fears of the dam's takeover by hostile forces or its physical collapse, because of soil instability under the structure, had concerned Iraqi and U.S. officials for years. If the dam failed, the resulting flood could cover Mosul and even Baghdad with several feet of water.

Smoke didn't worry about such momentous concerns, though. He took the road trip in stride. At one point he broke out in hee-haws when he noticed another donkey near the road.

"Have to wonder if he was yelling, 'Guess what! I am on my way to America,'" Terri wrote.

Early in the afternoon they reached Zakho. This town of ninety-five thousand sits near the Turkish border. Zakho sprawls along the Habur River, within sight of a Turkish mountain range. There they met up with the driver who would take over for the next leg of the journey. They headed for the border crossing—only to run smack up against a massive traffic jam.

Terri was shocked at the staggering line of trucks parked there, waiting to cross into Turkey. During her initial planning stages the driver had repeatedly assured her that crossing the border was not a problem. He did it all the time. He hadn't thought to mention that it could take up to five days to accomplish. The gate was a vital artery for trade between Kurdistan and Turkey. A thousand or more trucks cross the border there every day.

Terri had no intention of sitting in line for several days with a bunch of truck drivers. After waiting for two and a half hours she went off in search of the border office for KBR, the U.S. corporation that provided goods and services for Coalition forces operating in Iraq, among its varied business ventures. Terri had worked with KBR before, when she was involved in disaster relief efforts. Perhaps they could help her now.

She found the KBR office and explained her situation. The KBR folks were as surprised as everyone else to learn about Terri's mission. They had never heard of anyone taking a donkey across the border before. But they agreed to do what they could to help. A KBR representative accompanied Terri to the office of the top customs official.

Terri anxiously watched as the KBR rep and the customs official discussed the situation. She couldn't understand a word of the conversation other than what she picked up in body language. "The raised eyebrows, smiles, head shaking and laughter kept me wondering if we were going to be good to go," she wrote.

To her relief the customs official cleared Smoke to leave Iraq. Terri also received permission to move to the front of the line, ahead of hundreds of waiting trucks. Not only that, but KBR staff introduced her to a U.S. military liaison officer who was on duty at the border. He agreed to accompany the group through the Turkish border checkpoints if needed.

Terri and Ameer went to collect Smoke. The donkey had spent the afternoon in a nearby garage, resting and entertaining a cluster of neighborhood children. Now it was time to load him into the truck that would take him to Istanbul.

But another spring rainstorm had broken out. Terri and Ameer were soaked by the time they had the little donkey settled in again. They fed Smoke his dinner and then found a truck stop, where they ordered dinner, dried off, and warmed up.

By the time they finished eating, the rain had stopped, and they headed out. The entourage drove past truck after truck after truck in the staggering line. At last they reached the head of the line—which didn't exactly mean first among all. It just meant joining about a hundred other trucks that were also at the head of the line. Once there the group was stopped by a police officer, who said the driver would need to get another stamp on his documents.

"These people are big into stamps," Terri wrote. "Our driver left us in the truck and went to get the stamp. That was 45 minutes ago. It is now almost dark and there are no lights. Not sure how long we will have to wait."

At last the driver returned. The mini-convoy headed out. It was more stop than go, halting at four more checkpoints, as officials demanded to see their documentation.

"As we made our way through the Iraqi border crossing we drew a crowd each time we stopped," Terri wrote. "No one can believe we would want to take an 'ordinary' donkey to the U.S."

It had taken seven tedious hours, but at last all the needed stamps were purchased, the travelers' visas were stamped, and the truck was allowed to depart. Goodbye, Iraq. Hello, Turkey!

And hello, Turkish border checkpoints. Terri braced herself for the next round of inspections. "As we crossed into Turkey we were met by a young man, again a serious look on his face. As our driver explained our situation, a smile began to appear on his face, followed by laughter. I could just hear him saying, 'You've got to be kidding!'"

He kept the traffic waiting as he walked to the back of the truck and peered in. Then he called out to another soldier, who came over. "Before we knew it we had a crowd of soldiers standing at the back of the truck, signaling their approval with thumbs up."

The truck crawled forward until it reached checkpoint number two. Again a crowd gathered. Terri was feeling positive until a man worked his way through the onlookers to the truck. He asked Terri if she spoke English. She said she did, and he delivered his message. No need for interpreting body language this time.

"Donkeys," he told her, "cannot enter Turkey from Iraq."

Terri stayed calm. She launched into her spiel, explaining that she had documentation to show all the blood work that had been performed on Smoke in Irbil and the test results showing a clean bill of health. Then her driver took over the discussion with the border official. Eventually, the official allowed the group to pass—after the driver made it worth his while. "It appeared that money spoke," Terri concluded, "thanks to our driver who has the kind of experience that comes in handy during times like this."

At the third checkpoint officials removed the travelers' luggage from the truck and ran it through a security scanner. Ameer and the driver went inside to talk to more border control officers. Terri waited outside with Smoke. It was 10 p.m. when the customs official delivered the bad news.

A veterinarian would need to examine Smoke and his paperwork. But by now the veterinarian had gone home for the night. Smoke would need to cool his hooves until Wednesday morning. Terri couldn't accept the notion of being stopped now, when she felt so close to reaching her objective after a day spent inching forward. She decided to call in the troops, in the form of U.S. Army Maj. Daniel Barnard.

Barnard was what's known as a foreign area officer. He had attended graduate school and was trained in multiple languages, including Arabic and Turkish. During his current deployment he was assigned to the Defense Attaché Office at the U.S. embassy in Ankara. He was immersed in the Turkish culture, and his primary role was to serve as liaison to the Turkish Special Forces.

Because of that Barnard's circumstances differed from those of most Americans deployed to the war zone. The majority of troops lived on huge U.S. bases, like Camp al Taqaddum. They spent their time surrounded mostly by other Americans or allied troops, eating American food and communicating in their native language. By contrast Barnard was the only American embedded with a Turkish Special Forces unit in Silopi, Turkey. He lived and worked with Turkish soldiers, eating meals with them, sharing their quarters, and talking with them in their language, day in and day out.

Barnard viewed Silopi as the frontier. It is in the middle of nowhere, miles and miles from any major hub, almost off the grid. Rugged mountains surround the town. The region's foothills turn green with the spring rains, a contrast to the dusty plains of Iraq and standing out against the starkness of the largely barren mountains. The Habur River runs through a mountain pass to form a natural border between the two countries at Silopi. A set of two large bridges spans the river at the border crossing, which is called the Habur Gate in Turkey and the Ibrahim Khalil International Port on the Kurdish side.

Although Barnard was the sole American embedded with the Turkish unit, he did have some American neighbors: a small U.S. Army logistics unit was based in Silopi. The unit took care of the occasional U.S. convoy that traveled through. This tiny outpost was similar to a small hotel, with rooms and a dining hall where soldiers could eat and sleep. Barnard, however, was the senior officer on the border, and because of his work he frequently crossed back and forth across the border. So when the KBR guys needed help with a border issue, they went to Barnard, even though it wasn't exactly his job.

By the time Terri called Barnard to tell him she had been stalled, he had retired to his quarters. But he agreed to return to the customs office to see if he could help. Barnard talked to the officer on duty, but the customs official wouldn't budge: Smoke must wait to see the doctor. There would be no passage into Turkey tonight.

After spending more than eight hours in stop-and-go traffic and at checkpoint after checkpoint, Terri couldn't bear to think of backtracking to Iraq and then repeating the same, painfully slow path the next day. Besides, Barnard was optimistic that the veterinarian would clear Smoke for entry into Turkey. So Terri, Ameer, and Ahmed, their driver, got their passports stamped, and Barnard escorted them to a nearby hotel. They left Smoke settled in the truck outside the customs building, where he could spend the night safely.

Back in Omaha it was still midafternoon on Tuesday. John had begun the day filled with anticipation. Smoke was finally beginning the journey to his new home. John's lengthy struggle to be reunited with his long-eared friend was paying off at last. He stayed glued to his computer and his cell phone during much of the day, hanging on the occasional dispatches from Terri, as she delivered updates from halfway around the world.

He rejoiced with every checkpoint success and worried over every delay. He kept his friends, family, and followers in the loop through Terri's blog updates. At midafternoon Omaha time Terri called to say she was stalled until a veterinarian could see Smoke.

John looked for some way he might be able to help from Omaha. He asked Terri how to contact the customs official. She told him the official's name but didn't have a phone number. He emailed Tülay at the Turkish embassy in Washington. Maybe she could pull some strings, he thought. But she didn't reply,

It was before dawn that Wednesday in Omaha when John's

cell phone rang, jarring him awake. Terri was calling again. By then it was around noon at the Turkish border. Terri and Barnard had taken Smoke to see the customs office veterinarian. After waiting for an appointment, they had finally seen the doctor. Once again Terri found herself trying to read body language as Barnard and the veterinarian talked. It didn't seem to be going well—and it wasn't. The doctor informed Barnard that no animals from Iraq had been allowed to enter Turkey since September 2003, six months after the war started. Terri was baffled—she hadn't discovered news about a ban while researching her trip.

With that setback they returned to the customs office. They arranged to meet with the top customs official, and Barnard pleaded Terri's case. The Turkish official was sympathetic. But rules were rules, he told Barnard. And Smoke was not going to be the exception. Not on this conscientious bureaucrat's watch.

Terri was crushed. All those hours working through the lines of traffic, the numerous border stops, the repeated explanations given to customs officials—and now she had to make the painful call to John to announce failure.

She told him about the ban on Iraqi livestock, prompted by concerns about transmitting diseases to healthy Turkish animals. She would most likely have to return to Iraq with the donkey to await developments. But for now she would spend the night in Silopi, still hoping against hope that an exception to the ban would be made.

John thought back to his conversations with Tülay at the Turkish Embassy. He had felt so sure at the time that she recognized the value in her government's cooperation in letting Smoke travel through Turkey. He wondered if he had simply misinterpreted bureaucratic indifference, but she had seemed so responsive when he met her. And when he contacted her before Terri left Irbil, Tülay had replied promptly with some guidance and a word of caution, even though Terri hadn't heeded it.

Despite his frustration John was in too far to quit. There must be something he could do, he thought. He rolled out of bed and went downstairs to fire up his computer. He looked up the telephone listing for the U.S. Department of Agriculture at the U.S. embassy in Ankara, Turkey, and was soon on the line with Samet Serttas, a Turkish employee. "Hello. This is Colonel John Folsom calling from Omaha, Nebraska, in the States. I need your help with something," he told Samet. "We are trying to take a donkey from Iraq through Turkey so we can get him to the United States."

Silence met him from the Ankara end of the line. It wasn't every day that someone took a donkey on an international journey. John started from the beginning. He launched into his story, telling Samet all about how he had met Smoke, how the Marine Corps had adopted him, how he had returned home but couldn't forget about Smoke and wanted to be reunited with him. He explained that Terri and Smoke had been stalled at the Silopi border, even though they had proof the donkey was healthy. "As far as I know, all the required blood tests have been completed," he said. "I would appreciate whatever you could do to work with the Turkish government so the donkey can cross the border to get to Istanbul."

John didn't know it, but he wasn't the only one tying up the embassy's phone line that day to talk about Smoke.

9.

Donkey Diplomacy

Lt. Col. Lloyd Freeman was busy at his desk in the U.S. embassy in Ankara when a staff member dropped in. "You need to call down to Silopi," the staff member told him. "Something is up."

"Silopi?" Freeman asked, surprised.

What could be happening in that quiet corner of the country? he wondered. Not that Silopi had always been quiet. Back in July 2003, soon after U.S. forces first entered Iraq, a tense incident had unfolded near this Turkish border town. A unit of the U.S. Army's 173rd Airborne Brigade Combat Team had inadvertently captured a group of Turkish Special Forces, after storming an Iraqi compound in the town of Sulaymānīyah, southeast of Irbil. The Turkish military had Special Forces operating quietly in the region, both to monitor the area and to conduct operations against Kurdish rebels. Although the U.S. Central Intelligence Agency knew about the Turks operating in the area, that information had not been shared with the 173rd.

When the "Sky Soldiers" captured the Turkish unit, which included a colonel and two majors, they followed standard military procedures for handling detainees: covering their heads with bags to subdue them and prevent them from gathering useful intelligence. After photos were published showing the soldiers, heads bagged, the Turkish public erupted in outrage. The controversy roiled the diplomatic waters for months. The United States and Turkey had been allies for decades, but after this incident, combined with several other missteps on both sides, the U.S.-Turkish relationship took a nosedive.

Diplomatic efforts churned at the highest levels in an attempt to normalize relations. One of the initiatives the United States took to prevent future mishaps such as the confusion over the Turkish capture was to station a liaison officer—an LNO in military lingo—at Silopi. He would be embedded with the Turkish Special Forces unit so the two sides had direct communication.

In the early years of the war, Freeman knew, the liaison officer had led a pretty exciting life, traveling throughout northern Iraq on missions and being fairly integrated with his Turkish military hosts. By 2011, though, things had settled down significantly. So what, he wondered, could possibly be happening now in Silopi that would require the attention of the Defense Attaché Office at the U.S. embassy in Ankara? Freeman picked up the phone and returned the call to the liaison—Maj. Daniel Barnard.

Barnard attempted to explain the situation. He was trying to help a stranded American, he told Freeman. This woman represented the Society for the Prevention of Cruelty to Animals International, and she had shown up at the Habur Gate. She was trying to bring a donkey across the border from Iraq into Turkey, so she could take it cross-country to Istanbul and then fly it to the United States. But the Turks wouldn't let the donkey in, and Barnard had run out of strategies. Since this involved a stranded American, he thought it might call for embassy attention.

Freeman listened incredulously. This story couldn't be legitimate. And even supposing it was, how was any of it his problem? "Is this some kind of joke?" he challenged Barnard.

"No, Sir," Barnard insisted. "It's on the level."

Freeman asked Barnard to go over everything again. And again. Finally, he was satisfied that Barnard wasn't pulling his leg. He accepted the notion that there really was an American woman at Silopi, and she really did need help getting into the country with a donkey. The bit about Istanbul made sense to him, too. This international city was the only port in the region that could handle the air transportation of livestock.

But he was still baffled about why the LNO had contacted him, of all people. What was Freeman supposed to do about it? He was a defense attaché, not an agricultural officer. Livestock issues were not in his job description, even if they did involve stranded

Americans. "Just why," Freeman challenged Barnard, "is any of this my problem?"

"Well, you see," Barnard explained, "the donkey belongs to a Marine colonel. He apparently was formerly in charge down at TQ."

With that the picture came into clear focus for Freeman. As the Marine Corps attaché at Ankara, it was his job to take care of all Marine Corps issues. So the donkey problem, as crazy as it sounded, had now become Freeman's problem.

He collected Terri Crisp's contact information from Barnard and called her at the Iraqi border. She went over her story with him from the top and explained that the Turkish customs officials had declared that Smoke couldn't cross the border. Even though she was confident Smoke had been tested properly and was free from disease, she couldn't get them to make an exception.

"I am not surprised," he told her. "The Turks are sticklers for procedure and bureaucracy."

Exactly what he could do about the tangle wasn't immediately clear. Freeman had been stationed in Ankara since August 2008—arriving, coincidentally, about the same time John had deployed to Camp al Taqaddum. Freeman enjoyed his work at the embassy. It required a combination of quick thinking and common sense. But until now it hadn't required knowledge of livestock importation issues.

Freeman headed over to the Political Section to track down the chief political-military officer. No, traveling donkeys aren't exactly political, and they typically aren't military. But after twenty years in the State Department the chief POL-MIL must be able to point Freeman in the right direction, he figured. So he dropped in and explained his unusual problem. Sure enough, after chuckling at the donkey story, his colleague sent him down the hall to the Agricultural Attaché Office.

Not every U.S. embassy around the world housed an Agricultural Attaché Office, but the embassy in Ankara did. This embassy was one of America's largest and had a full contingent of federal agencies represented. Freeman occasionally wondered whether the Agricultural Attaché Office in Ankara had outlived its usefulness. After all, Turkey was by now a relatively developed nation. Its leaders took pride in their ability to manage the nation's agricultural sector without foreign assistance. But luckily for Freeman, the office was still considered necessary.

Once in the office he was referred to an LES—that's "locally employed staff" to the uninitiated. These local employees are minor yet vital cogs in the embassy machinery. They know the local culture, they speak the local language, and most important, most have been on the job long enough to know many of the local government officials well—and that's a big plus in dealing with international affairs. The particular LES that Freeman was connected to happened to be Samet Serttas—who had already been primed by John's phone call. Freeman laid out the problem as described by Barnard, and Samet hit the phones.

By late Wednesday afternoon Samet thought he had pinpointed the problem. After consulting the Turkish Ministry of Agriculture, he concluded that the main reason for the ban on Iraqi livestock appeared to be a concern about screwworm.

Screwworm is a nasty little fly whose maggots burrow into the healthy flesh of animals, including horses and donkeys, and feed on it. Eventually, the parasites kill the livestock. Screwworm was a significant problem in Iraq. Neighboring countries such as Turkey were vigilant in working to keep the parasite from infesting their own healthy livestock. And they had no documentation showing that Smoke had been tested and vaccinated for the parasite.

Samet briefed Freeman about what was required—if they had hopes of getting an exception to the livestock ban. Then Freeman contacted Terri. In addition to the testing and vaccination the Turkish government needed two letters, he told her: one from her organization and another from the U.S. Department of Agriculture. The Turks wanted assurances that Smoke was just passing through—and that if the Turks did agree to let him enter, he would be welcome in the United States once transportation was arranged. They weren't about to let a donkey into the country and then get left holding its feedbag. Freeman also reached out to John in an email, introducing himself and letting him know that the U.S. Marine Corps was now on the job.

John quickly grabbed his phone and called Freeman.

"This is great news! The Marine Corps is involved! Now maybe we'll make something happen," he told the attaché, with his booming laugh. "Let me tell you about Smoke the Donkey."

He launched into his story, regaling Freeman with his yarns about how he met the donkey, Smoke's life at Camp al Taqaddum, and how his unit had adopted the donkey. He also bent Freeman's ear with his displeasure over the bureaucratic red tape that was now preventing Smoke from entering Turkey. Freeman assured John his office was doing everything it could to help.

In the meantime Terri got to work in Silopi, following the instructions from the embassy. She reached out to Dr. Ellen Buck, the equine import specialist at the U.S. Department of Agriculture's National Center for Import and Export in Riverdale, Maryland. They had communicated during the winter when she first began planning her road trip. John had also contacted Buck in 2009, so the veterinarian was already familiar with Smoke's story.

Recognizing the time pressure Terri faced, the veterinarian responded quickly. Before the day was out, she wrote the needed letter, confirming that the U.S. Department of Agriculture would indeed allow Smoke to be "presented for importation." But the Turks were far from alone in being cautious about letting animals enter their country. The Americans had their share of red tape, too. Dr. Buck spelled out the intricate requirements in the letter she sent to Freeman:

April 6, 2011

General Directorate of Protection and Control
Ministry of Agriculture and Rural Affairs
Ankara, Turkey

Dear Sir or Madam:

This letter is to confirm that the United States Department of Agriculture, Animal and Plant Health Protection Service (USDA APHIS) will allow "Smoke," a grey donkey jack, to be presented for importation into the U.S. Upon arrival into the U.S. "Smoke" will be quarantined at the New York Animal Import Center for testing and examination.

"Smoke" must be accompanied by government-endorsed health certificates representing 60 days of residency prior to his export to the U.S. The health certificate should include a complete description of the animal and attest that, to the best of the endorsing official's knowledge, the donkey has:

(a) Resided in the exporting country for 60 days immediately preceding importation to the United States. [Note: If that has not been the case, then the official veterinarian from each country where the horse has been during the 60 days prior to importation into the United States must issue the health certificate reflecting the time the donkey has resided there.]

(b) Not been in a country where contagious equine metritis (CEM) is known to exist, nor has had any contact with horses or donkeys, by breeding or in any manner exposed, from such a country, for the 12 months preceding exportation.

(c) Not been on a premises where African horse sickness, dourine, glanders, surra, epizootic lymphangitis, ulcerative lymphangitis, equine piroplasmosis, equine infectious anemia (EIA), contagious equine metritis (CEM), vesicular stomatitis, or Venezuelan equine encephalomyelitis has occurred during the 60 days immediately preceding exportation, nor have any of these disease[s] occurred on any adjoining premised during the same period of time.

(d) Not been vaccinated for any diseases during the 14 days immediately preceding exportation.

(e) Been inspected and found to be free of contagious diseases and insofar as can be determined, exposure thereto during the 60 days immediately preceding exportation.

(f) Been inspected and found free from ectoparasites.

If you require any additional information, I can be reached by email. . . .

Sincerely,

Ellen Buck, DVM
Equine Import Specialist
National Center for Import and Export

In New York the SPCAI staff drafted a letter, as well:

General Directorate of Protection and Control
Ministry of Agriculture and Rural Affairs

SPCA International is working with Retired Colonel John Folsom to get a donkey that was the mascot for his Marine unit from Iraq to the United States. This donkey has a great importance to Colonel Folsom and his men. When SPCA International was asked to assist in the transport, we first made sure that Smoke was in good health and able to travel. Working with the Director of the Central Veterinary Laboratory in the Ankawa District of Erbil, Kurdistan, we were able to get the donkey tested and examined by a veterinarian. Once we received a clean bill of health, we proceeded to work on a plan to get the donkey to the United States. As the details of the plan were worked out, the donkey remained quarantined from other equine for a period of 60 days.

Our plan is to transport the donkey by truck to Istanbul, Turkey where he will remain for no more than 10 days, quarantined during this time from other equine. He will then fly on Lufthansa to Frankfurt, Germany and then on to New York City. Upon his arrival in the United States, he will be transported to the USDA/APHIS quarantine stables to assure compliance with all entry requirements. USDA/APHIS has been notified of our plan. They have offered their assistance, recognizing too the importance of this donkey and the unique nature of this mission.

SPCA International is requesting that the Turkish Ministry of Agriculture allow the donkey to transit through Turkey, as we have no other option to get the donkey to the United States. We can assure you that during the donkey's transit to Istanbul, he will remain in an enclosed vehicle. SPCA International understands the importance of reducing the spread of diseases carried by animals and would in no way endanger people or other animals.

Thank you for considering this request.

Sincerely,

JD Winston
Executive Director
SPCA International

Barnard found rooms for the night for Terri and her companions at the Army installation. Smoke spent the night under a military tent. Thursday brought hope for Smoke's supporters. Freeman hand-delivered the letters from Dr. Buck and JD, as promised. And Barnard was confident. "We've come this far," he told Terri, "so giving up is not an option."

Barnard had put a lot of time into this donkey mission, and—truth be told—he had been none too happy about it at the beginning. When the folks at KBR had initially told him that a stranded American needed his help, he was frustrated to discover he was being dragged into a border hassle over a donkey. His function as the liaison at Silopi was to provide a go-between for the Turkish general who commanded the country's Special Forces and the American division commander in Mosul as they worked on a variety of missions.

Much of Barnard's work was classified and, therefore, shrouded in secrecy. He might be writing to the American general and then briefing the Turkish general on certain developments. Or arranging meetings between U.S. and Turkish brass. Or communicating with the Iraqis. Or arranging meetings or working issues for various diplomats. But donkey diplomacy? That most definitely was not on his task list. But he knew he was the only person in this rugged frontier town who could even attempt to help Terri. And he admired her persistence in trying to get the donkey across the border.

His role was time consuming. Each time the group tried to cross the border, he needed to accompany them. When they communicated with various customs officials or the Turkish veterinarian, it was Barnard who had to set up the appointments—and that chore alone could consume hours of his time. He sat in on every meeting, providing translation services. And in this part of the world every meeting involved taking time to drink tea and observe other cultural niceties, as well as discussing the issues at hand.

Eventually, Barnard came to appreciate the significance of the Smoke mission and why John felt so strongly about not leaving the donkey behind. Besides, now that Barnard had "raised the flag" at the U.S. embassy, there was no turning back. So instead of spending his days arranging meetings between key military officials to discuss classified business, he was talking livestock issues with customs officials.

Oddly enough, even the donkey problem involved careful diplomacy—on both sides of the Turkey-Kurdistan border. On the Kurdish side the border officials were baffled about why anyone, even an American, would go to so much trouble over a donkey. Just as John had discovered years earlier, the donkey was a lowly beast in the Arabic culture. Donkeys are pressed into

Donkey Diplomacy

heavy service by the poorest of farmers—those who can't afford machinery to haul loads. So who would care about any donkey, let alone one particular donkey? Barnard found it difficult, if not impossible, to translate for the Kurds and Iraqis the emotional attachment that the U.S. Marines had placed on Smoke. "Why don't you just buy a donkey in America? Why do you need this donkey?" they would ask again and again.

Of course, they knew that sometimes you just had to shrug your shoulders at the strange behavior of Americans. But the resistance went deeper than that. Many Iraqis and Kurds wanted fervently to go to America themselves. When they tried, they ran up against significant red tape, battling immigration requirements and government restrictions. Yet here were these Americans, going to all this work, not for human beings, but for what they saw as an insignificant beast of burden.

By contrast the Turks mostly found Smoke's saga funny. Certainly the Turkish soldiers with Barnard were highly amused by the story, and they teased him about it every chance they got. As for the Turkish border officials: they didn't object to the animal crossing the border. They all expressed goodwill to the Americans in the various meetings and tea-drinking sessions. The customs officials and veterinarians and all the other officials were professional and polite in their behavior.

Another difference: On the Iraqi side some officials might be more willing to look the other way with the proper enticement. But the Turks were conscientious about following their governmental rules. And without sanctioning from the top of their government ladder, it was made quite clear that Smoke wasn't going anywhere.

Back in Ankara Freeman was working through issues, as well—or at least trying to. Freeman was astute enough to know that if a U.S. veteran wanted to take a donkey from war-torn Iraq to the Land of the Free, it was going to capture some media attention. It was time, he decided, to fill in the embassy brass. The embassy at Ankara was between ambassadors at the moment.

Francis J. Ricciardone Jr. had just been appointed—so recently, in fact, that he was still awaiting confirmation by the U.S. Senate. Absent a sitting ambassador, Freeman turned to the number two: Deputy Chief of Mission Doug Silliman.

Freeman delivered his report to Silliman at the next country team meeting. During these gatherings the heads of all the embassy sections and any U.S. government agencies represented at the embassy met to report on their issues of the day. The ambassador or deputy chief of mission chaired the meeting and provided guidance as needed. The topics were usually serious in nature. So Freeman's report on Smoke livened up the meeting considerably. Silliman told Freeman that importing or transiting an Iraqi donkey to or through Turkey would likely require significant work. He could foresee plenty of bureaucratic traps to run. But everyone at the meeting recognized what members of the military were going through during the war. They all rallied behind Smoke's heartwarming story, up to and including Silliman.

While Freeman wrestled with the diplomatic dilemma, Terri and Ameer spent Thursday killing time—grooming Smoke, taking him for walks, and feeding him treats. Just before 5 p.m. Barnard arrived. "I need the license plate for the truck," he told Terri. "How soon will Smoke fly out of Istanbul to the United States once we get him there?"

The visit raised Terri's hopes that a resolution was in the works. Half an hour later Samet emailed Freeman to say that a letter to allow "transit movement" of Smoke would be sent Friday from the Ministry of Agriculture and Rural Affairs. Freeman was pleased. "I've accomplished a few things in my life, but something like this—well, you just can't put a value on experiences like this," he told Samet.

On Friday morning Terri settled into what had become her temporary "office"—the dining hall at the U.S. Army post. She fired up her Blackberry and sent colleagues and followers her morning update. "I awoke at 5 a.m. to the sound of pouring rain and the question of whether Smoke would sleep in Iraq or Turkey tonight," she blogged. "Major Barnard is meeting with the Turkish Customs Officials at 9:00 a.m. this morning to make sure the approval letter has been faxed from the Ministry of Agriculture and Rural Affairs to the border. We are waiting for Major Barnard's arrival and another 'thumbs up.'

"Smoke is definitely ready to travel. He sounded the wakeup call at 5:00 a.m. this morning, hee hawing to say it was time for someone to bring him another apple or his breakfast of oatmeal. Smoke's presence has been a real morale booster for the troops and the KBR employees in this isolated corner of Iraq. Once again Smoke is doing what he is good at—making people laugh."

It turned into another day of waiting. Smoke waited for Terri. Terri waited for Barnard, who waited for Freeman. And Barnard and Freeman both waited for the Turks to fax the formal letter of approval to the border.

By afternoon they learned that a second signature was needed, from the deputy director of the Turkish Ministry of Agriculture. But it was getting late in the day, and once the letter finally reached the border offices, it would require attention from the veterinarian before the group could cross the border. About 4 p.m. the embassy reported to Barnard that the letter was being sent. He dropped his regular work once again and checked in with the customs office. But no letter was found. More waiting.

About 6 p.m. Freeman finally discovered why no letter had been faxed. The deputy Turkish agricultural director had decided against signing anything to allow Smoke into the country. And without that vital signature there would be no border crossing for the little donkey. The team had truly hit a dead end this time.

To: John Folsom
From: Lloyd Freeman
Date: Fri, 8 April 2011
Subject: letter

Sir,

Bad news. At the last minute the Deputy Director of
Ministry of Agriculture did not sign the letter . . . it will
not be approved. Smoke is stuck for now. Only thing
we can do now is regroup on Monday and brainstorm
a way towards a plan B. We need any agency/entity that
is interested in this to weigh in. Only way forward now
is for some kind of pressure from within Turkey to get
Smoke through.

If you have any ideas send them my way . . . we are
working on it still.

R/S

Lt Col Freeman

Freeman had also alerted Barnard about the deputy director's
decision. Barnard had dutifully found Terri and delivered the
news. The border crossing was off for now. Smoke, it was clear,
would need to retreat. Ahmed, the driver, would take him back
to the farm outside Irbil, where he had been kept before. Meanwhile Terri and Ameer would move forward, crossing the border
into Turkey, driving to the city of Mardin, and catching a flight
from there to Istanbul. spcaI had connections with another animal advocacy organization, called Shelter Volunteers for Animals Association. The shelter, with the Turkish acronym of bgd,
wanted to help. And Freeman had offered to schedule a meeting
between Terri and the deputy director of the Ministry of Agriculture. Perhaps if she appeared in person, she could persuade
him to help reunite John and Smoke.

Terri and Ameer headed for the border stations to enter
Turkey—only to confront another roadblock. Ameer's visa was
no longer usable, he was told. It turned out that his paperwork
was good for a single trip into Turkey. Had everything gone
smoothly, that would have been enough. But back on Tuesday
evening, when they discovered that Smoke needed to be examined by a Turkish veterinarian, Terri and Ameer had crossed
the border to spend the night. Now his visa had expired—even

Donkey Diplomacy

though border officials had assured them at the time that he could reenter.

Terri appealed to Barnard for help. He used all his diplomacy to appeal to the border officials. But while the Turks were sympathetic, they could do nothing, they told him. Their computerized system couldn't be overridden. Ameer would need to go home and start over.

On Saturday the little group broke up. Ameer and Ahmed headed back to Irbil with Smoke. Terri stayed at the border, where she had Internet access and could continue making plans.

Freeman had hinted to Barnard that perhaps the Ministry of Agriculture would respond to public pressure. Barnard passed along the hint to Terri. She quickly began brainstorming her next move with her colleagues. The staff had been living and breathing Smoke issues all week. Now, taking Freeman's advice, they decided to start a petition drive to create public pressure in hopes that would influence the Turks. Stephanie Scott, the group's communication director, contacted the group's webmaster. The two spent the weekend writing the computer code so Stephanie could roll out the petition drive as soon as possible.

Back in Irbil, when the Turkish consulate opened for business on Sunday morning, Ameer was there, waiting to turn in his new visa application. This time around he requested a multientry visa that would last six months.

He picked it up Monday afternoon and once again made the three-and-a-half-hour drive to the border. This time he and Terri knew what to expect. Not only did they know what to do, but everyone along their path knew them. They were the "donkey people," and everyone along the way wanted an update on Smoke. Without the donkey in tow the crossing went more smoothly. Terri and Ameer spent the night in Silopi. They rose before dawn Tuesday to make the three-hour trip to Mardin in time to catch their flight to Istanbul.

In Ankara Freeman continued pressing the case for Smoke to pass into Turkey. Along with sorting out whether it was possible to cut through the red tape of the Turkish bureaucracy, Freeman also found himself at the center of considerable attention at the embassy. After his briefing at the country team meeting, word of Smoke's story spread quickly. It seemed that everyone in the building now knew about Smoke—and they all wanted updates. In fact, so many members of the Foreign Service staff and other embassy personnel began asking Freeman for the latest donkey news that he had been sending out group emails to save time.

Not that he had a lot to report. Negotiations were under way with the Turkish Ministry of Agriculture. But they weren't going well. The ministry remained reluctant to provide a waiver for Smoke's paperwork. The agricultural officers continued to worry about the threat the donkey could pose to Turkish livestock if he wasn't appropriately inoculated. Freeman found himself consulting Silliman repeatedly for advice. At one point Silliman himself engaged the Turkish Ministry of Foreign Affairs for advice and assistance on getting Smoke into the country.

By Tuesday Stephanie was ready to send out her news release announcing the petition drive on Smoke's behalf: "In an effort to help convince the Turkish Minister of Agriculture and Rural Affairs that it is more than safe to allow 'Smoke' passage out of Iraq through Turkey to arrive in New York City, SPCA International is calling on donors and supporters to petition the Turkish authorities in order to bring Smoke to the U.S. The Iraqi Donkey was rescued in 2008 by Ret. USMC Col John Folsom and his Marines at Camp Taqaddum, brought back to good health and soon became the unit's mascot and friend."

The release went on to quote Terri about Smoke's health, and it urged readers to follow daily updates on the organization's webpage and to sign a petition "demanding Smoke's passage through Turkey from Iraq." In addition JD Winston, in the SPCAI New York headquarters, sent out a plea directly to followers on the organization's email list:

Smoke Is Stuck

Remember Smoke the donkey?

Retired Marine Colonel John Folsom emailed you in
February about bringing his buddy Smoke from Iraq to
Nebraska to be a therapy donkey for wounded warriors.

I knew his journey would be dangerous and fraught
with risks. But, I never thought I'd be writing you today.
Frankly, I wish I didn't have to.

Last week, Smoke started his trip from Iraq to
Nebraska.

We carefully planned every step of the trip. First,
we'd drive Smoke across the border into Turkey and then
north to Istanbul where he'd fly to Paris and on to New
York.

As I write you, the Turkish government is denying
Smoke entrance. The Deputy Turkish Minister of
Agriculture changed his mind and told us Smoke
cannot pass.

There's no time to waste. spcai staff is on their way
to Turkey to try to persuade the Ministry to reverse their
decision. We need to show them how important Smoke
is. He was there for our Armed Forces in Iraq. It's our
turn to be there for him.

Will you sign this petition right now telling the
Turkish government to "Let Smoke Through!"?

Your signature will help us make the case to the
Turkish officials. I know if we band together, we can
change their minds!

Thank you for your support and for your quick
response.

Sincerely,

JD Winston
Executive Director
spca International

Word spread through news outlets and animal advocacy groups and among email groups and on Facebook. Care2 News Network was among the organizations that tried to help, distributing the story to its millions of members. "Please Take Action!" it urged followers. Donkey supporters quickly signed the petition and sent funds. The "Smoke Is Stuck" email alone prompted seven hundred donations to help pay for Smoke's passage. Thousands of signatures started pouring in from across the United States, with a sprinkling from other countries.

Wednesday and Thursday passed. Freeman tapped a translator on staff to help prepare emails sent from advocacy groups and Smoke supporters to provide to the Turkish government. The groups all urged the Turkish minister of agriculture to reconsider his rejection of Smoke. One of them came from BGD, the shelter in Istanbul that was working with Terri. "I wish I was translating more stuff like this rather than unmanned air vehicles, tanks and aircraft," Selin, the translator, told Freeman that Wednesday. "Thanks for sending this to me."

Freeman persuaded the Ministry of Agriculture to agree to a meeting with Terri the next week. But on Friday afternoon Samet fired up his computer. The impasse had been broken.

> To: Freeman, Lloyd; Guido, Deborah; Witmer, Kami; John Folsom
> From: Serttas, Samet
> Date: Fri, 15 Apr 2011
> Subject: very good news
>
> We convinced Ministry of Agriculture to write letter to allow transit movements of smoke. Letter is now signed and sent to Habur gate.

Exactly what had persuaded the Ministry of Agriculture to concede was unclear, although Freeman told Barnard afterward that the Ministry of Foreign Affairs had become involved and made the breakthrough with the Ministry of Agriculture. The deputy minister of agriculture duly signed the letter of approval, which was faxed to the Habur Gate border offices. Barnard visited personally the next day to confirm its arrival. By this time Barnard was almost as relieved as Terri and John. While he had come to feel compassion for the Smoke mission, it was also consuming a significant amount of time, seriously impeding his other work. "There are some great supporters of Smoke at the border that want to see our now famous donkey clear this hurdle and be on his way," Terri told her followers. "We will be so happy once we get word Smoke has left Iraq behind—once and for all."

Terri made arrangements for Ahmed to take Smoke from Irbil to Istanbul and began to harbor hopes that Smoke could be eating American-grown hay by the end of April. She met with the founders of BGD and told them the good news. "These dedicated women were as excited as we were to learn over the weekend that the efforts to get Smoke into Turkey had been successful. We will be going with them this weekend to the local Ministry of Agriculture to make sure we do everything necessary to be able to get Smoke moved out of Turkey as quickly as possible," Terri wrote on the blog. "It feels good to be moving forward again and not taking steps backwards."

She and Ameer also visited K9 Akademisi, the facility where Smoke would stay. Ameer knew Göktan Eker, the owner of K9 Akademisi, through his work at Reed Inc. The company used specially trained dogs in its demining work, and Eker trained such dogs. He had agreed to shelter the donkey at his kennels, nestled in the green hills outside Istanbul. Smoke would be comfortable there—it would be like staying at the Reed kennels, back in Irbil.

Early on Tuesday, April 19, Ahmed picked up Smoke at the farm and set out for the border. Smoke had gotten to rest up for ten days before his second big road trip began. They reached Silopi about 8:30 a.m. and met up with Barnard, who escorted them through the various checkpoints. Even though Smoke's passage was now sanctioned, the crossing was tediously slow. Shortly before 6 p.m. Terri notified her blog followers that Ahmed and Barnard were at the customs director's office at the border, waiting for the final paperwork. "The official is saying a customs import fee of $500 has to be paid for Smoke to cross the border into Turkey which is not something we had expected to pay," she wrote. "At this point though we will gladly pay the fee if it means Smoke will be able to enter Turkey."

The journey continued to grind along. Each step of the way border officials had a friendly greeting for the little donkey. People and trucks might be forgettable, but not so a little donkey—a little donkey who was about to become the first animal from Iraq to set foot in Turkey with the sanctioning of the Turkish government since the beginning of the Iraq War.

It was nearly 10 p.m. when Terri passed along the long-awaited news: "We did it! Smoke is in Turkey!"

10.

Turkish Delight

Ahmed and Smoke spent a long day on the road Wednesday, traveling the thousand miles from the border at Silopi to Istanbul. They turned their faces to the west, leaving behind the rugged mountains of eastern Turkey. And they left behind, too, the country of Smoke's birth, the desert land that was once called Mesopotamia, seat of the ancient Sumerians and Babylonians.

Now Smoke was crossing Turkey, the great crossroads of East and West. This land has been influenced by one culture after another in its long history, including the Hittite, Thracian, Hellenistic, and Byzantine civilizations. The Seljuk Turks introduced the Turkish language and Islamic religion to the area in the eleventh century. They were followed by the Ottoman Turks a few centuries later. After peaking in the 1600s the Ottoman Empire dwindled slowly until World War I, when it aligned with the Central Powers of Germany, Austria-Hungary, and Bulgaria. The Central Powers' loss in the Great War spelled the demise of the Ottomans.

The secular Republic of Turkey was born in 1923. It has thrived in modern times: Turkey's economy now ranks among the top twenty in the world, with a mix of agricultural, industrial, and service sectors. In Turkey, as in Iraq, the vast majority of residents are Muslim. But while three-fourths of Turkish residents are ethnic Turks, the same proportion of Iraqis are Arabs. Kurds make up roughly a fifth of the population in both countries.

The road west took the travelers through green countryside, past rivers, lakes, and rich farmland, a contrast to the arid landscape of Iraq. Their route angled northwest across the Anatolian Plateau and skirting Ankara, the modern capital of Turkey.

Smoke didn't stop to visit the U.S. embassy or the seat of the Turkish government, where dozens of staff from both governments had worked so hard to help the little donkey enter the country.

But that's probably just as well. Lt. Col. Lloyd Freeman was ready for a breather from Smoke issues, although he had loved seeing the press coverage surrounding Smoke's triumphant entry. "Esek diplomasisi!" or "Donkey diplomacy!" one headline read, and Turkish television reporters showed footage of "Mr. Smoke."

Smoke had been fortunate, Freeman figured, because he was dealing with the Turks, who love animals. A lot of other countries in the region might not have been willing to bend their rules for a lowly donkey. But even now he knew the battle was only half over, and he braced himself for the next phase of Smoke's journey.

Ahmed and Smoke finally reached Istanbul and made their way to K9 Akademisi, the kennels where Smoke would stay. Early Thursday Terri left her downtown hotel and set out with Ameer to see Smoke. They walked to a Metro station, took the train to a ferry station, and crossed the Bosporus, the strait that separates Europe from Asia. From there they hopped another train and then caught a taxi for the final leg. They were rewarded with the sight of a very happy Smoke—who was even happier when Terri took him for a walk.

The hilly countryside was covered with green vegetation, and Smoke took full advantage of this donkey version of Turkish delight. When he had his fill, he settled down on the cool grass for a much-needed nap. He was exhausted after standing in a truck for two long days on the trek from Irbil. Little did he know he was violating Turkish regulations as he grazed. In the world of Turkish transportation regulations Smoke fell under the category of cargo. And he was in transit, since Turkey wasn't his final destination. Under the regulations all cargo in transit must be stored in a warehouse or stay on the truck it rode in on. Cargo should certainly not be roaming the countryside, let alone pilfering Turkish grass.

While such rules make sense for farm goods and machinery,

they don't work for donkeys. So Terri and Ameer loaded Smoke back into the truck, reluctantly, and headed for the customs office at Ataturk airport to explain their problem. They spent the next two hours in stop-and-go traffic—and spent the four hours after that in stop-and-go negotiations with customs officials.

Terri headed up a small entourage: Ameer, Ahmed, and Safak Asparuk, security manager for MNG Airlines. Terri had arranged for MNG, a cargo airline, to transport Smoke from Istanbul to Paris. Safak would be Terri's interpreter and customs office tour guide for the day. The entourage soon added another member: Taner Demir, a friendly customs attorney who rallied behind Terri's cause.

Together the group walked the length and width of the customs office, telling one official after another why they were there and what they hoped to accomplish. They even met with the customs director himself, urging him to agree that Smoke couldn't be stored like a box of car parts, as Terri put it. "Figuring out how to maneuver government agencies in a foreign country is a skill Ameer and I have acquired since our journey with Smoke began," she told her blog followers later. "The one important thing to remember is that when you walk through the door of these agencies you better bring your patience and lots of it."

But it wasn't Terri who was doing the talking. Safak and the attorney, and sometimes Ahmed, negotiated with the customs officials in Turkish, gesturing, arguing, explaining. All Terri could do was read their body language and tone and wait for a translation. It wasn't that the officials were unfriendly. In fact, the customs director greeted their request with pleasant smiles. But his employees were unbending as they insisted that all the proper steps be taken.

Smoke's retinue filled out a raft of government forms and handwrote letter after letter of explanation. They wrote and rewrote the letters, amending them until the customs manager in charge of Smoke's case declared them acceptable. Terri signed them—and so did Safak, which struck Terri as strange, but she didn't hold up the proceedings further by asking for an explanation.

It wasn't until afterward that Safak explained she had promised to be held jointly responsible if anything went wrong. If Smoke didn't leave Turkey within the six-day transit limit, or if he spread disease to any Turkish animals, both Terri and Safak would be fined significantly. Terri was astonished that Safak would take such a risk.

While that ended one battle, another remained: the customs manager refused to let Smoke stay at K9 Akademisi until customs inspectors had visited and confirmed he wouldn't come into contact with other livestock. Terri was happy to comply, but by now it was nearly 6 p.m.—closing time—and the inspection couldn't be done until Friday. Well then, the manager declared, Smoke must stay in the truck in the customs office parking lot. At that all Smoke's supporters protested. Absolutely not, they vowed.

More talk, more pleas, more phone calls. Finally, after Terri managed to move up a Friday-afternoon appointment at the Ministry of Agriculture to 9:30 a.m., the customs manager relented. Smoke could return to the kennels, she said—but only if he stayed in the truck and only if the inspection was done immediately after the meeting at the Ministry of Agriculture.

Smoke's champions reluctantly agreed, deciding at least it would be better than leaving him in an airport parking lot all by himself. The manager signed the last of the paperwork, and the weary warriors beat a retreat.

Friday brought another ferry ride across the Bosporus for Terri and Ameer. They had arranged to rendezvous with Asli Varlier Pelit, one of the founders of BGD, the Turkish animal shelter. The three of them caught a taxi to the Istanbul offices of the agricultural ministry. They arrived in time for their 9:30 a.m. meeting with a manager and explained their purpose: to find out what paperwork was needed to get Smoke out of the country. The manager smiled—it was clear that the publicity about Smoke had preceded them. He explained the agricultural requirements. Terri was relieved to hear that for once the process didn't sound as complicated as she had expected.

She and her retinue explained that they needed the ministry to authorize Smoke's stay at the dog kennels and to send the proper documentation to the customs office. The manager agreed to have his staff examine the kennels and send his authorization. Compared to Thursday's marathon battle, this was a tea party, and the group celebrated over lunch. That afternoon Terri emailed Dr. Buck with an update and asked for help with an equine import form.

By now Terri had made a major change in the transportation plan. She had discovered that MNG Airlines didn't transport equines. That was a huge blow since Safak had told her the airline would not charge for the transportation. Terri informed Dr. Buck she now planned to ship Smoke on Lufthansa, routing through Frankfurt and then to JFK in New York. She had arranged a flight for April 28, the following Thursday. She figured that was the earliest Smoke could leave since he needed to remain in Turkey at least seven days to confirm he was free from screwworm. She knew she needed to fill out an import permit application and asked Buck if she could help direct her to the form.

The veterinarian, who had been following Smoke's story, wrote back, saying she was glad to hear Smoke had made it to Turkey. She provided the information Terri had requested about the import permit application form and told her about another required document, a "declaration of importation" form that needed to be filled out in duplicate for customs officials. Buck also asked whether anyone had made reservations for Smoke at the New York Animal Import Center. If not, she said, it would need to be done as soon as possible to ensure there was room at the inn, so to speak. Terri hadn't known about the second form or the need to reserve a spot at the quarantine center. She reached out to John for help in making arrangements.

John filled out the import forms and contacted the quarantine center. The veterinarian he talked to, like Buck, already knew all about Smoke, who had now become major news across the equine world.

Back in Istanbul the Turkish agricultural official gave his

permission for Smoke to stay at K9 Akademisi, as long as the site passed inspection. He faxed the required documents to the customs office at the airport. But by the end of the business day the documents hadn't reached the appropriate customs manager. After observing the pace of Turkish red tape at Silopi, no one was terribly surprised by this. But without the blessings of the customs office Smoke was stuck on the truck, and Ahmed was stuck in Istanbul.

On Saturday Safak stopped by the customs office several times, hoping for an update. After making inquiries, she was directed to the agency's fax office, where she found stacks of documents waiting for delivery. She painstakingly dug through the stacks until she uncovered the paperwork from the Ministry of Agriculture and then hand delivered it to the customs manager and to several other officials for their signatures. Finally, the manager was satisfied and arranged for a site inspection.

Smoke's quarantine arrangements were deemed satisfactory, and it was time for farewells. Ahmed waved goodbye to Terri and Ameer and gave Smoke a final pat before climbing into the truck for the long drive back to Irbil. Smoke stretched his legs, sniffed the air, and began to enjoy his new, albeit temporary, digs.

John notified friends and supporters Saturday that Smoke's travel plan looked like a go. His friend Lisa had agreed to loan him a pickup truck and horse trailer. If all went well, he could pick up Smoke on May 2 at the New York quarantine center. Then he and Smoke would head for Fredericksburg, Virginia, for a "meet and greet" en route to Omaha. It was a happy weekend for Smoke's supporters on both sides of the Atlantic.

The happy bubble didn't take long to burst. Dr. Dale Weinmann, a veterinarian at the quarantine center in New York, called Monday. He told John he was concerned because he didn't see evidence of a health certificate or any documentation showing that Smoke had been pretested for certain diseases, which was an integral step. Weinmann urged the use of a customs broker to make sure the proper procedures were followed, because importing an equine was so complex. Who did Weinmann recommend? Paul Weygand.

John emailed Terri, relating Weinmann's concerns. "What we don't need is for Smoke to arrive at JFK and then find out he's going to be rejected," he wrote. "Not good. We're too close."

The more John thought about what Weinmann had said, the more frustrated he felt. He had been asking SPCAI for months to get professional guidance as they waded into the unfamiliar territory of importing a donkey. He had contacted Terri's boss, JD Winston, back in the winter, before Smoke had been captured, about hiring a professional broker. He knew that Terri would work hard to get Smoke out of Iraq, and he was grateful for the group's help. But he worried they were out of their depth, and he wanted to make sure nothing would go wrong. JD hadn't been enthusiastic at the time. His organization was budget conscious, and he was worried about additional expenses. John, however, was adamant. "Either hire Mersant or there's no deal," he had told JD.

Terri had told him before she left Irbil that Paul would be hired. Yet here they were, a month later, and it still hadn't been done. But at this point it was no longer optional, and the organization acquiesced to hiring Paul as broker. Once he was formally employed, he quickly shot off an email, detailing a list of questions and requests: What health papers would Smoke be traveling with? He needed the correct certificates from both Iraq and Turkey, Paul pointed out. What flights had been arranged? What health tests had been conducted? Did they have the appropriate documentation and forms? Who would be responsible for the costs?

Terri told him she had the Iraqi health certificate and was planning to get the Turkish health certificate on Wednesday. She filled in Paul on Smoke's Lufthansa travel plans and confirmed that SPCAI was covering the costs.

One point on Paul's checklist that Terri knew she hadn't done: provide blood samples to an official U.S. Department of Agriculture lab to screen for the diseases Paul had detailed. These were the same diseases Buck had told Terri about back in January. Terri had been working under the assumption that this work could wait until Smoke was in New York. Even now she wasn't convinced it was necessary. "Smoke has a limited time in Turkey and there is not time to do it here," she told Paul.

John wasn't satisfied with her response. He contacted her New York office and talked to Stephanie, who touched base with Paul, questioning the need for the testing. Stephanie relayed the bad news to Terri: there was no way around it. They would have to get Smoke's blood work tested before he was shipped to New York or run the risk of him being put down if anything went wrong. It would take approximately one week for the tests to be processed at the USDA lab. So Smoke wasn't going anywhere for at least seven days.

Terri contacted Lufthansa to change flights and discuss the details of shipping the donkey. She was relieved to talk to someone who was knowledgeable—and someone who spoke English. She found out the weekly schedule for cargo flights and learned that Smoke would travel in a stall. But she was startled to discover that Smoke couldn't travel unaccompanied. Until now, based on information from MNG Airlines, she had assumed she could put the donkey on a flight and wave goodbye. This development wasn't good. Dogs and cats were stacking up back in Irbil, so to speak, and she felt pressure to wrap up this mission. Since Ameer lacked the proper visa, she emailed John. "So, how about coming to Istanbul?" she asked him, explaining the situation.

While she waited to hear back, Terri touched base with Paul. She filled him in on Smoke's travel itinerary, but Paul continued pressing her on his primary concerns: getting the blood samples and the Iraqi health certificate.

Then John checked in. "This is doable," he said of making the trip.

"How soon do you think you could get to Istanbul?" she asked. "Ameer and I will not leave until you get here and both you and Smoke are on your way. Ideally, doing this on Saturday would work for us."

Time out on that timeline, replied Paul, who had been copied on the email. "I assume you are speaking of Friday, 6 May, at earliest?" he asked.

Terri, of course, didn't mean May 6 at all. She had been forced to push back Smoke's departure time again and again. By now this mission was taking much longer to resolve than she had ever imagined. Under her original schedule Smoke would have flown to New York by April 14. Yet here she was, still in Istanbul in late April, and all she could see were roadblocks—and dollar signs. Her budget kept blowing up, pressure from her home office was building, and she couldn't understand why these tests—which she had considered optional—should bog everything down.

To: Paul Weygand
From: Terri Crisp
Date: Tuesday, April 26, 2011
Subject: RE: New Information

Hi Paul:

We cannot wait here until May 6. This mission has ended up costing a fortune. The blood samples are being done today as I indicated in my earlier email. If we get them sent to the U.S. tomorrow by FedEx as quickly as possible the lab should have them by Friday at the latest. If Smoke left on Saturday or maybe next Tuesday he would arrive in New York right about the same time or after the blood work got there. Could he not be quarantined in New York until we got the results? If anything came back positive, which I would be real surprised if they did and he had to be euthanized, he would be euthanized here in Turkey anyway.

I will send the lab work now. I have to run downstairs and have the hotel send it.

Thanks!

Humanely,

Terri Crisp

John was surprised that someone who professed a love for animals was callous enough to shrug at the possibility of euthanization. The idea that Smoke might be put down as a result of his quest had never occurred to him. His main concern had always been that if the donkey were left in Iraq, he would live a short, miserable life—or perhaps become lion food at the Baghdad zoo.

"The point is we DO NOT want to even put him on an aircraft before we KNOW the blood samples are negative," Paul told Terri emphatically. "If he arrives here and the samples are POSITIVE, he will be refused entry. There is no point importing him without the pre-test. When he arrives in the U.S., he is taken to the quarantine where he will be held while he is tested officially AND IF HE IS POSITIVE HE WILL NEVER LEAVE QUARANTINE. I don't know how to say this strongly enough, but he must not be shipped until we know the blood tests are negative."

The problem was that, unlike most animals being imported, Smoke had no home to return to. Turkey had barely let him in the first time, and if the blood tests turned up evidence of disease, no other nation was likely to allow him in, even en route to somewhere else. In a very real sense, Paul thought, Smoke would become a donkey without a country.

Terri succumbed. "Then I guess we have no choice," she wrote back. "How long does it normally take to get the results from the time the blood is shipped?"

While Terri finally accepted the notion that she needed to slow down, John was ready to jump. "When would you want me there?" he asked her.

"We have to see what the timeline is for the blood test results," she told him.

"I may 'lead turn,'" he told her, using fighter pilot terminology, "and be there this Monday. That's what I am planning based on Paul's assessment of blood sample turnaround time."

"Let me first confirm we can get the blood samples sent tomorrow my time," she wrote back.

"My plan is to depart on Saturday for Istanbul," he informed her. "I need to be there anyway, so I'm coming. Fares are low right now."

She made one more try. "I would still wait until after we get the blood sent and FedEx can tell me when it will reach the lab. This is the peak season in Istanbul and hotels are not cheap. With the way things have gone there could still be delays. I think now that we are dealing with Lufthansa things will happen the way they are supposed to."

She could have spared her typing fingers. Now that John had decided to go, there was no slowing him down. For one thing he needed time to make arrangements. If he was going to book a flight, the sooner the better. He also needed to borrow a truck and trailer to transport Smoke to Nebraska after leaving the quarantine center in Newburgh, New York. And he had to allow time to drive said truck and trailer to the East Coast on the way to Istanbul. Practical considerations aside, John loathed indecision. He was a man of action. On top of all that his intuition told him things were not as they should be in Istanbul, and he felt the need to be on the ground. He began studying airfares and searched around for other ways to help the cause.

Donita Eickholt was sitting at her desk that Tuesday at the National Veterinary Services Laboratories in Ames, Iowa, managing the usual volume of work, when the phone rang. It was a coworker, transferring a call from the "Chime Line," the general phone line for callers who don't know the specific office they want at the U.S. Animal Plant and Health Inspection Service.

"Someone wants to import a donkey from Iraq," the coworker told Donita and handed off the call.

"Serology, this is Donita," she told the caller.

As a laboratory program assistant Donita helped direct people who needed to submit samples to test for animal diseases. She had been working at the lab since 2006, and she knew her role well. She prepared to run down her usual list of questions. What kind of animal are you calling about? Are you importing, exporting, or planning interstate travel? What kind of testing have you already done? Instead, the fifty-four-year-old found herself bombarded with questions and demands from the gruff stranger on the other end of the line. Within a minute Donita concluded she was dealing with a prankster.

His name was John Folsom, he told her. He was a retired colonel, he claimed, trying to import a donkey from Iraq. Now he needed to get the animal's blood tested. He wanted to find out just what tests would be required. And he was in a hurry.

The caller told Donita he was from Omaha, just a couple hours down the road from Ames. In fact, he told her, he knew exactly where the laboratory was. He described a white farmhouse just to the north of it, on the other side of Interstate 35. He was right, which surprised Donita so much she peeked out her office window, wondering if he was out there and if he knew where she was.

But she set aside her suspicions and dutifully explained the requirements for sending in the blood work. She asked if he was working with a broker, which she advised. The broker would get a permit to send the serum samples to the lab and handle other details. John explained the tight timing involved. But when she began pressing for more details, John became impatient. He wasn't one for minutia, and her questions seemed unnecessary to him. "Just get on your computer," he said, "and look up 'Smoke the Donkey.'"

Donita thought about Dr. Beth Lautner, the laboratory director. Dr. Lautner had strict rules, including this one: no unauthorized computer use during working hours. But Donita's primary motivation in her work was to help people, whether she was dealing with a wealthy businessman importing a million-dollar racehorse or a family farmer trying to sell livestock. And this caller had practically commanded her to sign onto the Internet. "All right, hold on," she told him, thinking to herself, *I am probably going to get fired for this one.*

She reluctantly called up a search engine and typed in "Smoke the Donkey." To her surprise she found herself looking at a news article with a photograph of a man and a donkey.

"Do you see a guy there in a uniform?" her pesky caller asked.

"Yes," she replied.

"Well, that's me!" he told her.

By now the call had lasted twenty-nine minutes—she had timed it—and she was still half wondering whether this whole thing was a joke. "Okay, I'll have to check into it," she said. "I'll get back to you."

Donita hung up and sat there, thinking about her puzzling call. If this man was serious, she thought, she needed to figure out how to talk to him. She was dealing with a colonel, and she was certain he was used to giving orders, not taking them. She thought of Patricia in the director's office. Patricia was military. Maybe she could help. So Donita poured out her problem to Patricia and asked for advice. Patricia told her she needed to be direct with the colonel and not "beat around the bush." Just give him the facts.

By now Donita was burning with curiosity. When she went home that night, she powered up her own computer and searched for "Smoke the Donkey." Up popped the James Sanborn article she had glanced at in the office. His *Marine Corps Times* article from January had been redistributed by *usa Today*. She studied the photograph of the man in uniform and read the caption: "Former Marine Colonel John Folsom, left, is trying to arrange to get Smoke the donkey to the usa through an spca International program." Then she found a mid-April update in the *Marine Corps Times*, when Turkish authorities let Smoke enter the country.

"Oh, yeah, it's true!" she cried out. "It's him!"

14. Veterinary staff in Irbil struggle to get a blood sample.
COURTESY OF SPCA INTERNATIONAL.

15. Terri Crisp, Smoke, and Maj. Daniel Barnard at the Turkish border.
COURTESY OF SPCA INTERNATIONAL.

16. Smoke on the road in Iraq.
COURTESY OF SPCA INTERNATIONAL.

17. Dr. Kenneth Davis inspects Smoke's teeth at the Animal Import Center. COURTESY OF DEBRA DAVIS.

18. Smoke and John are reunited at last, May 14, 2011.
COURTESY OF DEBRA DAVIS.

19. Alan and Debbie Nash throw a party for Smoke in Warrenton, Virginia. COURTESY OF JOHN FOLSOM.

20. Donita Eickholt (*left*) and Sara Albers meet Smoke outside the National Veterinary Services Laboratories in Ames, Iowa. COURTESY OF DONITA EICKHOLT.

21. Annie the horse welcomes Smoke the Donkey to Miracle Hills Ranch & Stables. COURTESY OF ASSOCIATED PRESS.

22. John and Smoke at the Take Flight Farms fundraiser at Bar Hills Farm, July 27, 2011. COURTESY OF JOHN FOLSOM.

23. Staff Sgt. Matthew Shelato is reunited with Smoke at the Pentagon, November 2011. COURTESY OF JOHN FOLSOM.

24. John and Smoke greet crowds at the Veterans Day Parade in New York, November 2011. COURTESY OF JOHN FOLSOM.

25. Smoke and Jack Folsom with Marines at the New York City Veterans Day Parade, November 2011. COURTESY OF JOHN FOLSOM.

26. Smoke receives Nebraska Humane
Society award. With him (*from left*):
Vietnam veteran Chuck Faltin and his
wife, Gale, with Take Flight Farms;
Sunny Lundgren (award named for her
parents' pet); and Judie Olson, a Friends
Forever guild founding member.

27. Smoke's first snow, December 3, 2011.
COURTESY OF JOHN FOLSOM.

28. Smoke charms crowds at the International Equestrian Show, April 2012. COURTESY OF JOHN FOLSOM.

29. Smoke with Mike Appleby, of the U.S. Cavalry Association, at the International Equestrian Show, April 2012.
COURTESY OF JOHN FOLSOM.

11.

Trouble in Istanbul

As soon as Donita hit the office Wednesday, she emailed her supervisors, telling them about the call from John. She confessed she had initially thought the call was a prank but then had determined the caller was legitimate: he really was trying to import an Iraqi donkey with U.S. military credentials. She listed the tests the donkey would need and explained that this was a rush job.

"He indicated that a member of the team would be drawing and submitting the serum to us hopefully by Friday. I did give him the information as far as how long the results would take," Donita wrote. "As a member of Customer Service Working Group and as a part of the Government I feel compelled to pass this information along to ask if there is anything that we could do on our end."

In Istanbul Terri was struggling to get Smoke's blood drawn. Like everything else in Turkey this was turning into a headache. She had confidently told Paul the serum sample would be in the mail Tuesday. But Tuesday had come and gone, and no donkey blood had been collected. She returned to the Ministry of Agriculture to ask if an equine vet there could draw the blood. Finally, she was able to arrange an appointment for Thursday.

By now she had changed her mind about John's travel plans. After telling him to hold off, she pressed him to hurry up. "Hi, John. We cannot get the blood drawn until tomorrow and shipped," she emailed him Wednesday. "Do you have a flight booked?"

"Yes. Arriving Sunday afternoon. I'll see if I can change it to Tuesday," he wrote back.

"Tuesday will probably be too late," she replied. "We are still hoping to get him out Tuesday but it may be Wednesday."

John had selected a flight departing Saturday from JFK and arriving in Istanbul on Sunday. He asked Terri where they should meet, but she didn't respond. She was busy at the Turkish Ministry of Agriculture, trying to pull together the paperwork she thought Smoke would need. Asli, the local animal advocate, had gone along as interpreter.

Meanwhile the transportation professionals were getting acquainted and talking shop. Paul emailed Müge Özgenç, the Turkish freight forwarder for Ekiptrans Ltd. who was working with Terri. Paul was hoping the blood tests would be completed and results would be back by early the next week. He explained that John would accompany Smoke as the "groom." Müge told Paul that, at Terri's request, she had booked a flight for Tuesday, May 3, and that Lufthansa would send a container from Germany to Istanbul.

"I know Terri is very anxious to ship Smoke here, but we are waiting for blood samples to be tested before he can ship," Paul responded. "At best, we will not have results until Tuesday afternoon (23:00 local time Istanbul), 3 May, so this flight booking might be too early."

Müge agreed. If the transport container arrived in Istanbul and then Smoke tested positive for disease, Lufthansa would still charge the container fee. And since Lufthansa flights routed through Frankfurt, the European requirements for live animals would also have to be met and additional permits obtained. She decided to cancel the booking.

They talked over the long list of documents required for Smoke's trip, copying Terri on their emails. Among them were the transit permits required by the European Union, a health certificate from Iraq and another from Turkey, a U.S. transit permit and a veterinary certificate to be signed in Germany, a groom declaration for John, and a copy of his passport.

They compared notes on whether certain forms were absolutely required or substitutions could be made. Müge pressed

Paul for a health certificate from Turkey for travel to Europe or the United States. Paul didn't have that. But when Terri returned to her hotel that afternoon and caught up with the email chain, she assured them she had gotten the document. "It is at the Turkish Ministry of Ag," she emailed Paul and Müge. "Will try and get a copy today."

In the wooded hills north of Omaha John stood outside Lisa Roskens's well-appointed stables. An Exiss stock trailer had been hooked up to a red Silverado 2500 pickup truck. Lisa was loaning him the truck and trailer to haul Smoke home once he and the donkey landed in New York. John circled the rig, staring at it and marveling. The gooseneck trailer was sixteen feet long— easily large enough to carry four horses. All he had to carry was one short, two-hundred-pound donkey. It was like borrowing a bus to pick up a toddler. Not that he was complaining—he was grateful for Lisa's generosity.

It was about 5:30 p.m. on Wednesday, and the sun was still relatively high in the spring sky over Omaha's version of horse country, in the rolling hills north of the city. John was packed and ready to hit the road. As the day had progressed, he had grown increasingly anxious about how much time it would take to drive the truck and trailer halfway across the country, and he wasn't about to miss his Saturday flight. He was leaving tonight.

Lisa's stable manager, Dot, had the truck ready to go with a full tank of gas. She threw a bale of hay in the back, and John headed out.

As he crossed Iowa on Interstate 80, John's mind churned, thinking about all the coordination still needed to get Smoke home. He called Donita from the road and again talked over exactly what the lab needed and what would be done when the blood arrived. He was impressed with this government employee from Iowa, who was so willing to go out of her way to help him. She explained that the typical turnaround time for most of the tests Smoke needed was three to four working days. And normally such tests are run only on weekdays. But Donita was petitioning to see if the director's office would expedite testing for Smoke. She asked John to let her know when he arrived in Turkey so she could alert the testing team.

Farther down the highway John's cell phone rang. It was Brad Mulcahy, a human-interest producer with the television show *Jimmy Kimmel Live*. Mulcahy had heard about Smoke's story from a friend of a friend of John's. He wanted to know whether John would be willing to take the donkey to Los Angeles for a taping. John was flattered. But first he had to get Smoke across an ocean.

Thursday brought hopeful news. Terri emailed to say that after trips to two veterinarians, Smoke was at long last getting his blood drawn. And Donita checked in from Ames: her bosses had signed off on weekend testing. Just think, the National Veterinary Services Laboratories staff was on standby to test the blood of a humble stray from Iraq. This humble stray was still newsworthy, too. Owen Thomas, a deputy editor with the *Christian Science Monitor*, had been exchanging emails with John. Thomas had seen a recent story on Smoke in a New Zealand publication and wanted to update *Monitor* readers about Smoke's journey to America. John arranged to send along photos and provide information for a story.

John arrived in Fredericksburg on Friday, as scheduled, and dropped off the truck and trailer with his friends Craig and Gena Pirtle. Craig would drive him into Washington the next day to catch a train north and would store the rig on his acreage until John was back in the country.

In Istanbul Terri was frustrated. She had collected the blood serum from the Turkish vet that morning. But after requesting a FedEx pickup, she waited and waited for the driver to arrive. By the time he finally showed up, it was late in the day—so late that it was now impossible to deliver the serum to the lab in Ames before Monday. That dashed any lingering hopes for Terri's cross-your-fingers Tuesday-departure plan. Still, she put a positive spin on the developments for her blog followers: "This week has ended with another major accomplishment. After working for three days to get blood drawn from Smoke . . . we finally succeeded. When I handed the package with the serum in it to the FedEx driver I was ready to celebrate with another major hurdle overcome."

But other hurdles remained. Terri finally understood after talking with Lufthansa that additional paperwork was needed to satisfy German authorities. She realized she would need to return once more to the Ministry of Agriculture. She made plans to go back Monday, with Asli as her translator.

The weekend would bring a changing of the guard for Smoke: Ameer was leaving Istanbul on Saturday to return to Irbil. He could finally get back to his job at Reed, after being gone most of April with Terri. As Smoke's new friend left, an old friend was on the way. "Smoke is still doing fine," Terri wrote on her blog. "Little does he know he is in for a big surprise this weekend. John Folsom, Smoke's friend from Iraq, is arriving in Istanbul on Sunday. . . . I can't wait to witness that reunion."

On Saturday morning Craig drove John to Union Station in Washington DC to catch an Amtrak for New York. As the train crossed the Hackensack River in New Jersey heading northeast, John could make out the skyline of lower Manhattan. He was struck not only by the cityscape but by what was missing: the Twin Towers of the World Trade Center. It wasn't a surprise, of course, but the gaping hole reminded him of how the nation had been forever changed by the terrorist acts of 9/11.

After arriving at Penn Station, he transferred to the Long Island Rail Road and rode to the Jamaica station in Queens on Long Island. Once at John F. Kennedy International Airport he checked his orange Nautica bag and made his way to the departure lounge. He thought about his whirlwind trip and how, less than a week earlier, he had had no notion of a trip to Istanbul. Now he was looking forward to finally seeing Smoke, after two years' separation, and excited about visiting this storied city. He loved to explore new places and regretted only that he couldn't take his family along.

John unzipped his well-traveled leather business case. He called it his "Jump CP," military jargon for a commander's mobile command post. All he needed was an electrical outlet and Internet connectivity, and he could work from anywhere. He pulled out his laptop to catch up on email and read the latest news. He had also packed a copy of *The Korean War*, by Donald Knox, and the Bible he never traveled without. A friend from flight training had given him the Bible in 1984. Its worn leather cover was a testament to his travels to four continents and during twice that many deployments.

Hanging from the bag was another special possession: a hamsa key chain. This hand-shaped amulet, popular in both Islamic and Jewish cultures, had been given to him years earlier by Rachel Lapan, the mother of his good friend Irit Ehrlich. The hamsa is inscribed with a prayer that beseeches God to protect the traveler from evil. Israeli-born Rachel had made John promise he would never travel without it. John is no more superstitious than the next helicopter pilot. The way he figured it, carrying the hamsa couldn't hurt.

John thumbed through his brand-new passport, its empty pages waiting to be stamped in foreign lands. He thought about the coming adventure and mused about trips he had already taken or wanted to take someday. The Lufthansa Airbus 340 took off at 6:11 p.m. He whiled away some time by studying a moving map that tracked the plane's path. As darkness settled in over the Atlantic, he thought about what might lie ahead and then dropped off to sleep.

After a short layover and change of planes in Munich John landed at Ataturk International Airport about noon Sunday, Istanbul time. He quickly cleared customs, exchanged some dollars for Turkish lira, and caught a taxi to the Günes Hotel, where Terri had booked him a room.

The Günes was a disappointment. It was clean and respectable, and the staff was nice and quite accommodating. But the hotel smelled of stale cigarettes and disinfectant, and the décor had a 1960s feel. Terri had told him it was four miles from the airport, but that hadn't meant much to John at the time. Situated in an ordinary, commercial-residential section of the city, the Günes was miles from the tourist center, where he had assumed he would stay—the Sultanahmet area was in the heart of the city's shopping district and within easy walking distance to famous landmarks such as Hagia Sophia and the Blue Mosque.

He found an email from Terri waiting when he settled in to his small second-floor room. "I am so glad you finally made it to Istanbul. It will be great to be a part of your reunion with Smoke and to work together to finally get you and Smoke on a plane to the States," she wrote, providing directions to meet her at a Starbucks the next morning. "Call if you need anything. Looking forward to finally meeting you."

He was disappointed Terri hadn't offered to meet him at the airport. He had hoped she would show him around the city or at least meet for dinner. Instead he dropped off his gear and headed out on his own. Rather than talking to Terri over kebabs at a local eatery and catching up on donkey developments, he ate alone at a nearby Burger King.

He returned to the Günes and spent the evening scouring the Internet for news and sending emails home. There was no television in the room. The quiet was broken at intervals by the muezzin's call to prayer from the mosque just up the street. Muslims answer five calls to prayer each day: at predawn, midday, afternoon, sunset, and night. It was 4:53 p.m. when John heard the afternoon prayer call from the nearby İnce Minareli Cami. In quick succession other muezzin issued their calls from other mosques in other neighborhoods. The calls were nearly in sync, but not quite, each beginning a moment or two before or after another. The calls rippled across the city, giving the effect of a continuous echo. To the Presbyterian from Nebraska it had a fascinating effect. He heard the call again at 8:01 p.m. and at 9:40 p.m., before turning in for the night.

Early Monday he walked downstairs for breakfast and learned that the world had changed a bit more overnight. The lobby television was tuned to CNN, and the anchors and commentators were busy with wall-to-wall coverage: President Barack Obama had just announced that a special unit had killed Osama bin Laden in a fortified residence in Pakistan. The news didn't surprise John. The U.S. military had been looking for the al Qaeda leader for nearly ten years, so it was only a matter of time until they found him.

As John watched the developments, he reflected on how fitting it was that he was here. Nothing happens in isolation, he thought. Here he was, watching the news of Osama bin Laden's death from Istanbul. Why was he in Istanbul? To retrieve a donkey he had befriended in Iraq. Why had he been in Iraq? Because the United States had invaded in response to the al Qaeda attacks of 9/11. Who was the leader of al Qaeda? Osama bin Laden. So in a roundabout way he was in Istanbul because of bin Laden. And now bin Laden was dead.

John's Marine Corps training kicked in. He considered his potential vulnerability as an American in a Muslim city, fresh after the attack in Pakistan. As one small protective step he decided his razor would stay packed up after today. Beards and mustaches were the norm in this part of the world, and a clean-shaven man was sure to stand out. And he would definitely be on alert to any danger as he moved around the city. In some ways, he decided, perhaps he was better off at the Günes Hotel, after all, rather than being in a typical tourist area.

After breakfast John walked to the nearby Merter Metro train platform and followed Terri's instructions. He took the Metro as far as Zeytinburnu. There he caught the Kabatas tram to the city center. He was impressed with the tram, which travels on a track running down the center of the city's main thoroughfares. The twenty-first-century technology looked out of place as it snaked slowly through the narrow, crowded streets, past the nineteenth-century architecture of the old Ottoman Empire. The tram had standing room only on this workday morning. He got off at Sultanahmet and walked to the Starbucks near the Faros Hotel.

Terri was there as promised. But they didn't have a substantial meeting or a satisfactory one, from John's perspective. He had expected her to begin handing off all her information to him so she could head back to Irbil and her dog rescues. That was the urgent appeal that had brought him here and what she had told him as recently as Sunday. But rather than share information, Terri kept a firm hold on it—literally. She carried a raft of paperwork and documents that were obviously related to Smoke but kept it clutched against her chest much of the time. It began to sink in that this was Terri's show, and he was simply along for the ride.

He had assumed from her Sunday email that they would start the day by visiting Smoke, but Terri told him that was impossible because Smoke was staying way out in the country. She said it would cost too much and take too long to get there. Instead, she told John, they needed to visit BGD, the animal shelter where Asli worked. Terri and John made their way to a ferry terminal on the south shore of the famous Golden Horn in the Eminönü district, the center of the ancient city of Constantinople. The ferries ran every twenty minutes, providing an inexpensive way to travel from the European side of Istanbul to the Asian side. John enjoyed the boat ride and soaked in the panoramic, unobstructed view of the city. He spotted a glimpse of what he thought must be the famous Hagia Sophia. Over the centuries this beautiful, ancient structure had served, in turn, as an Eastern Orthodox cathedral, a Roman Catholic cathedral, and a mosque, before becoming a museum in 1935.

They spent a few hours at the shelter for some reason not made clear to John. Afterward Terri and Asli headed out to visit the Ministry of Agriculture to get a Turkish health certificate. They didn't invite John to go along. Instead he roamed around the city by himself for an hour or two, sightseeing before returning to the Günes Hotel. Terri was now telling him Smoke could leave "on or about May 6." But he wasn't sure whose approval was still needed. The Turkish agricultural officials? The Germans? Terri didn't fill him in. He sent Paul Weygand a quick note.

To: Paul Weygand
From: John Folsom
Sent: Mon, 2 May 2011
Subject:

Paul . . .

Do you know what is going on?
 I don't have a warm and fuzzy feeling.

Thanks

John

Terri wasn't sharing much, and what she could have shared was just another dose of ice-cold reality. She had hit yet another roadblock during the visit to the Ministry of Agriculture. The ministry official she and Asli met with informed them he didn't need to sign the Turkish health certificate because Smoke wasn't from Turkey—he was merely in transit. After they pressed the official, he consulted with higher-ups. In the end the Turks concluded that, yes, they could sign the health certificate. But they doubted the Germans would accept it because Smoke had originated in Iraq. And without proper paperwork the Germans wouldn't let Smoke into Frankfurt.

That left Terri staring two looming deadlines in the face. The first involved Smoke's Iraqi health certificate. Ahmed had gotten it April 18, the day before he left Irbil to drive the donkey to Istanbul. The certificate was valid for fifteen days, meaning it would expire on May 3. The next day. Then there was Smoke's Turkish transit permit. Customs officials at the airport had eventually agreed to let Smoke remain in Turkey for fifteen days. If he lingered beyond that, then Terri and Safak Asparuk, the helpful security manager for MNG Airlines, would be fined. That clock would run out on May 7—Saturday.

All that explained why Terri was so insistent on getting Smoke on a flight that week. Now, after getting the latest bad news about the Turkish paperwork, she considered her options and decided it was time to play the diplomatic card. She sent an SOS to Lt.

Col. Lloyd Freeman in Ankara. Her lengthy email brought the attaché up to speed on all her difficulties and asked for his help.

This was the news Freeman had been dreading—but half expecting to hear—ever since the logjam had been cleared at Silopi: Smoke was stranded again. He realized that the biggest hang-up at this point was satisfying German travel requirements. He promised Terri he would explore options with Lufthansa and touch base with the contacts he had in Germany.

The team in Turkey woke up Tuesday to the best news it had heard in a while: Smoke was officially disease free. FedEx had delivered the serum to the National Veterinary Services Laboratories in Ames by midmorning Monday, as promised. Thanks to Donita's advocacy and the blessings of the laboratory's top brass, the lab team treated the job with high priority, expediting tests that typically took three to four working days to complete. Instead the lab turned around all four tests within twenty-four hours. By the end of Monday Dr. David Kinker, head of the serology department, had sent the preliminary results of three of the tests to Mersant International. But the news from Iowa was tempered by the looming deadlines on the key documents. Terri laid out the issues in a morning email to Müge, copying John and Paul.

"It was great to wake up to the news that Smoke's blood test came back negative. This certainly confirms that our donkey is in good health," Terri wrote. "So, how do we move forward to satisfy the Turkish and German officials?" She explained what she had learned from the Ministry of Agriculture and noted that Smoke's Iraqi health certificate and Turkish transit permit were both on the verge of expiring.

"In order to get a new health certificate from Iraq the vet technically has to see Smoke and we obviously are not taking him back to Iraq. Plus, we could not even get him into Iraq at this point, I don't think, without a valid health certificate," Terri told Müge. "It is Lufthansa and the German officials we have to satisfy at this point. With your experience and contacts at

Lufthansa do you have any idea how we can do this given these unique circumstances?"

She also asked Müge for clarity about just when Smoke had a flight reservation. Terri thought he was leaving May 6, Friday. But John had told her Monday night that according to Müge the flight was scheduled for May 7, Saturday, which Terri had now explained was the last day Smoke could get out of Turkey without heavy fines being imposed. But Paul had told John that next Thursday, May 12, was more likely. "We really need to get this clarified and keep all information going through me as I am the coordinating person for the entire operation," Terri wrote. "So, can you clarify whether Smoke does have a reservation and when it is? I just want to get us all back on the same page."

In a follow-up email to the group, Müge brushed past the scheduling questions and focused on clarifying exactly what paperwork was needed to satisfy the Germans. "With Lufthansa, this transit permit is a must along with health certificate as they stop over in Germany," she wrote in her broken English. "For the moment I am thinking very hard what can be done. . . . Do you think you can get this transit form of Lufthansa from Iraq now?"

The emails made clear the hard reality confronting the group: deadlines were looming, the Germans were demanding the proper paperwork, and the Turks weren't budging. Terri blamed everyone in sight.

> To: John Folsom
> From: Terri Crisp
> Date: Tue, 3 May 2011
> Subject: Flight
>
> Hi John:
>
> Well, things are not going well. I am fed up with the incompetence of the officials here. I have tried my hardest to make this work but we are spinning our wheels and getting nowhere. It's one step forward and 10 backwards. I don't know what to tell you. Now I am

being told that because Smoke has no health certificate
he is stuck. I have spent all morning trying to sort
things out and come up with new solutions and each
time I do, I hit another roadblock. Now there are new
problems with getting the stall here from Frankfurt.
I feel like I am dealing with people who stepped into
a new job and have had no training. It is frustrating
beyond belief. And, I am tired of getting information
through interpretation and having to explain the same
things over and over again. I am now also being told by
Muge that Smoke has to go back to the airport. There
are no facilities there to house a donkey or a horse. I
can't have Smoke tied up in a parking lot for days. This
is why I wanted you not to fly here until we were 100%
sure we had everything completed. I am going to talk
to my boss when he gets in this morning to see what he
recommends.

Humanely,

Terri Crisp

John was incredulous that she was now complaining that he
had traveled too soon, after she had urged him to keep his Saturday flight. "Tuesday will probably be too late," he remembered
her telling him while he was still back in Omaha. "We can do
this. Let's meet and put our heads together," John urged her.

"You and I cannot make it happen," she fumed in a follow-up
email. "It is in the hands of government officials who don't have
a clue what they are doing which is really alarming! My fear is
we will not get Smoke to the U.S. and so many people are waiting for that to happen. I am also facing some serious fines and
possible jail time now for not getting Smoke out of here within
the time customs allotted. . . . This has become a very, very
expensive endeavor that SPCA International just can't afford and
it may cost me my job."

So far she had spent more than five thousand dollars just to get

Smoke from Irbil to Istanbul. She had been racking up roughly hundreds of dollars a day plus incidentals since arriving in Istanbul three weeks earlier. And the big transportation costs were yet to come—the overseas cargo flight would cost thousands.

But Smoke's defenders weren't about to wave the white flag. What followed was a multinational, transatlantic brainstorming session. Seemingly under attack by an army of bureaucrats, the allies began firing emails back and forth, in a disjointed, rapid-fire assault. Ready at their battle positions on the right flank:

—John, in his room at the Günes

—Terri, across town at the Acropol Suites and Spa

—Müge, at her Ekiptrans Ltd. office, across the Golden Horn, to the north of the two Americans

—Freeman, from the U.S. embassy in Ankara

And on the left flank:

—Paul, at his Mersant International office in Long Island, New York

—JD Winston, at spcai headquarters in Manhattan

It was reminiscent of a Marine Corps unit under attack by an overwhelming enemy. In a last-ditch effort to keep from being overrun, the warriors sent their ammo flying everywhere.

Paul to Müge, Terri, and John: "Have the Turkish authorities signed any health certificate? We need a U.S. health certificate. . . . I can speak to my German agent but I think they will insist on a transit certificate."

Müge to Terri, Paul, and John: "No good news unfortunately. Turkish vet didn't sign the docs that Lufthansa required as it's entered in Turkey as transit. Also Lufthansa informed us yesterday saying that Germany has no stall available to be sent to Istanbul before the 6th of May. So we had neither stall, nor transit health certificate for Germany."

John to Terri: "Saw the latest email from Müge. Question: If the hang-up is that this is a transit issue, could you persuade someone at the Ministry of Ag to show Turkey as the country of origin? Just an idea."

Terri to John: "We are getting the Iraqis to complete the form. It is in the works now. Ameer is coordinating it."

John to Freeman, Terri, and Paul: "We can solve this problem by getting the Turkish government to recognize Smoke as a citizen. Problem solved."

Freeman to John, Terri, and Paul: "The issue is Lufthansa needs a health certificate. I'm sure we can pay for a Turkish vet to examine Smoke and certify him. I'm not in Istanbul. Can we try this?"

John to Freeman, Terri, and Paul: "Lloyd . . . The Iraq health certificate expires today. . . . If it expired after the stall arrived here, there would be no problem. It's a date thing. One way to solve this is to get a local vet to certify Smoke and make Turkey the country of origin and not Iraq. Then, the Iraq health certificate is a non-issue. Import Smoke into Turkey, export him to the States. That's it in a nut shell."

Terri to John, Freeman, and Paul: "This is not possible as Smoke is in the customs system as a transit animal and they have copies of all his paperwork. Presenting a new health certificate from Turkey to customs at the time of Smoke's departure would not be valid for that reason. There is not a simple solution."

John to Terri, Freeman, and Paul: "It can be changed. It only takes a government official to do it. Smoke has attracted enough worldwide interest that someone in Ankara can make that call. We're up against an arbitrary date. If that document had a date stamp of 31 May 2011 this would not be an issue."

Freeman to John, Terri, and Paul: "Hold on . . . we are talking to Lufthansa."

John to Freeman: "Smoke needs to become a citizen of Turkey. Game, set, match."

Freeman to John: "I inquired into that. It's possible . . . but will take five weeks."

John to Freeman: "What I need is a Marine KC-130 with a couple of young captains up for an adventure at the controls."

Freeman to John: "We are working with the German Embassy now . . . will let you know what we find out."

John to Freeman: "Disregard. We may have a solution. I will send the email to you once I have it. BLUF [bottom line up front]: the Germans will allow Smoke to transit if he was a military mascot. Can you put that on letterhead without jeopardizing your career???"

Freeman to John: "Hell yeah I can."

John to Freeman: "You da man, Man!"

Freeman to John: "Do I need to draft a letter? . . . Tell me what to do."

John to Freeman: "I sent you something from Lufthansa."

Freeman to John: "Is Terri on board?"

John to Freeman: "Terri will be fine. I would like you to sign it. It will be something that goes with all the other memorabilia."

Suddenly, Paul called a cease-fire. He had heard from his German agent, Heike Schmitz. She worked for Peden Bloodstock, a horse transportation company, in Mülheim an der Ruhr, in northwest Germany.

> To: Paul Weygand
> From: Heike Schmitz
> Date: Tuesday, May 03, 2011
> Subject: Donkey from Iraq in transit through FRA
>
> Good news! We will get a transit permit through FRA [Frankfurt] for that donkey. Just couldn't believe it.
>
> I must apply for a special transit permit, in writing of course.
>
> Send the vet all details, please send me whatever you have got so far, blood tests, identification, health certificates etc., full info about the donkey, name, age, sex, etc.
>
> We must clearly state on all paperwork that this is a mascot of the Army as only in this case we will get the permit.

Usually only the importation of registered horses from Turkey is allowed.

Need to give the exact name etc. of the battalion or how you call it. Final destination in the USA etc.

Please see what you can send me and I will get it started . . .

Mit freundlichen Grüßen,

Kind regards,

Heike Schmitz

This development confirmed John's confidence in Paul—and underscored his growing uneasiness about Terri. The head USDA vet in New York had told John there was no one better in the business than Paul. Terri clearly wasn't a fan and considered Paul arrogant and pushy, but John trusted Paul, who provided results. John was still bewildered about why Terri hadn't had Smoke's blood drawn for testing much earlier. If the blood tests had been done in a timely manner, the expiration date on an Iraqi health certificate would have been a nonissue.

Yet he realized that he needed both Terri and Paul to succeed. The last thing he wanted was to have Terri fired, leaving him with a stranded donkey. He sent a note to her boss, expressing confidence he was far from feeling. "JD . . . Terri has done a tremendous job on this mission. She deserves a great deal of credit. This had to be her toughest and most grueling assignment. But, she never gave up," he wrote. "This was tremendously expensive, but the American people love the story and your work to make Smoke's coming to America a reality. They will no doubt show their appreciation to SPCAI for their generosity. . . . It's a great story and millions are watching."

The promise of a permit from the Germans was a huge accomplishment. But Paul warned everyone they couldn't relax yet. The next step was getting the Turkish government to sign off on a demand by the Americans: the USDA required an import health certificate before Smoke could enter the country. "MUST have the Turkish authorities sign the attached U.S. import health certificate for the time he has resided in Turkey," Paul emailed.

John and Terri arranged to meet at the Starbucks at 10 a.m. Wednesday and then tackle the Ministry of Agriculture to get this all-important certificate signed. Asli couldn't go along to interpret this time, although she was available by phone if needed. John was determined to succeed. "I do not intend to leave Turkey without Smoke," he emailed Terri. "We did not come all the way here to fail. There are millions of people who are interested in what we are doing and I have no intention of telling them that we failed."

On Wednesday morning they met at the coffee shop, as planned, and headed to the Ministry of Agriculture. Terri and John walked down the hall to a small office and were greeted by a heavyset man with a mustache.

Terri explained what she needed and handed the official the simple one-page form to sign and stamp. The form contained seven blanks to fill in with Smoke's vital statistics, such as his name, species, sex, date of birth, and country of origin. The official needed to certify when Smoke had arrived in Turkey, that he had received a clean bill of health from a veterinarian, and that he hadn't been vaccinated during the fourteen days prior to export. He further needed to verify that Smoke had, "insofar as can be determined, not been on a premises where African horse sickness, dourine, glanders, surra, epizootic lymphangitis, ulcerative lymphangitis, equine piroplasmosis, Venezuelan equine encephalomyelitis (VEE), equine infectious anemia (EIA), contagious equine metritis or vesicular stomatitis has occurred during the sixty (60) days preceding export to the Unites States." His signature would also confirm that Smoke carried no ectoparasites and hadn't been "in a country where CEM is known to exist, or had any contact, breeding or otherwise with horses from such a country, during the twelve months preceding exportation."

The official looked over the form and then responded calmly that he would not sign it. Terri kept pressing him, rather forcefully, it seemed to John, telling the official she needed to get the form signed. He kept declining. "It is not in my computer," he told her repeatedly, in very precise English.

The more insistent the American was, the more passive the Turk became. John watched the two and wondered why Terri hadn't learned from her experience at the border that bullying tactics didn't work on Turkish bureaucrats. He hadn't been involved in the many meetings Terri had since arriving in Istanbul and couldn't properly appreciate how thin her patience was running by now. But he thought back to his own experiences over the years with officials in Islamic cultures—Indonesia, Malaysia, Egypt, and Iraq. He knew it didn't pay to get pushy. When U.S. military personnel pressed their Iraqi counterparts too hard, for example, the Iraqis shut down, clammed up, and refused to budge. He was pretty sure that an assertive American woman who did not appear to understand this culture was not going to get anywhere.

John thought of all the meetings he used to have at East Camp Habbaniyah. Brig. Gen. Ali Haider Abdul Hameed, who commanded the Iraqi Army unit there, would always begin a meeting with a cup of chai and a smoke. Maj. Daniel Barnard, the U.S. Army liaison officer who had helped Terri navigate the Turkish border for Smoke at Silopi, also recognized the importance of respecting customs. He spent long hours in meetings with the Turkish border officials. He knew it was important to Turks to take the time to relax, drink a cup of tea, and observe other cultural niceties before launching into serious discussions.

John also remembered how he and Isaam had negotiated with the sheik for the return of Smoke. After the sheik asked for thirty thousand dollars, they backed away rather than pressing the issue. When Isaam eventually reengaged the sheik, he did so in an offhand manner, suggesting an alternative solution rather than making demands.

Now, as John watched the diplomatic standoff with the agricultural official, it was clear to him that Terri didn't understand the culture. He thought he might be able to help. If he explained that Smoke was a military mascot and what Smoke meant to the Marines, perhaps he could work on the official's sympathy. He began to speak—but Terri quickly checked him with an upraised hand. John knew that in the Islamic culture women simply didn't treat men like that. By cutting him off, she was embarrassing him in front of this Turkish official. The meeting continued for a time but ended with nothing accomplished. "It is not in my computer" were the last words they heard as they left.

John was furious. He walked ahead of Terri, not speaking, as they retreated to a nearby café. By now he had lost all confidence. He strode past the café, fuming, and turned into a nearby alley. He paced for a few minutes, his mind racing as he wondered how everything had gotten out of control. He had spent a lot of money coming to Istanbul, and they weren't getting anywhere, he thought. With time running out, he desperately wanted to find some way he could help.

Then he thought about Heike Schmitz.

12.

Now Boarding for Frankfurt

John stood in an alley in the middle of Istanbul, frustration fueling his anger. He saw all the work and worry he had poured into this mission over the past nine months going to waste, unless some way could be found to cut through the seemingly unending bureaucratic tangle. One unexpected problem after another kept cropping up—problems that, as far as he was concerned, wouldn't have been problems at all had Paul Weygand been hired at the outset.

Now John felt driven to do something—anything—to help get Smoke out of Turkey by Saturday, whether Terri wanted his assistance or not. Perhaps Heike Schmitz could help. After all, the need to satisfy the Germans' requirements was now front and center. And Heike was Paul's German agent for transporting horses. Besides, she had been helpful already. He decided he needed to talk to Heike.

He pulled out his phone, where he had stored contact information for everyone involved with Smoke's journey. He scrolled down to Schmitz and punched in the number. He was familiar with Germans from a sixteen-month deployment in Stuttgart, early in the Iraq War. He admired their tendency to be methodical and precise but knew they were sticklers for rules. He also considered Germans to be great animal lovers—it was not uncommon to see them take their dogs along on public transportation or even into restaurants. John hoped to play to Heike's sympathy. He didn't realize Heike had just deflected another request to work on Smoke's problems. Müge had notified her that morning that the Turkish veterinarian had refused to sign the document Lufthansa needed.

Heike's employer, Peden Bloodstock, handled horse transportation and logistics for the world's traveling equine elite. Every day was a busy day for Peden Bloodstock, and this had been a particularly hectic day. "Thanks for your call and email," Heike had written back to Müge. "I will deal with this shipment later today as I am extremely busy with another shipment right now and need to get it done as horses arrive tomorrow. Thanks for your patience."

Now here she was, fielding another plea to help this donkey. Once John had Heike on the phone, he launched into the story of Smoke and the importance of speed in helping him leave Turkey. The conversation was one-sided: all John's. He told her tales of Smoke in Iraq, of how the donkey helped military families connect during war, of how Smoke was a battle buddy for the troops. He tried to explain why he was so determined to get the donkey to the United States.

John paced back and forth in the alley as he talked on and on. He felt like a defense attorney, delivering a summation to the jury in a murder trial. After a while he decided he had found not a sympathetic ear but simply another disinterested party, bound by bureaucratic rules. But that was far from the case.

When Heike had first heard about Smoke's story from Paul, she'd had two thoughts. Thought one: "Great story!" Thought two: "It will never be possible to get the sweet little thing through Europe!"

Now, with John on the phone describing Smoke's life and problems in more detail—well, her two thoughts didn't change. She loved the story of the donkey and what John was trying to do. But she knew that the odds of shipping Smoke through Europe were slim. Heike had been in the horse-transportation business for nearly forty years and had worked with Paul on U.S. shipments for almost as long. She had landed in this line of work almost by accident. She was a young foreign-language correspondent in Dusseldorf in 1972, but with a newborn daughter she was looking for a job closer to her hometown of Oberhausen. One opened up with a company that shipped horses, and she took it. Since then she had become an expert on government rules for equine transportation. She was well aware of the strict European Union rules and regulations for importing animals. And an unregistered Iraqi donkey traveling from Turkey was a big red flag.

Heike could tell how desperate John was, but she firmly explained what he already knew: If Smoke's paperwork was not in order, a layover in Germany—or anywhere else in the European Union—was *verboten*.

"But," John blurted out in desperation, "Smoke has his own Facebook page!"

There was a pause on the other end of the line. "Smoke has his own Facebook page?" Heike asked, incredulously.

"Yes! You can look it up!"

More silence as Heike searched the Internet. "Smoke has his own Facebook page!" she told him excitedly.

Heike's demeanor transformed. Here she was, soaking in the Facebook page. Studying Smoke's photographs. Reading his fan comments. Discovering he had hundreds of followers. Seeing links to news articles about John and Smoke. This obviously was no ordinary donkey—he was famous! All of a sudden Heike made time for Smoke.

She placed a call to Dr. Andrea Göbel, the border inspection veterinarian at the Frankfurt airport. Dr. Göbel had nearly twenty years of experience as a state veterinarian at the airport and knew the work inside and out. The two had a long discussion, in which Heike reviewed everything she knew about Smoke, including his paperwork problems. Dr. Göbel was sympathetic to Smoke's dilemma and asked to see all the documents Heike could provide about him. Heike followed up with an email to the veterinarian, attaching the documents and formally requesting a special transit permit.

"He is the mascot of U.S. Army," she wrote, confusing the Marine Corps with the Army. "You can even find Smoke the Donkey on Facebook including various reports about him and his journey until now. . . . Smoke and Colonel Folsom are now in Istanbul. . . . Both are waiting desperately to be able to fly to the USA . . . .

"Lufthansa requests a European Union health certificate which must be issued by the Turkish authorities, but the Turkish authorities refuse to do so.

"All parties concerned and involved would be extremely grateful if you would agree to a special exception and issue a special transit permit for the little donkey, please."

She emailed John to let him know she had talked to the veterinarian and asked if he could get a letter from the U.S. embassy about Smoke. "I'm Smoke's fan on Facebook now of course," she wrote.

She soon sent an update. "Seems I'm on a good way. I referred the Facebook site to the airport vet."

Like Heike, Göbel was starstruck. Smoke quickly gained another friend. "I'm trying to get Smoke through the European Union!" she posted on Facebook.

"Peden Bloodstock is looking forward to receive your approval & permit. Thanks a mil!" Heike replied.

"Border Inspection Post Frankfurt Airport tries its best to get Smoke through the European Union," the doctor posted a minute later.

When Heike saw the posts, she smiled. She was confident Smoke would get his special permit.

On Wednesday morning in Turkey's capital Freeman got to work, writing the requested letter under an embassy seal.

> Embassy of the United States of America
> Defense Attaché Office
> Ankara, Turkey
> 4 May 2011
>
> To Whom It May Concern
> Subj: Designation of Smoke the Donkey as Official Mascot to Camp Commandant, 1st Marine Logistics Group, Camp Al-Taqaddum, Iraq

1. In August of 2008, a donkey was found by a group of Marines near the Al-Taqaddum Iraqi Military Base outside of Baghdad, Iraq. The Marines retrieved the donkey, cared for it, and subsequently adopted the animal as their mascot and named him Smoke.

2. Col John Folsom, USMC, was the Camp Commandant for 1st Marine Logistics Group based at Al-Taqaddum and designated Smoke as an official mascot of the base in 2008. He has led an effort over the past few months to bring Smoke back to the United States to serve as a therapy animal for the disabled. His efforts have been supported by the Society for the Prevention of Cruelty to Animals [International] and he and the [SPCAI] have received international recognition for their humane efforts to bring Smoke to the United States. [SPCAI] has worked tirelessly over the past few years to bring hundreds of working animals from Iraq back to the United States as part of their efforts to provide humane care for animals that had served with the U.S. military during Operation Iraqi Freedom.

3. Any assistance you can provide in helping to transport Smoke to the United States would be greatly appreciated. The point of contact at the U.S. Embassy in Turkey is Lt Col Lloyd Freeman, U.S. Marine Attaché.

Lloyd D. Freeman
Lt Col USMC
Marine Attaché

The letter was forwarded to Heike—whose sharp eye soon spotted a problem.

"There must be a mistake somewhere," she emailed. "In the letter it says Smoke the Donkey was found in 2008 but in all health certs his date of birth says 2009." Terri, it turned out, had gotten Smoke's birth date mixed up from the beginning on the paperwork she obtained in Iraq and Turkey.

"I hope we haven't got another problem on our hands," Paul replied. "Perhaps the letter could be brought into agreement with the date of birth on the sole existing health certificate we have seen? I think the Germans would be disinclined to sign a permit if there is a discrepancy in the age of the animal."

Late in the day Heike reported in again. "Herewith attached the transit permit via Frankfurt/Airport for Smoke the Donkey—I will send you a translation for the special requirements in a while but didn't want to wait too long to give you these good news." She attached an email from Dr. Göbel. It was in German, but the message was perfectly clear to the Americans. Even without a signature from the Turks on a health certificate, even with conflicting birth dates for Smoke, the transit permit had been granted.

"Now we're cooking with gas . . . let's get Smoke airborne," Freeman wrote.

"Ditto!" Terri chimed in.

It was Paul who put a damper on the festivities. Despite obtaining the special transit permit from the European Union, there was still the matter of that nagging requirement by the U.S. government: a valid health certificate, signed by Turkish authorities. "We still need to try to get the health certificate signed," he reminded everyone. "If the Turks absolutely won't, then we have to go to NCIE [the U.S. National Center for Import and Export] or higher and plead our case. I don't see this as insurmountable but it would ease things tremendously if we have it."

Paul sent a revised health certificate form, with a birth date that conformed to the other paperwork. He changed the information to state that Turkey was the country of export, not the country of origin. Terri sent Freeman the contact information for the Turkish agricultural official she had been dealing with. Freeman, in turn, sent a note asking his staff to work with the ministry. "I hope we can close this out soon," he wrote. "I don't want Smoke moving into Park Vadi Evleri," he joked, referring to his own high-rise apartment building in Ankara.

But his request hit a dead end. "The Turkish side said there is nothing they can do, so any new paperwork will have to come from Iraqi authorities," agricultural attaché staffer Rachel Nelson told him.

"Turkey," Freeman informed John and Terri, "will not be signing anything."

By then it was Wednesday evening. John was in his room at the Günes. Despite the day's progress he wondered whether they would ever get Smoke out of Turkey. Terri sent him an email, trying to make up after the disastrous visit to the Ministry of Agriculture.

To: John Folsom
From: Terri Crisp
Date: Wed, 4 May 2011
Subject: Update

Hi John:

Did you make it back ok? Sorry for another challenging day. I did talk to Muge and she said that things are coming together. She is feeling optimistic. The permit from Germany is a very big step forward. She also said there is still a good possibility Smoke could fly on Saturday. The stall has been ordered so let's hope it arrives tomorrow or Friday.

Asli can take us to see Smoke tomorrow. So, let's see where things are first thing in the morning. Why don't I call you at 8?

Hang in there. Smoke is so worth the effort!

Humanely,

Terri Crisp

A couple of hours later she emailed again. This time she caught him entirely off guard. He stared at the brief message in astonishment.

To: John Folsom
From: Terri Crisp
Date: Wed, 4 May 2011
Subject: Flight

Hi John:

I got someone to cover the missions in Iraq so I can fly back to the U.S. with Smoke. If things do not work out on Saturday I can fly home with him hopefully on Tuesday.

Humanely,

Terri Crisp

The only reason John was in Istanbul was to escort the donkey to New York because Terri had dogs and cats stacking up in Irbil. Now she was free? He had really been looking forward to being reunited with Smoke and to the adventure of making a transatlantic flight as the donkey's groom. But Terri was pulling the Turkish rug out from under him.

Disappointment mixed with other emotions: John worried about being away from home and work for so long. He felt guilty about all the money he was spending. And he was stressed about keeping Lisa's borrowed horse trailer and truck for so much longer than intended. He suspected that Terri wanted a triumphant arrival at JFK Airport so that, after all the time and money she had spent on Smoke, she could present her boss with a "mission complete" moment.

He emailed back, pointing out that he couldn't exactly return home to Omaha anyway, since he had the truck and horse trailer parked on the East Coast. "Departing on Saturday does no good if he arrives at JFK on Wednesday. I still need to get him from USDA quarantine," John wrote.

Terri brushed past his concerns. "Ok, so when are you planning on leaving?" she replied. "I need to start working on getting the necessary paperwork completed so that I can fly with Smoke now."

This drawn-out business with Smoke was bothering Freeman. He sat at his desk at the U.S. embassy on Thursday morning, his brain churning. He had continued to update the embassy's country team about Smoke's progress—or lack of progress—as the stay in Istanbul stretched on. Interest in the little donkey remained high among embassy staff. There was even talk of throwing a "Wheels Up" party in his honor—standard fare in the State Department when a visiting VIP successfully departs. And Freeman was determined that this mission would be successful. He had found himself in many strange situations during his assignment to Turkey, and he had always found a solution to the problem at hand. With all his experience he prided himself on understanding how things worked in this country. He also had a deep knowledge of how bureaucracies operated.

Suddenly, something clicked. Maybe, the attaché thought to himself, just maybe they could use his knowledge of this Byzantine bureaucracy to their advantage as they tried to resolve the impasse over the import health certificate. He called Terri. "Am I right in thinking that all you need is a stamp on that document?" he asked her. "Is that right?"

"That's right," Terri agreed.

"Okay, then I know our path forward," he told her. "Go get the document stamped."

There was a pause as she digested what Freeman had said. Then the light bulb went on. This health certificate wasn't so much a requirement to get Smoke out of Turkey as it was to get Smoke into the United States. The Germans simply wanted to see a stamped, signed document, but the Turks wouldn't cooperate. Terri agreed to get a signature on the document and produce a stamp that looked official enough to pass muster. She contacted John to let him know what Freeman had suggested. She also informed him she wasn't able to arrange a visit to Smoke that day, after all, which further disappointed John.

"I'll hang here today, but I would like to see Smoke tomorrow," John told her. "Let me know if we can go."

He called Freeman himself to talk things over. He thought the stamp idea sounded resourceful. "After all, it's only a signature and a stamp," John said.

Freeman told him the important thing was to get Smoke to

the United States and stop battling with the Turkish bureaucrats. "Let's deal with our bureaucrats. They speak English," Freeman said.

At midday John packed his minimalist luggage and checked out of the Güneş. The room had been reserved only through Wednesday night, and the busy hotel couldn't accommodate him beyond then. He collected his orange Nautica bag and his leather "Jump CP" and took a taxi across town to the Arena Hotel.

He was impressed as he checked in with Farouk at the front desk. The quaint Arena was housed in a stately, three-story stone building that had been converted from an Ottoman mansion. The rooms were smaller than those at the Güneş but nicer, with polished wood floors and elegant tile baths. The hotel restaurant overlooked the famous Sultanahmet tourist district. The real bonus: he was a two-minute walk from the Blue Mosque, the Hagia Sophia, and other prominent attractions.

John settled into his room and then strolled around the city a bit. His usual pleasure in exploring a foreign city was dimmed by his disappointment at being replaced as Smoke's traveling companion. He hadn't felt like a full participant since arriving. In fact, he felt more like a potted plant than a partner with Terri. His feeling of being shut out had culminated in the terrible meeting at the Ministry of Agriculture. His disappointment at coming all this way—only to leave without Smoke—turned to anger. Still, he knew that without the unswerving commitment and support of SPCA International, Smoke would never have left Iraq. John wasn't one to back down from a fight but saw no purpose in arguing about the travel plan. The most important objective was getting Smoke to the United States. So he endeavored to set aside his anger and disappointment.

Friday was his last chance to see Smoke before leaving Turkey. He emailed Terri on Thursday evening, suggesting they meet at Starbucks at 9 a.m. and head out from there. But Terri was too busy on Friday, arranging for her travel credentials, notifying everyone that she was taking over from John as Smoke's travel companion, and writing a report for the home office.

"I also need to revise the budget since we are way over what was projected," she told John. "JD wired money to Müge yesterday. It was $18,000. This was not an expense that was originally figured into the budget because initially MNG Cargo and Air France were going to transport Smoke and they were going to do it for free.

"I feel much better though that Smoke is flying Lufthansa and that I will be with him. MNG Cargo and Air France never asked for someone to escort Smoke."

Under International Air Transport Association regulations, though, horses and other equine must almost always be accompanied on flights, regardless of the airline, unless an animal is transported in a wooden crate in the lower deck—a stressful and somewhat risky experience. Fortunately Smoke would travel on the main deck, in a special equine container, with a companion to supervise his safety and provide help as needed.

With the visit to Smoke off the table John spent the day exploring more of the city. He walked the few blocks to Divan Yolu. This major street through Old Istanbul was once part of the imperial route to Rome, as laid out by Constantinople. John toured the Blue Mosque and walked past street peddlers selling fragrant roasted chestnuts. He passed coffee shops and bakeries and shops selling Turkish delight, the famous Turkish candy. He marveled at the beautiful wool rugs displayed by other merchants and walked across the campus of Istanbul University.

The city was filled with European tourists, particularly Germans. John's beard worked beautifully to help disguise his nationality: people approached him twice to ask for directions—in Turkish. He found Istanbul as charming and beautiful as he had expected. But he was largely going through the motions. He couldn't get over his disappointment about returning to New York empty-handed and without a single visit to Smoke.

The next day he caught a Lufthansa flight to New York, arriving at JFK late Saturday afternoon. From there he retraced his steps to Fredericksburg, staying with Craig and Gena Pirtle as he awaited developments. Although everything appeared to be falling into place at last, he was still on edge, half expecting the plans to collapse again.

"Good luck on Tuesday," he had emailed Terri Friday night. "The latest I heard is to 'get him on the airplane!' from a number of people, including State. Many people all over the world are watching Smoke's progress. I'll be one of them. If you don't leave on Tuesday, I need to know. . . . At any rate, if you need to get back to Iraq and he has to stay, we will work on a backup plan. At least he's closer here than there. Smoke is NOT going back to Iraq."

Terri assured him she would deliver Smoke "safe and sound— one way or another. . . . No more steps backwards."

Freeman, who considered Terri determined but fairly helpless when it came to dealing with bureaucratic setbacks, finally told her to stop worrying about the Germans and about Lufthansa. "If you've got the stamps, if they're letting you on the plane, get on the plane and go. They're not going to send you back to Turkey," Freeman had told her. "If there's a problem in the States, we'll resolve it in the States."

Terri confided in John that she hadn't been able to get a copy of the import health certificate from the Turkish Ministry of Agriculture. "Paul was concerned that if there was something wrong with it, Smoke could get stuck in New York," she told John. "My response to him was that I would much rather have Smoke stuck in the U.S. than to spend any more time here in Turkey. Dealing with Americans would be so much easier!!!!!!!"

Monday brought a flurry of last-minute checks by Smoke's support crew.

"Terri," wrote Donita Eickholt, at the USDA lab in Ames. "Did you get a Health Certificate from Turkey?"

"Yes," came Terri's reply, despite what she had told John.

Donita forwarded the exchange to John, on standby in Virginia. "Turkey did come through with a Health Certificate, so looking good!"

Heike touched base with Müge. "How are you? Hope you had a nice weekend. Is everything going as scheduled for Smoke's journey to the USA?"

"I am doing fine, many thanks," Müge replied. "We are getting ready for the big day :)))) We all hope that tomorrow all trouble for Smoke is ending and hopefully we will be sending him out of Istanbul to Frankfurt."

"Brilliant!" Heike emailed back.

The next morning Terri checked out of the Acropol Suites and Spa and made her way to K9 Akademisi. She said her thanks for the three weeks of boarding, loaded Smoke into a truck, and headed for Ataturk International Airport. She didn't have to tackle the job alone: her old travel companion, Ameer, was back in town. Terri had contacted him after Smoke's original Iraqi health certificate expired on May 3. Ameer had consulted the Kurdistan officials and managed to get a fresh certificate, stamped with a new date. But by the time the paperwork was completed, it was too late to mail the document and assure its on-time arrival. So Ameer hand delivered it.

They arrived at the airport customs building about 11 a.m. and were met by a crowd, including a number of Istanbul news reporters and camera crews. Smoke was a media darling by now, and everyone wanted to record his successful departure for America.

After wrapping up the press conference, Terri tackled the customs gauntlet. Müge was on hand to help, luckily—because it turned out they still lacked certain required signatures and stamps. Müge set off to satisfy the last-minute demands, driving from one office to another. The process took a grueling five hours. Terri and Ameer found a patch of grass nearby and took turns keeping Smoke company. It was a nice, cool spring day, with scattered clouds and a slight breeze—great weather for flying. Smoke spent the time grazing, napping, and graciously posing for seemingly hundreds of photographs as nearly everyone who passed by wanted to stop and record the moment.

Paul checked in with Müge one last time. "Is all okay with this shipment? Do you know if Terri obtained a health certificate from your veterinary authorities? I have not heard from her. I hope she has or there will be problems here," he wrote.

"I was at the airport since morning with Terri, all is done, the health certificate obtained from Iraq has been finally stamped & signed by the Turkish vets but I think they are idiots really," Müge wrote. "Anyhow, I hope there would be no problem at your end too."

Heike also emailed Müge. "Just to see if all is set and under control for Smoke leaving tonight."

"HAPPY END :)))) It's all done and finally Smoke is flying this evening as planned & booked along with Terri," Müge wrote back, copying Terri, John, and Paul. "He is really so cute, everybody at the airport today while waiting for the customs formalities loved him. He has lots of fans already. . . . Thanks a lot for everything and so glad to meet you all."

By about 4 p.m. Terri received word that everything was completed. Smoke had been cleared for takeoff by customs, the airport veterinarian, the Ministry of Agriculture, and Lufthansa. They made their way to the boarding area to load Smoke into his portable stall. Once again a crowd gathered to bid farewell to the famous donkey.

Terri kept her support crew informed as she and Smoke progressed.

> 9:25 p.m.: "I am on the plane and Smoke is about to be loaded. We are on our way!"
>
> 10:26 p.m.: "Smoke and I are aboard the plane and we are 15 minutes away from departing Turkey. Next stop Frankfurt then home!"
>
> 10:30 p.m.: "Wheels are up."
>
> 11:22 p.m.: "Just landed in Frankfurt. All is well."

Welcome to Germany, Smoke. *Willkommen.*

13.

Welcome to America

Any equine paparazzi waiting for the famous donkey to arrive at Frankfurt Airport didn't stand a chance. Once the plane from Istanbul landed, Smoke was treated something like a sheltered Hollywood star—actually, more like a sheltered Hollywood star with the plague. He required special treatment because he didn't fulfill all the regular health requirements of the European Union.

When his stall was unloaded onto the tarmac, Smoke was transferred immediately into a quarantine stall. This special thermo-controlled vehicle kept Smoke comfortable, while keeping him out of contact with any other animals. He was transferred in the special vehicle to the Lufthansa Animal Lounge. No chance to mingle—he was whisked away to a quarantine stable.

It wasn't just screwworm the EU veterinary officials worried about. Without a functioning veterinary administration operating in Iraq during the war, many animal diseases had risen to epidemic levels. Information about a number of other diseases endemic to Iraq wasn't even available to the World Organization of Animal Health. So, although Smoke received a waiver to pass through Germany, special precautions were required in order to protect European livestock.

Heike checked in with the airport vet from her office in Mülheim an der Ruhr. "Smoke is doing fine in the quarantine box at FRA airport," she told Terri, Asli, Müge, John, Paul, Donita, Safak, Freeman, and Barnard. "So glad to have been a small part of this movement."

The transit area in the animal lounge was closed to other animals during Smoke's visit. Staff members dressed in special protective clothing while handling him—head-to-toe suits, facemasks, goggles, gloves, and booties. His stable was partitioned off from the rest of the area. A veterinarian conducted a physical checkup, and officials examined Smoke's documents. Under the requirements his traveling stall had to be disinfected, and his droppings, litter, and fodder had to be contained, as well. But the staff took good care of Smoke during the thirty-hour layover.

Smoke didn't know it, but he was lodging in the world's largest transit point for live animals as they travel from here to there and back again. More than 110 million animals a year pass through the Border Inspection Point at Frankfurt Airport. In 2011 the busy facility would handle 1,374 registered horses by the end of the year. And one donkey.

On Thursday morning Terri and Smoke boarded a cargo plane and waved "Auf Wiedersehen" to Germany. Next stop: the United States of America.

Smoke landed at John F. Kennedy International Airport Thursday morning, New York time, to the e-cheers of his close group of supporters.

"Smoke is Home!" Terri emailed. "Just landed in New York and all is good."

"WOWWWSUPERRR," Müge emailed back. "Finally you are at home. Unbelievable indeed. Great, take very good care."

"Thanks for the good news!" wrote Heike. "Glad to hear Smoke & you had a good trip."

John, who was staying with the Pirtles in Virginia, began spreading the word. He sent a note to Robert Ruark, his commanding general back at Camp al Taqaddum, who by now was a major general—a two-star. "Great job, John, folks have sent me the articles already! You have done the impossible," said the man who first suggested that the Marines go capture a donkey.

John also put in a phone call to Freeman, thanking him over and over for his help. Freeman heard the news with pride. The way he saw it, Smoke was the "poster donkey" for the compassion of U.S. service men and women deployed overseas.

"In the middle of great conflict and death," the attaché told

John, "we always found the time to show compassion to God's creatures who no one else was going to love."

Back when Smoke was stuck at the Turkish border and Freeman first learned his story, he realized the donkey was part of the Marine Corps family. That meant the golden rule would apply: Marines don't leave Marines behind.

No major public fanfare accompanied Smoke's landing in New York. After all, he couldn't formally enter the United States until he cleared the traps at the USDA quarantine center. After animal health technicians at the airport loaded the donkey onto a truck and sealed it, Smoke headed out for the ninety-mile ride north to the New York Animal Import Center at Newburgh—the Ellis Island for immigrating equines and birds. In the course of a year roughly three thousand equines pass through this import center.

When Smoke arrived, the staff unloaded him and led him into the receiving barn. He was walked through a footbath filled with disinfectant designed to kill foot-and-mouth disease. Then his temperature was taken to check for fever. After that Smoke was checked into Barn 17, where he waited for the doctors to make their rounds. Dr. Jason Koopman and Dr. Dale Weinmann, the veterinarians on duty, duly stopped in. They checked Smoke's chart, confirmed that his temperature was normal, and looked him over. Was he perky and active? Did his eyes look clear? Smoke got a thumbs-up. The vets drew a blood sample to send to the National Veterinary Services Laboratories in Ames. To ensure scientific consistency, this single facility conducts blood tests on all the horses entering the United States from the three U.S. import centers: in New York, Miami, and Los Angeles. Donita had kept careful tabs on Smoke's travel progress, and the lab staff was expecting the delivery.

The docs looked Smoke over for external parasites. Bugs can be bad, particularly ticks, which can carry diseases such as the dreaded piroplasmosis, which can lead to fever and anemia, as well as jaundiced mucous membranes and labored breathing. Smoke was sprayed with a mild acetic acid—the active ingredient in vinegar—to kill any foot-and-mouth virus that could be present on his coat, a standard procedure. A high-pressure insecticide spray was next, to kill any bugs that might have come along for the ride. After all the poking and prodding and spraying, Smoke was left to relax.

Animal caretakers would monitor him carefully during his stay—stopping in at least twice a day to take his temperature, track how much food and water he consumed, and confirm that he was passing manure every few hours, a key sign of good equine health. Smoke's blood work was sent to Ames. The tests would take twenty-four hours to process. Meanwhile the doctors began looking over Smoke's paperwork.

John found out there was trouble afoot Thursday afternoon, when he emailed Dr. Ellen Buck in Maryland. He let her know Smoke had arrived. When she congratulated him, John asked whether she could get to Warrenton, Virginia, that weekend to attend a party being planned for Smoke.

"I'd love to meet Smoke if I can make it out there," she wrote back late in the afternoon. "However, we need to get Smoke out of quarantine first, and there's a problem."

Of course there was. That little dark trouble cloud seemed to follow Smoke wherever he went. The veterinarians had pored over the stack of documents that had accumulated as Smoke traveled from Irbil to Silopi, back to Irbil, back to Silopi, then on to Istanbul and to Frankfurt and now to New York.

There was the veterinary clearance document issued by Border Inspection Post, Frankfurt Airport, allowing Smoke to transit the European Union through Germany from Turkey. Check.

There was the official veterinary certificate from the Frankfurt Animal Lounge. Check.

There was the air waybill from Turkey to the United States, along with the shipper's certificate and the journey declaration, required whenever an animal is shipped from Europe. Check, check, check.

There was the U.S. import permit, signed by Dr. Buck. Check.

There was the May 4 letter from the U.S. embassy, signed by

Freeman, seeking assistance in transporting Smoke, and the April 15 letter from the Turkish Ministry of Agriculture allowing Smoke to enter Turkey, signed by the deputy minister. Good.

There were the May 3 lab results from the National Veterinary Services Laboratories in Ames. Check.

There was the veterinary health certificate from Irbil. The import health certificate from Iraq. The paperwork from the Areous Clinic in Irbil showing the results from the blood tests and veterinary examination. Check, check, and another check.

And there was the transit permit issued by Dr. Göbel, stating Smoke's arrival and departure times at Frankfurt Airport and instructions for his stay there, including required use of the special, thermo-controlled vehicle. Check.

But where, oh where, was the USDA import health certificate signed by Turkish officials? The one John, Terri, Paul, Müge, and Freeman agonized over for days? The one Terri said she would get signed and stamped by hook or by crook? The one she told Donita, just before getting on the cargo flight, she had obtained? The import health certificate, it seems, was AWOL.

The import center veterinarians alerted Paul and Dr. Buck. While Paul started hunting around for answers, Dr. Buck asked John if he could provide a statement from the Turkish Ministry of Agriculture covering Smoke's time there. Well, that wasn't going to happen. But he thought Terri had given a form of some sort to Lufthansa. Would that help?

"Even if we can't come up with the right form, I'm sure that an affidavit as to Smoke's care while he was in Turkey may do the trick," John told her.

Paul, meanwhile, reached out to Müge. "You have been so helpful. And of course he has arrived safely," he told her. "But we have nothing from the Turkish Ministry. Is it possible that you were given a health certificate for him? Terri has nothing, as far as I could see. Possibly one was sent but held in Germany? We have a problem now because we have an incomplete health record. All this work and it is not over yet."

Smoke, meanwhile, was oblivious to the document drama. He

had more interesting things to do. He loved it when the vets or animal caretakers came by for a visit. He followed them around his stall like a well-trained puppy. The staff found him extraordinarily friendly. It was unusual enough to see a donkey at the import center. Seeing one that responded to people instead of standing in the corner of the stall, sending out "I want to be alone" signals, was rare indeed.

Smoke was friendly to everyone, but truth to tell, he did like some people better than others. Take, for example, the two smokers on staff. He made fast friends with them, deftly nosing out any pack of cigarettes. But that was nothing compared to the guy who used snuff. Smoke caught one whiff and nearly knocked the man down with his did-you-bring-enough-for-everybody zeal. The staffer quickly opened his tin and let Smoke have a sample. Only then did Smoke back off a bit.

While Smoke was shaking down import center staff for tobacco, the search for documentation continued. Müge told Paul on Thursday that she didn't have a health certificate from the Turks. "Is there any chance that you can find a copy of whatever paper your Ministry might have signed for Terri?" he asked her. "Right now we have nothing from Turkey and our government vets are asking me to find it."

Müge reported back on Friday, sending him copies of all the pertinent documents she had. Eventually, the papers made their way into the hands of Dr. Kenneth Davis, who was back on duty Friday at the import center. Ultimately, it was his decision whether to sign the documents allowing Smoke into the United States. Weinmann and Koopman worked for him, and if anything went wrong, it would be his head on the chopping block. But Dr. Davis wasn't worried. Kenny Davis looked on Jason and Dale like his own sons. He had hired them and trained them, and he had complete faith in their integrity. And no veterinarian with integrity would let his emotions get involved with quarantine decisions.

The quarantine centers are gatekeepers for animal health—their diligence protects the nation's livestock from disease. And that's no small matter. If a sick animal gets past them and an epidemic breaks out, the damage can be widespread and costly. In 1987 officials in Spain had imported a shipment of African zebras without taking proper precautions. It turned out the zebras were carrying a strain of African horse sickness. While zebras sometimes survive the disease, horses never do. The resulting outbreaks led to several hundred horses dying or being put down. So as lovable as Smoke was, the USDA vets weren't about to sign off on his release unless they were confident he wasn't a health risk.

It was Friday afternoon when Dr. Davis called John to walk through the issues and the options available to the staff. The first option, if all else failed, was euthanasia—but that was the most extreme option and was never contemplated in Smoke's case. A more likely scenario, if the document problems couldn't be overcome, was to send Smoke back to Iraq. "That is not an option, either," John replied flatly. The doctor agreed.

A third option would be to extend Smoke's time in quarantine to sixty days, for precautionary reasons. That would be an expensive move, since a stay at the import center cost hundreds of dollars a day. Assuming no signs of illness broke out in those two months, however, the donkey would be allowed entry.

The most desirable option, obviously, was to release Smoke after the standard three days in quarantine. But the main concern of the conscientious staff was to do the right thing. The vets couldn't and wouldn't give the donkey preferential treatment.

Smoke, for once, was in luck. That luck came down to the Turkish government's ultra-cautiousness and love of stamps and the detective powers of Dr. Davis. As he pored over the documents in the donkey dossier, he discovered that the Turks had signed and stamped everything in sight.

The Turkish veterinarian had signed the Iraqi health certificate and stamped it. He had signed the veterinary examination from Irbil. The Turkish customs official had signed the letter stating that Smoke had remained under his control during the donkey's entire stay in Turkey. Dr. Davis was able to reconstruct Smoke's entire travel history by following the stamps. And that trail of stamps assured him of two things: Smoke had been out of Iraq long enough, and he had been kept properly segregated from other animals well enough, to make the staff confident that everything was in order.

Dr. Davis felt assured he was cutting no corners. Therefore, he declared, Smoke could leave quarantine Saturday morning, after the basic three-day stay. At long last the little donkey could escape from the red-tape jungle.

John and Craig Pirtle left Virginia on Friday afternoon and drove Lisa's truck and horse trailer north. On Saturday morning they pulled up at the quarantine center. John could barely contain his excitement as he checked in with Dr. Davis.

As it turned out, Smoke wasn't the only traveler being released that day. He was in high company: another man had arrived to pick up two Belgian warmbloods that had just arrived from Europe. These specially bred horses are internationally renowned for their skills at show jumping and dressage. They often sell for one hundred thousand dollars or more. The warmbloods had every right to look down their noses at Smoke. They didn't have much choice, frankly. At eighteen hands tall these heavily built horses were literally twice as tall as Smoke.

The day was such a special occasion that Dr. Davis's wife, Debra, had driven over to snap photos of the release. And she wasn't there to see the Belgian beauties. No, she was there to see Smoke.

Just then an animal caretaker led the donkey out of the barn. John stared as the donkey approached with ears erect, face forward. He found himself thinking vague, uncomfortable thoughts. This donkey looked somehow smaller and browner than John remembered. And furrier. John remembered Smoke being skinnier and more gray than brown. What if—after all the time, money, and agony spent over the last nine months—what if this was the wrong donkey?

The retired colonel peered down at the donkey, much as he had on that Sunday morning in Iraq in August 2008, and he suddenly relaxed. *He has been eating a better diet than I could ever provide*, he told himself. *And he has been living in a cooler climate than on the Iraqi desert. Of course he's not skin and bones anymore. Of course his coat has improved. Of course he's Smoke.*

The donkey peered back, much as he had on that first day at Camp al Taqaddum, looking up at the colonel with his bright, brown eyes. He showed none of the anxiety John had felt—the moment Smoke saw the colonel, he brightened up like a new penny. He was no longer a forlorn, hungry desert wanderer. Today he was confident, cool, and collected. *I'm a world traveler*, he seemed to be signaling. *I just crossed a continent. And here is my long-lost friend. I'm ready for anything!*

A rush of relief, gratitude, and joy overwhelmed John. Finally, after all this time, his battle buddy had made it to the United States of America. John and his long cast of supporters had been successful. He flashed a grin as he looked down at Smoke, and then he held onto his furry, gray head and gave his old friend a welcoming rub.

John and Smoke posed for pictures and chatted with the import center staff. Dr. Davis gave John a packet of paperwork and told him Smoke was in good health. When John asked for a professional assessment of Smoke's age, the veterinarian studied the donkey's teeth and put his age at four and a half to five and a half years old.

Then Smoke was loaded onto the big trailer—not without reluctance on Smoke's part—and they headed out, arriving in Fredericksburg that evening. Smoke met Craig's wife, Gena, and son, Zach. John walked Smoke to a pasture across the road and let him off his rope. The donkey took off, dashing up and over the hill. John stayed put, watching and listening. A few seconds later Smoke began braying like crazy. Then he came trotting over the crest of the hill, saw John, and charged down to greet him. It was just like old times.

Smoke snacked on the Virginia bluegrass and a few selections from Gena's flower garden. The next day they all drove the forty miles to the Warrenton home of Debbie and Alan Nash. Hillsborough was the name of their sprawling property. Warrenton lies in the heart of Virginia horse country, characterized by gently rolling hills and mile after mile of wooden horse fences that line mile after mile of green pastures dotted with grazing thoroughbreds. Hillsborough's Colonial-style main house had been built in the 1960s, but the handsome exterior featured two-hundred-year-old bricks from a dismantled Boston church.

After the Nashes bought the property, they built up a full stable of horses to support their shared love of polo and fox hunting. The Pirtles introduced them to John at a polo match in 2010. Alan and Debbie supported John's nonprofit group and fell in love with the story of Smoke. So when the donkey finally made it to America, they decided to throw a party. They had a spare horse paddock where Smoke could bunk down. Debbie invited friends they knew through polo or the Warrenton hunt community.

Thirty to forty of Fauquier County's finest attended Smoke's "Welcome to America" party, toasting him with Chardonnay and cocktails and listening to John's stories about Smoke's life and times. Miguel, the Nashes' groom, and his friend Ronald had given Smoke a bath and spruced him up for the special occasion.

John had invited Maj. Gen. Robert Ruark, his boss at Camp al Taqaddum, and retired Army Lt. Gen. John Sylvester, who served on the board of John's nonprofit organization. Two reporters were there to record the occasion. Joseph Morton drove down from the *Omaha World-Herald*'s Washington bureau, where he typically covered the kind of donkeys who frequent Capitol Hill. "Smoke the donkey must have thought he'd died and wafted up to heaven," Morton wrote, adding that partygoers bantered about whether Smoke had served in the Special Forces or military intelligence. Smoke "was pampered with carrots and more grass than he likely ever saw near Fallujah," reported James Sanborn with the *Marine Corps Times*, who had also written about Smoke back in January.

The polo crowd loved Smoke. At one point two pretty young brunettes, Amy and Rebecca, gave him simultaneous smooches on either side of his furry gray head. Ah, the Land of the Free: hay in every trough and a girl on every cheek.

Sylvester hadn't known quite what to expect when he met Smoke. He had seen plenty of burros over the years, but never a donkey. When he finally laid eyes on Smoke, he was taken aback. Somehow he had envisioned him as being much bigger and grander—not this stunted, zebralike critter with a stripe on his back. Sylvester also thought it was funny that all these people were fawning over Smoke, while Smoke was paying almost no attention to them. Instead he was gazing longingly at the neighbors: three long-legged, well-heeled polo fillies in the paddock just across the road.

Smoke couldn't keep his eyes off them. He suddenly started heehawing like crazy in his best donkey-about-town way. But the bray that erupted from this height-challenged foreign rake terrified the Virginia beauties. They fled, galloping up and over the little slope in their paddock. Once safely over the hill they turned in unison and stood side by side, three little heads timidly peeking over the crest of the hill. Poor Smoke was getting the cold shoulder, in triplicate.

When the party broke up, it was travel time again. Stephanie Scott at SPCAI had arranged for an interview Monday morning with WCBS-TV in New York. John wanted to avoid maneuvering a sixteen-foot trailer through Manhattan during the morning rush hour, so he arrived Sunday night and found a spot to park on an Upper West Side street. He slept fitfully in the truck cab, hoping no one would want to steal a horse trailer and a donkey. Smoke fended for himself in back, snacking on a box of Cheerios he had rooted out of its hiding place. John figured it out the next morning, when he opened the trailer door and found bits of yellow cardboard and Cheerios strewn everywhere.

John headed for the rendezvous spot at Seventy-third and Riverside Drive. Terri planned to meet him there with her boss, JD, and Meredith Ayan, the staff's executive assistant. Meredith had been responsible for creating the paperwork required for the Smoke mission, passing information between Terri and Paul, and keeping everyone apprised of developments. Meredith arrived earlier than the others and started looking for Smoke. He should be easy to spot, she figured—he had to be the only donkey on Riverside Drive. But just to be sure, when she found the truck, Meredith knocked politely on the window. "Are you John Folsom?" she inquired.

On this chilly, rainy morning, Lisa's big rig came in handy. WCBS reporter Don Dahler, his crew, and the SPCAI staff clambered into the spacious trailer. They made friends with Smoke, petting him and feeding him apples and carrots. Then Smoke started braying at the top of his lungs. The noise echoed off the trailer's metal walls.

After the news crew left, John thanked SPCAI. The nonprofit organization had kept its commitment to reunite him with Smoke, despite the unexpected delays, the many bureaucratic barriers, and the mounting costs. The original estimate of ten thousand dollars to get Smoke to America had ballooned during the stays at Silopi and Istanbul. The price had risen again when they realized they would need to pay for the Lufthansa flight.

And yet the costs would have been higher if not for the generosity of many involved in the adventure. Paul was amazed to see how many people were pulling for Smoke. The German authorities had granted a special exception to the European Union transit requirements. Lufthansa had charged a minimal fee for the special thermo-controlled quarantine stall. Peden Bloodstock had billed only two hundred euros total for its services, instead of its usual rate of six hundred euros plus the cost of the transit permit fee, airport veterinary fees, and stabling.

Mersant International had donated its services, and Paul's trucker had waived his $775 fee to take Smoke from the airport to the quarantine facility. Even the federal government had been helpful, and how often does that happen, for heaven's sake, Paul remarked. The USDA lab in Ames had donated its testing services both when Smoke was in Istanbul and again when he was at the quarantine center. And the import center had charged only four hundred dollars per day for Smoke's stay—the rate for a miniature horse, rather than the full equine price of about twelve hundred dollars a day. In all thousands of dollars in fees and services had been ultimately donated or waived.

Even with such generosity Smoke's journey was no bargain. Consider the costs of transportation by truck and plane from Irbil to Silopi, back to Irbil, back to Silopi, then on to Istanbul and eventually to New York; customs fees at Silopi and Istanbul; Turkish Ministry of Agriculture fees; hotels, meals, and airfare for Terri, Ameer, and Ahmed; drivers' fees; boarding costs in Istanbul; the quarantine center bill; fees and expenses for Ekiptrans Ltd. in Istanbul, Peden Bloodstock in Germany, and Mersant International in New York; and other miscellaneous expenses. In the end SPCAI spent between thirty-five thousand and forty thousand dollars to bring Smoke to the United States. Who footed the bill? More than nine hundred donors, who had responded to the agency's requests for help before, during, and after the journey. This was truly an amazing show of compassion and support for the little Iraqi donkey.

After saying goodbye to the crew from SPCAI, John and Smoke headed out, driving north to the New Jersey Turnpike and then west to Interstate 80, which would take them the twelve hundred miles to Omaha. They spent the night in Pennsylvania before continuing west through Ohio, Indiana, and Illinois.

The weather continued cold and rainy on Tuesday, and Smoke was miserable. The trailer was ventilated enough that some rain got inside. John covered Smoke with blankets, but they didn't keep him from getting chilled, wet, and cranky. When John stopped for gas, he opened the side door to the trailer to check on the donkey. Smoke kept his backside to the door, refusing to turn around. He was clearly miffed. "Okay, have it your way," John told him and closed the door.

"Heehaw, heehaw!" Smoke complained.

John opened the door again. There was Smoke, face forward,

ready to kiss and make up. "You are a big baby," John told him, rubbing his head affectionately.

John had sent Donita a quick note that morning, confirming that he and Smoke would arrive at the Ames lab at 9 a.m. Wednesday to meet their well-wishers. "I appreciate and thank you for all of your help! You and your colleagues at USDA have been great," he wrote. "I look forward to meeting you tomorrow!"

He pulled up on schedule outside the National Veterinary Services Laboratories and was surprised to see a crowd gathered. Front and center, of course, was Donita. She had organized a program, and nearly seventy-five staff members had come out to meet John and his battle buddy in person, including the lab director, Dr. Beth Lautner.

Donita had worked for days writing a speech for the occasion. But when she saw the red truck and horse trailer pull up, she felt weak in the knees. She stood there, speechless, while Dr. Lautner tugged on her arm, prompting her to begin her remarks.

Smoke's story held a very personal place in Donita's heart. When terrorists struck the United States back on September 11, 2001, she had been a supervisor and lead recovery technician for the American Red Cross Tissue Services. Appalled by the terrorism she desperately sought some way to help, some way to heal.

She thought closure would come when she worked to get clearance to waive the national no-fly order so that human tissue could be delivered to New York to help victims of the attacks. But it didn't. She thought she would find closure that fall, when she helped to sort and load semitrailer after semitrailer of donations for U.S. troops. She didn't.

She continued working with the Red Cross, urging families who had lost a loved one to donate tissue to help others in need. While the work gave her satisfaction, something was still missing. When the program changed hands, Donita took a job with the laboratory in Ames, still with the goal of helping others. Then the phone rang on April 26, 2011, and a gruff-voiced man started talking about a donkey he wanted to import from Iraq. She soon embraced his mission and spent countless hours, sometimes staying awake at night, trying to help him. When she awoke Sunday morning, the day after Smoke left the import center in New York, she finally felt a sense of relief.

"Our first conversation consisted of many things, but we both agreed that things happen for a reason, and if it was meant to be then it would be," she told John. "I now have closure in what has been a long personal journey. And I have your phone call and Smoke to thank for that."

Now here was Smoke in person, and Donita was overwhelmed. Her well-rehearsed speech was left unsaid. All she could think of was how that April phone call had become more significant than she first realized and how proud she was of the lab staff's teamwork. John thanked the staff for its efforts, and everyone took turns meeting Smoke. Donita indulged him with double treats—both apples and carrots.

Then it was time to load Smoke into the trailer for the final 175 miles of the journey. Early that afternoon John crossed the Missouri River and continued on to Miracle Hills Ranch & Stables in the rolling hills of Fort Calhoun, north of Omaha. Gale Faltin, executive director of Take Flight Farms, had issued a press release about Smoke's arrival. The *Omaha World-Herald,* the Associated Press, and the local television stations covered the occasion. The cameras were lined up, waiting, and Gale was giving her press spiel. She was just wondering when John would arrive when she heard the boompita boompita boomp of a truck rumbling along the gravel road. Here came the colonel, with Smoke in tow.

John pulled in to the small parking lot, climbed out, and opened the trailer door. All anyone could hear was Smoke, braying at the top of his lungs. Everybody was laughing, and all the cameras were pointing at Smoke. John lowered the gate and escorted Smoke down to his waiting paparazzi.

The resident horses rushed outside to their runs, curious about the commotion. Annie, a white beauty who bunked in the first stall, poked her head over the fence. No skittish Virginia filly this one. She and the Iraqi ladies' man touched noses in a priceless, welcome-to-Nebraska moment.

After the pictures, videos, and interviews were over and the visitors dispersed, it was time for one more ride in the trailer. John and the Take Flight staff had agreed that Smoke needed a quiet spot to become acclimated to his new home and to rest after his exhausting journey. John once again loaded Smoke into the trailer and delivered him to an "undisclosed location." Then John returned Lisa's truck and trailer and headed home, eighteen days after leaving on what he thought would be a weeklong trip.

Wednesday brought another day of news articles, continuing a wave of press coverage that had begun when Smoke left Istanbul. Newspapers, blogs, and broadcast outlets ran Smoke's story in languages including English, German, Russian, French, Italian, Spanish, Arabic, Turkish, Portuguese, Japanese, Korean, and Chinese. An Associated Press article published Sunday was distributed across the country and internationally. "It took 37 days and a group of determined animal lovers, but a donkey from Iraq is now a U.S. resident," the AP article read.

Reuters tapped Omaha stringer David Hendee for its report, which was published across Europe and beyond. "Smoke the Donkey's long odyssey from Iraq to Omaha gives new meaning to the U.S. Marine Corps motto 'semper fi,'" wrote Hendee. "For Retired Marine Colonel John Folsom of Omaha, the Latin phrase—'semper fidelis' in full—for 'always faithful' has become 'semper fi(nally).'"

As National Public Radio reporter Eyder Peralta put it: "The story of Smoke is pretty sweet." Peralta later blogged: "As has happened with the Bronx Zoo cobra and, more recently, its peacock, Smoke, the donkey that befriended U.S. Marines in Iraq, now has his own Twitter and Facebook pages. Except that unlike the Bronx Zoo cobra and peacock, Smoke's accounts seem earnest and, well, real."

A talked-about appearance on the *Jimmy Kimmel Show* never panned out—John thought Smoke had done enough traveling for a while. But John was a guest that week on *The Mark Levin*

Show. His ten-minute chat with Levin about Smoke's story was distributed to more than three hundred radio stations nationwide.

Smoke's "undisclosed location" happened to be the home of Lyle and Sherma Seitzinger. Their daughter, Karman De Luca, who lived down the road a mile or two, was a volunteer equine specialist with Take Flight Farms. She had learned at a staff meeting that Smoke was heading for Nebraska and needed a place to stay.

Eventually, Smoke would move to Miracle Hills, where the Take Flight equine therapy program was based. But everyone thought it would be wise to keep this newcomer away from a barn environment for a while. John and the Take Flight staff also worried Smoke might attract too many visitors or, even worse, someone intending mischief. Karman talked to her parents, who already boarded two of her horses. Lyle and Sherma graciously agreed to take in Smoke if Karman provided most of his care. Gale was grateful for the offer—sure enough, the Take Flight phone lines were soon flooded with calls from people asking to see Smoke.

Smoke's stable mates were Dakota and Cowboy. Dakota got along just fine with Smoke. But Cowboy was a different story. Horses in a herd establish a hierarchy, and Cowboy had always been number three or four. But Karman had recently sold her number-one and -two horses, making Cowboy top dog. And the new boss was, well, kind of bossy. When he wanted to discipline Dakota or Smoke, he didn't quite know when to stop. That didn't sit well with Smoke, who was fully intact and had the hormones and aggressiveness to prove it. Karman knew it wasn't the best mix, considering Cowboy was a "late-cut stud," with lingering male hormones.

When Cowboy got annoyed with Smoke, he came at him with his teeth bared, ears pinned, and tried to run him off the property. Smoke, for his part, felt no qualms about biting or kicking out at the big boss in a "get-out-of-my-space" kind of way. Cowboy was just as pushy with Dakota, a gelding, as he was with Smoke. So Karman moved Dakota in with Smoke, and they quickly became friends. They hung out every day, grazing and relaxing together. When Smoke felt playful, he would nibble on Dakota's neck or ears—or whatever else the short guy could reach.

Karman discovered before long that Smoke had a very precise body clock. And he was particular about mealtimes. "If you were on time with his meal, you received a fifteen-second braying welcome," she told John. "Any later, and you would hear about it!"

Usually Lyle took care of the horses' morning meal, but if he wasn't around, Karman stopped by. One day she was on breakfast duty, but she was running half an hour late after getting her daughter on the school bus. Knowing she would get a chewing out, Karman set her cell phone to record before she hopped out of her Toyota RAV4. Smoke spotted her from about one hundred feet away.

"I received a forty-eight-second donkey diatribe," Karman told John. "We started using it as one of our favorite ring tones. Got a lot of startled looks in the grocery stores and doctors' offices when our phones rang!"

Given Smoke's haphazard upbringing, it wasn't surprising he didn't have the most civilized manners. For starters Karman discovered that he had not been trained to walk with a trainer on a lead rope. While he would follow John, not everyone had John's "command voice." It was time to teach Smoke some etiquette.

But Smoke didn't agree. When someone tried to lead him, either he planted his feet and refused to budge, or, worse yet, he tried to bite and kick the poor victim approaching with a lead rope. Karman knew it would take consistent effort to break Smoke of his bad habits. She gathered a crew of volunteers and created a daily training schedule. One handler would lead and control the donkey's direction and speed, while the other would use a flag to "encourage from behind" and redirect him when he tried to bite handler number one. After about three weeks the work paid off. Finally, someone other than John could help get Smoke to and from appointments with the farrier and the veterinarian and to therapy sessions at Take Flight Farms.

Teaching Smoke to tolerate having his feet touched was harder yet vital to his health. In Iraq the rough desert floor naturally maintained Smoke's feet. But in the soft soil of Nebraska his hooves would soon grow out of control unless a farrier filed them down every six to eight weeks. So he needed to stand quietly and let someone touch and lift his feet. Karman did her best, but Smoke remained leery. She eventually called in the Marines—a.k.a. John—for backup. Karman taught him how to work with Smoke, and from then on John took over the training. Finally, the donkey decided that if this foot-holding nonsense was all right with the colonel, it was all right with him. Most of the time, anyway.

One day Karman and a volunteer had just wrapped up a session on "how to lead on a lead rope." The volunteer mentioned how her horses loved getting their ears stroked. Karman's horses barely tolerated having their ears touched, so she was curious about the technique. To illustrate, the volunteer cupped Smoke's ear in her hand and gently stroked the inside, from the base to the tip. Both women were surprised when Smoke suddenly snuggled up against the volunteer, leaning into her side and gazing blissfully at her. Longears, it seems, love to be stroked.

Lyle and Sherma's kitchen window and sliding glass doors gave a clear view of the horses, and the family was in the habit of checking up on them whenever they were in the room. There was Cowboy. There was Dakota. But wait, where was Smoke? Time and again they rushed outside, only to find Smoke lying down, soaking in the sun, or standing completely motionless, becoming all but invisible against a backdrop of soil and grasses. Such camouflage is part of a donkey's natural defense against predators. The family soon learned to look for a tail swish or an ear flicker before panicking. Except by then Smoke had figured out his favorite trick: sneaking out.

The Seitzingers' fencing was geared to keep in large horses, not small donkeys. They had a "human gate" beside the buildings, a gap too narrow for a horse but wide enough for a person. And, as Smoke discovered, wide enough for him. He also found out that the cables on the pasture fencing were spaced far enough apart that he could slip his head and shoulders through. Then all he had to do was lift his feet over the cable, and voila! Out of donkey prison!

Smoke, being the friendly type, used his freedom to visit the neighbors' horses. He wasn't sneaky about it, loudly announcing his presence every time. But, just as when he was back at Camp al Taqaddum, he would eventually get ratted out. The neighbors put a rope on him and led him back home.

Despite Smoke's escape artistry Karman felt comfortable letting him and Dakota roam freely when she stopped by to visit or do chores. One day she was in the barn, fixing a bridle. She set her tools on the ground to keep them handy—a pair of pliers, a screwdriver, and a hole punch. Smoke strolled in and started nuzzling around, which was fine. But then Dakota wandered in to see what was going on. The big guy started to get in Karman's way, so she pushed him out of the barn and then went back to work. Except then she couldn't find her screwdriver. She searched the area thoroughly and came up dry. Just then Smoke gave a short "haw" sound over by the barn door. Apparently he couldn't muster a full heehaw—with that screwdriver in his mouth.

Karman headed his way, and Smoke took off for a good game of "catch me if you can." After running about twenty-five yards, he dropped the screwdriver in his excitement. But he looked pretty proud of himself. John laughed when he heard the story. He told Karman that Smoke had learned that game in Iraq: he confiscated one of the Marines' tools one day and dashed off.

At Karman's recommendation Smoke was gelded in early June, which helped tone down his aggressive behavior. That was a must if he was to work closely with people without being dangerous. The summer passed happily. John visited him nearly every day, unless he was traveling for work.

A coming-out party for Smoke was held July 27 at Bar Hills Farm, the home of Lisa and Bill Roskens. The cocktail reception was a fundraiser for Take Flight Farms. Plenty of loyal Take

Flight fans attended, along with active-duty and retired military. But what excited Lisa about the party was the large number of guests from fairly high up in Omaha's social strata. She marveled at Smoke's ability to interest people from across the socioeconomic spectrum.

Smoke was, in her opinion, one cool guy. He had had a rough start in life and had gone through a terrific ordeal getting to America. But he didn't let it faze him. It seemed he had never met a stranger, and he loved to schmooze people of all types. And they responded to him. A professional photographer was staged in a small tent during the party, and guests were invited to get their portrait taken with Smoke. Afterward Lisa couldn't think of a single person who declined the invitation—even those who had arrived without the slightest intention of participating.

After the photo session ended, Smoke was free to mingle. He worked the tables like a pro. He would cozy up to a group, plop his chin down on the table, and wait for the petting to begin. Then he moved on to the next group. After a few partygoers shared their hors d'oeuvres with him, he started working the plates, as well as the tables.

In August John decided Smoke should make an appearance at the Nebraska State Fair. He called livestock assistant Kelly O'Brien, who was intrigued. But she told John he would have to stay with Smoke during the eleven-day event in Grand Island, 150 miles west of Omaha. John couldn't commit that kind of time, so he dropped the idea. But Kelly didn't. She talked to her boss about what a great idea it would be to have Smoke at the fair. She offered to take care of the donkey herself, and he gave his permission. Kelly called John with the news. So, once again, John borrowed Lisa's truck and horse trailer, and he recruited Karman to help him get Smoke settled in. Off they went to Grand Island.

Smoke had a high-visibility stall, at the entrance to the sheep barn and just across from the birthing pavilion—a wildly popular attraction, with its growing stock of baby animals. Nearby was the poultry show—with all the raucousness of clucking chickens, quacking ducks, and gobbling turkeys. It would be a wonder, Kelly thought, if poor Smoke got any rest at all. But she did what she could to make him comfortable, keeping his stall clean, providing him with fresh hay and water, and taking him for regular walks. The two bonded nicely. And the fair crowd loved him. Kelly figured the bulk of the 333,000-plus visitors passed by his stall at some point during the fair.

After Labor Day Smoke headed back to Lyle and Sherma's, and life settled down to a regular routine. But when the weather turned cooler in October, it was time to move to Miracle Hills. Off to the next adventure for little Smoke.

14.

Spreading His Wings

Smoke settled into his new home in the number-one stall. It was right next to the parking lot—the same stall where Annie, the big white mare, had been staying when he first visited the stables in May. Every stall on that side of the barn featured an outside run, so Smoke could pop outdoors whenever he wanted. From there he could watch the occasional traffic rumble by on the gravel road or greet anyone who stopped by for a visit. And he had plenty of visitors.

Brenda and Jim Sheets had been boarding horses at Miracle Hills Ranch & Stables since 2002. They also offered riding lessons, birthday parties, horse camps, and trail riding. With all that activity Smoke had lots of people-watching to keep him busy, and plenty of thoughtful visitors remembered to bring him a treat. He became something of a celebrity in the rural neighborhood.

Miracle Hills sits on high ground in the rolling, wooded hills of Washington County, and those hills looked beautiful when Smoke arrived, decked out in their autumn colors, all golds and browns and reds. But Smoke was more interested in social relationships than in scenic vistas.

John stopped by nearly every day. He put Smoke on a lead rope and walked him down through a ravine and up a hill to a fenced-in pasture. Then the rope came off, and Smoke grazed and stretched his legs and got in a good run. Smoke also spent a lot of time with Brenda, who worked at the barn frequently, tending the horses, giving riding lessons, and doing upkeep. Brenda soon fell into the habit of giving Smoke the run of the barn whenever she was there doing chores.

John described life at the stables on Smoke's Facebook page.

He dubbed Smoke Brenda's "trustee" and posted messages about how the donkey was helping her with her chores. In other words, he ate whatever hay fell off the hay wagon and any leftovers the horses dropped on the floor. John adopted Smoke's persona on the page, posting photos and videos and writing about barn life.

More than two thousand people "friended" Smoke, men and women ranging in age from teenagers to retirees and hailing from twenty-six countries that spanned the globe: North and South America, Europe, Asia, Australia, and Africa. "Smoke" regaled his fans with stories about his animal friends—Buddy the Dog, Dolly the Goat, and Oreo the Cat, not to mention the fifteen to twenty horses in residence. But while Smoke tried his best to blend in with the horses, they saw right through him, and they were not amused.

His relationship with the horses at Brenda's barn wasn't as awkward as in Virginia, where Smoke had terrified the polo ponies. But it wasn't close to the camaraderie he had enjoyed with Dakota at Lyle and Sherma's place. He was a donkey, and the barn horses treated him like an outcast. Brenda didn't feel comfortable turning Smoke out into the pasture with the bigger horses. She was worried they would bully and hurt him.

Instead she introduced him to her miniature horses, Taffy and Domino—a brilliant move. Before long Smoke and the little horses were fast friends. When it was their turn to play in the pasture, they loved to romp. That meant running, kicking out their heels, biting, and rearing—all in the name of fun. To Brenda they were like boisterous little boys on the playground.

While Smoke loved his equine chums, he was mostly a people person. He looked forward to visits from children and adults who stopped to chat or give him a treat. And he got excited whenever he saw John or Brenda pull up outside the barn, greeting them with a special "heehaw!"

Brenda had been around horses and other animals much of her life. She knew that every animal has its own distinct personality, and she loved Smoke's laid-back attitude. He was no saint,

One day, after several sessions, a group of veterans gathered once more at the arena with Gale and the therapists. It was time for the at-war and at-home session. The therapists had set out a variety of props—hula hoops, Frisbees, orange cones, the white standards used for horse jumps—as well as military gear, such as boots, duffel bags, helmets, and fatigues.

The veterans were asked to arrange one end of the arena to look like home, placing all the fun props inside a big circle. The other end of the arena was set up to represent deployment, with orange cones and fences arranged to form a narrow lane entering the area, reflecting the structure of military life. Once that was finished, they were told that Smoke and the horses had just gotten their orders. It was time to deploy. The group was instructed to move the animals into the deployment area without touching them. They got to work, and the "unit" was deployed fairly quickly. Not a problem.

Great job, they were told. Now it was time to come home. They just needed to move the animals to the other end of the arena, once again without touching them. This time, the veterans glared at the therapists. "Oh, no," they groaned.

They set to work reluctantly. They struggled and struggled to get the horses to budge. After half an hour only one horse had gone "home." What was the difference? Gale thought the horses were picking up on the veterans' own emotions about returning home. By the end of the session the veterans had gotten the horses out of "deployment," but the horses refused to go into the circle that represented home. Instead they just stood on the outside. A couple of the veterans spoke up. That's exactly the way it is with us, they said. You go home, but you can never really go back to where you were. You always feel like you're on the outside, looking in. Soon members of the group were opening up about their feelings and frustrations.

Sessions like these taught Gale how special equine therapy was—and how Smoke was such an integral part of the experience. Take Flight held roughly a session a week at Brenda's barn. If members of the military were involved, Smoke was sure to take part, whether it was family therapy or psychotherapy, no matter what the issues were.

He was also popular during youth sessions. In addition to hosting school groups, Take Flight worked with at-risk youths of all ages. They might be struggling with eating disorders, substance abuse, criminal behavior, or other issues. Regardless of the issues or the age of the kids, everybody liked Smoke. Whenever children went to the barn, they got to choose which animals to work with. "Smoke! We want Smoke!" was a popular plea.

Smoke had a big job to do, and he embraced it. His involvement gained him a full-page presence in the organization's 2011 annual report, which dubbed him "one of Take Flight's most important staff members." Another page displayed children's artwork, which featured Smoke prominently. "We were humbled by the opportunity to help Smoke adjust to his new home and to introduce him to his new job as a therapy/learning animal," the report stated. "Smoke's story is a source of inspiration, especially for service members who may share similar stories. Although many consider Smoke an 'honorary Marine,' we have found that his story and personality resonate with most people, and he has become a powerful part of our programs."

When November rolled around, it was travel time again. Veterans Day was nearing—Smoke's first in the United States. This year it would carry the special date of 11-11-11 and would mark the tenth anniversary of the September 11 attacks. John decided Smoke should march in the annual parade in New York City. The event is called America's Parade, and John considered Smoke to be America's donkey, so what could be more fitting? He applied for a parade entry on behalf of Wounded Warriors Family Support and was accepted.

As long as Smoke was visiting the East Coast, it seemed like a great opportunity for a twofer by visiting the Pentagon. John put in a call to Col. David Lapan. They had been stationed together in Hawaii as young lieutenants and had met up again in 2005, when they both deployed to Iraq with II MEF (Forward). Now

Lapan was director of the Department of Defense Press Office. John asked Lapan if Smoke could visit the Pentagon on November 10. That date marks the Marine Corps birthday, celebrating the founding of the Marine Corps in 1775. Marine units always commemorate the occasion with birthday cake and often hold a Birthday Ball, which entails many traditions and much pomp and circumstance.

Lapan thought the birthday visit was a great idea. He did a battle handoff to Army Lt. Col. Robert L. Ditchey II, who coordinated public affairs activities at the Pentagon. Special event? Ditchey was the point guy. Special visitor coming? Ditchey made the arrangements. He had handled activities as diverse as an all-day radio broadcast, direct from the Pentagon, to a bagpipe performance by a Canadian military band. But he had never had to deal with a via—a very important animal. "Oh, man, how am I going to do this?" he asked himself when he heard the news.

Nobody in the press office had heard of livestock visiting the Pentagon. There were the working k-9s with the Force Protection Agency. And maybe Defense Secretary Leon Panetta's pet dog stopped in now and then. But nothing of the barnyard variety— not even the Naval Academy's goat mascot or West Point's Army mule mascots.

Hosting an event at any military installation involves a lot of logistics. It gets even more complicated at the headquarters for the U.S. Department of Defense, given the high-security environment, especially in the post-9/11 era. And, generally speaking, Pentagon types are trained to worry—risk assessment is their business. Ditchey knew they could easily turn down a great idea simply because they were worried about something going wrong. He walked through the possible objections to Smoke's visit. Who's going to clean up after him? What if he gets loose? What if he bites or kicks someone? What if some woman has a shiny object in her purse and Smoke goes all ptsd?

But he forged ahead, placing a call to the Facilities Management Office. He explained that a retired Marine Corps colonel, the founder of a nonprofit group called Wounded Warriors Family Support, was planning to visit. He thought that would set a good tone. Then he explained that the colonel wanted to bring along a special guest. A donkey. A donkey named Smoke. At that point the woman in the Facilities Management Office burst out laughing. But Ditchey's tactic worked—she didn't say no.

The next step was getting an event permit. That involved a vetting process: a security review, followed by a safety review, followed by a policy review. It took a couple of days before Ditchey got the green light.

With everything in order John and Smoke headed out from Omaha on Tuesday, November 8. Smoke had his very own trailer by now—a modest two-horse affair that John could pull with his Ford Explorer. On the way to Virginia John routed through Lexington, Kentucky, to fulfill a promise to visit Big Ass Fans. This ceiling-fan manufacturer had a donkey mascot, Fanny, and supported donkey causes—such as contributing to the SPCAI effort to bring Smoke to the United States. After a quick stop in Lexington John and Smoke set out for Warrenton, Virginia, where they spent the night with the Nashes. When John explained his trip to Debbie Nash and her mother, Barbara French, they made an impromptu request: Could they tag along? They thought the parade sounded like great fun. "Sure," John said. "Why not? You can help out with Smoke."

The group headed north on Thursday morning, reaching Arlington about lunchtime. They made their way to a parking lot near the Pentagon to rendezvous with Lieutenant General Sylvester. One of John's board members, Sylvester lived in the Washington DC area and wanted to be part of the Pentagon visit—pretty nice of the Army to help celebrate a Marine Corps occasion.

Getting into the Pentagon took some doing, even though Ditchey had done his preparation work well. It was just that, typically, Pentagon visitors report to the Visitors Center. Typically, as in always. But that wouldn't work for Smoke, who couldn't exactly walk in the front door. Instead John was directed to the delivery entrance, where force protection staff inspected the trailer and the visitors. That went smoothly enough, but then there was a hang-up in the press office. Under the strict security rules John couldn't stay at the entrance. He had to leave the Pentagon property, find a place to park, and wait. When he got the green light, he once again drove to the delivery entrance, once again underwent the security inspection—and once again learned there was a holdup.

At one point Sylvester spoke up. "Here we've got a retired general and a retired colonel trying to get into the Pentagon with a donkey, and we're getting a hassle over it like we might be potential terrorists," the general boomed.

The gate guards laughed. But it didn't stop them from finishing their inspection. It took three tries before Smoke and his entourage were finally escorted onto the property. They drove slowly through the special tunnel that leads into the Pentagon's center courtyard, known informally as ground zero. They circled the courtyard and found a shady place to park. John led Smoke out and arranged his Wounded Warriors Family Support blanket. Ditchey met the group there with the fifth member of Smoke's contingent. Helen Donnington, a supporter of John's nonprofit organization, lived in Boston. But Helen, like Debbie and Barbara, had thought the trip sounded like fun and had come to help.

For Ditchey this was game time. From the standpoint of a public affairs officer, or PAO, a day without glitches is a good day. And Ditchey was on special alert today because he was the designated horse handler. In PAO parlance a horse handler is anyone escorting a general—otherwise known as a thoroughbred. The term, which dates to cavalry days, is a nod to generals' military breeding, as well as to the tendency of many generals to be, well, high-maintenance. And the way Ditchey saw it, he had two thoroughbreds on his hands: Sylvester the General and Smoke the Donkey.

News of Smoke's visit had spread mostly by word of mouth, but he also attracted the attention of any Pentagon workers who had stepped outside for some fresh air over the lunch hour. Many came over to meet Smoke and then stayed to hear John tell his stories. Ditchey, who knew nothing about donkeys, was surprised at how docile and lovable Smoke was. That allowed him to let down his guard somewhat and focus instead on Sylvester. He recognized the general immediately—he had worked in European Command when Sylvester was chief of staff there from 2002 to 2004, and he well remembered the tall man with the deep command voice. Ditchey's decision to concentrate on the general must have been how he missed the finger episode.

John was chatting with a woman when she decided to touch Smoke on the muzzle with her fingers. Perhaps Smoke thought she was handing him a treat. In any case he wrapped his teeth around one of her fingers—and held on. The woman tried to keep calm. "My finger. He's got my finger," she told John quietly, yet with a note of alarm.

As Smoke held on, the woman kept pointing out the obvious to John, still quietly, but with increasing urgency. "He won't let go. My finger. He's got my finger."

John felt terrible. He quickly thumped Smoke on the jaw. "Smoke! Let go!" he ordered sternly.

Smoke relinquished his catch, John apologized profusely, and the woman went off, nursing her bruised digit. That was the only glitch of the day, though. Smoke was a model visitor otherwise. A number of people stopped by who had met Smoke in Iraq—a testament to what a small universe the Marine Corps is. They were surprised and pleased to see him again and lingered to reminisce with John about their deployment at Camp al Taqaddum. Among them was Staff Sgt. Matthew Shelato, the senior enlisted in the First MLG PAO office. He had taken Smoke for walks and let the donkey graze on his tomato plants.

As folks returned to their offices, they spread the word about Smoke, prompting others to go out and see the donkey for themselves. Before the event wrapped up a couple of hours later, 150 to 200 visitors had stopped by to meet and greet the little donkey. That included a couple of the gate guards, who were curious about their four-legged delivery.

After the birthday visit wrapped up, John thanked Ditchey, dropped off Sylvester at his truck, and prepared to hit Interstate 95 for New York with the rest of his entourage. But everyone was hungry, so Debbie directed John to one of her favorite bistros near the Kennedy Center, next to the Watergate. She and Barbara and Helen stocked up, collecting bread, cheese, and other goodies, along with a bottle or two of wine to go—but only three glasses. John was the designated driver. While they were making their selections, Debbie bumped into some friends having a late lunch. When they heard about Smoke, they all insisted on going outside and being introduced.

With provisions in hand the entourage was ready for the road trip. They made their way through Maryland and Pennsylvania. But by the time they hit New Jersey, the food was gone, and "the girls" were hungry again. John pulled off I-95, and they spotted what had the appearance of a biker bar, with a parking lot big enough to accommodate the trailer. The bar was filled with locals, who quickly made friends with the travelers. When they found out about Smoke, they roared. "Bring him into the bar," they urged John. "We want to meet him!"

A dark building plus a noisy crowd plus a tired donkey didn't add up to a wise idea, by John's calculations, and he declined. But he compromised by inviting them outside instead. So the crowd trooped out the door, much like the well-heeled group at the Kennedy Center bistro, and met America's donkey.

The next stop was LaGuardia Airport to pick up John's son, Jack, who had flown in from his Chicago-area college to help out with the parade. They found a hotel in Queens with ample parking for the trailer, got Smoke settled for the night, and turned in. The next morning they headed out to line up for the parade. But when they reached the Queens Midtown Tunnel, the Port Authority police pulled over the truck for an inspection.

The officers looked over the full house in the crowded Explorer—John, Jack, Debbie, Barbara, and Helen. Then they turned back to John. "What's in the trailer?" the officers demanded.

"A donkey," John replied. "Do you want to see him?"

"A donkey?!" they snapped. "No, we don't want to see no donkey!"

They waved him on without a backward glance.

John tried to reach his designated staging area, but the streets off Fifth Avenue, the parade route, were jammed. The annual parade involved more than 250 groups and twenty thousand people from across the country: military units, Medal of Honor recipients, veterans groups, nonprofit groups, youth groups, civic groups, businesses, and select high school marching bands. There were floats and military vehicles. And this year there was a donkey.

John finally gave up and parked where he could, and the tiny parade unit made its preparations, which consisted of once again draping the Wounded Warriors Family Support camouflage blanket on Smoke's back. The parade began at 11 a.m., and off they went, slipping in between a Navy band and a Korean band. While the contingent was tiny, it soon drew attention from the crowds lining the sidewalks. "Look! There's Smoke!" people shouted. "Hey, it's Smoke the Donkey! He's from Iraq!"

John was surprised by the number of people who recognized Smoke, and he was delighted with their warm response. He thought of New Yorkers as being hard-bitten, even off-putting. Yet here were all these people, treating Smoke as if he were a hometown hero. Smoke's handlers zigged and zagged from one side of Fifth Avenue to the other as onlookers called them over, wanting to pet Smoke. Then, with the Navy band and the Korean band marching on, they hurried to catch up to their adopted spot in the parade.

Smoke was in his element. He unerringly picked out soldiers along the way and made a beeline to greet them, grabbing at the cargo pockets on their BDUS, or battle dress uniforms. That's where John used to keep treats, as Smoke well knew. He also tried to wheedle a cigarette or two from the smokers along the route.

The parade made its way up Fifth Avenue, past such landmarks as the Empire State Building, the New York Public Library,

Saks Fifth Avenue, and St. Patrick's Cathedral. Finally Smoke and his entourage reached the reviewing stand. His name was announced from the podium, and Smoke marched past the VIPs and the television cameras. The parade route ended shortly afterward. The little contingent made its way south again, this time sharing the city sidewalks with shoppers and the general public. Some people stopped to chat, curious about what a donkey was doing in Manhattan.

Debbie was impressed with how well Smoke behaved in this environment of skyscrapers, bands, big-city crowds, and traffic. Parents pushing strollers fearlessly rushed up behind him, wanting to give him a pet. That scared Debbie to death—what if he kicked out and nailed a toddler? But he was good as gold, basking in all the attention.

The group finally made it back to John's Explorer and piled in, exhausted and hungry after the four-hour parade. They drove around until they found a pizza place with a parking spot directly outside. Smoke was content to dine in the trailer. Afterward the parade pals broke up. Debbie, Barbara, and Helen planned to make their own leisurely way home. John was eager to begin the long drive back to Nebraska—after a side trip to the Bronx. Jack was an avid Yankees fan, and the Folsom boys both wanted to see the new Yankee Stadium, opened two years earlier. Then they headed for New Jersey, Pennsylvania, and points west. Thus ended Smoke's tour of New York—the biggest apple he had ever taken a bite out of.

They made a pit stop in Hubbard, Ohio, early Saturday afternoon. While John filled the gas tank, Jack took Smoke for a walk on his lead rope. Then John pulled the Explorer to the side of the parking lot and guided Smoke back into the trailer. Jack stood at the rear, holding the donkey in place. But as soon as John took off Smoke's halter, the escape artist made his move. Doing a quick about-face, the four-legged used-to-be-jack pushed the two-legged Jack out of the way. The donkey was on the lam once more.

He trotted north on U.S. 62, craning his head to pick up

scents, with Jack behind him, running as fast as he could. John got a slower start but took off running with the halter. A passerby who saw John's predicament was kind enough to offer him a ride. John gratefully accepted, worried either that Smoke would bolt in front of traffic and get hurt or that some trigger-happy small-town cop would show up and shoot the donkey.

The area was mostly rural, with a few buildings nestled among woods and open fields. John's escort pulled ahead of Jack and the donkey. But the car was in the northbound lanes, and Smoke was running on the other side of the four-lane divided highway. At one point the highway curved off to the east, while Smoke kept heading due north. John thanked his benefactor and hopped out. Then, as quickly as Smoke had started his run, he stopped.

His nose had led him to some well-kept lawns outside a handful of homes on the outskirts of Hubbard. John approached Smoke cautiously, expecting him to take off again. But Smoke just stood there looking at him, as if to say, "What's all the fuss? Can't a guy get a bite to eat?"

Jack arrived on the scene as John was putting Smoke's halter back on. Smoke had run nearly a half-mile from the gas station. Back they went, at a slower pace. Smoke climbed into the trailer with no objections. He had had his fun. They arrived at Jack's college apartment in Woodstock, Illinois, by Saturday evening and spent the night.

On Sunday John and Smoke hit the road once more. America's donkey was headed home.

15.

Of Fans and Fanfare

Brenda was worried. Smoke's East Coast trip had been wildly successful, but within a day after he returned home, she could tell he wasn't feeling quite himself. On Tuesday morning he didn't rush over to see her, the way he usually did when she dropped off his breakfast. He just stood there in the number-one stall, with his head down, his hay untouched. When he finally did walk around, his movements were slow.

She kept an eye on him to see if he would snap out of it, but by evening Smoke was lying down in his stall. Brenda called John. She told him how Smoke was behaving and suggested he call the vet. John contacted the Nebraska Equine Veterinary Clinic, and Dr. Michael Thomassen made an emergency "barn call." He observed Smoke's lethargic behavior and noticed decreased gut sounds. Colic until proven otherwise, he concluded. This catch-all phrase for abdominal pain is the "C word" of horse health. Colic can signal a major problem for equines, which have very sensitive digestive systems.

Thomassen sedated Smoke and pumped some mineral oil and water through a tube from the donkey's nose to his stomach to treat a possible digestive problem. When equines start getting dehydrated, they draw fluids from the large colon, which acts as a water reservoir. That leaves only dry feed material in the GI tract, creating an impaction, or blockage. The doctor left the donkey to rest overnight and returned the next morning. Smoke was still quiet, and the single pile of manure he had passed overnight contained no oil.

He decided to take Smoke to the clinic and run some tests. Blood work revealed a significantly elevated liver enzyme level—

his GGT level registered 73, when 24 was on the high end of normal. Dr. Thomassen started him on IV fluids, oral fluids, antibiotics, and anti-inflammatory medications. By late Wednesday Smoke began passing oil, and on Thursday he was put back on feed. His GGT level had dropped to 66. He was cleared on Friday to return to the barn.

Smoke's first snowstorm came a week later. The weather had been sharply colder and overcast for a few days, but on Saturday, December 3, the sky really closed in. Snow began falling by late morning and kept on coming for the next twelve hours. The desert native was not impressed. When John took him for his daily walk, Smoke tucked his furry head down as snowflakes swirled and blew around him. Smoke moved gingerly along the fence line, slipping into camouflaged holes now and then and clearly perplexed about this suddenly stark, wet landscape, with no familiar grass in sight. He soon had enough and turned back. Thank goodness for dry, heated barns.

The veterinary staff continued to monitor Smoke's blood work. By December 8, his GGT had dropped to 48, well on the way to normal. Within a week, though, John was calling the vet again.

This time John suspected he knew the cause. In making his rounds of the barn, Smoke had stumbled across a notebook. Seemed like as good a snack as any. He ate most of it before being discovered. The donkey was soon moping around. All he wanted to do was lie down. John called the clinic for an appointment. It was almost a month to the day after Smoke's first episode with colic.

Dr. Mike Black, one of Dr. Thomassen's colleagues at the equine clinic, saw Smoke this time. He ran blood tests to assure himself that Smoke's liver wasn't acting up again, but the GGT level was down to 44. Dr. Black sedated Smoke and pumped mineral oil and water into his stomach through a nasogastric tube, just like the first time around.

Smoke responded quickly. By later in the day he was eating small amounts of hay. The veterinarian kept him overnight but deemed him well enough to go home the next day. John and Brenda kept a close eye on Smoke after that. His notebook-nibbling days were over.

As the cold weather set in Smoke spent more time inside, so John decided to make a modest adjustment. Smoke's stall gate was horse-height—too tall for the donkey to poke his head over. So John installed a stall guard, canvas webbing that attached to the sides of the stall door. Smoke was much happier when he could once again keep an eye on barn comings and goings.

With Christmas approaching, John decorated Smoke's stall with a festive wreath. The daily mail brought cards, letters, and gifts from Smoke's friends. Among them were a donkey carving, a book, a bag of donkey chips, and a donkey Christmas tree ornament.

John kept Smoke's Facebook page fresh with videos from his walks with Smoke and with information about donkey adoption efforts. "Smoke" bragged that with his growing list of friends, he would slowly but surely overtake Justin Bieber in Facebook popularity (score: Bieber 38,000,000, Smoke 2,148). And he cracked very bad donkey jokes. For example: A donkey goes into a local ice cream shop and asks for a chocolate mint milkshake. The man brings the donkey the milkshake and says it will cost ten dollars. After the donkey pays him, the man says, "I've never seen a talking donkey in here." The donkey replies, "With these prices I'm not surprised."

No worries, Justin. Even Smoke's friends suggested that he keep his day job: being cute.

In January Smoke was drawn into a donkey controversy. Donkey advocates in Texas were outraged that park rangers at Big Bend State Park were rounding up and killing donkeys that had wandered across the Rio Grande from Mexico to graze in the park. State wildlife officials argued that the donkeys were damaging habitat being nurtured for native species. Donkey advocates argued that donkeys didn't damage the habitat at all and that there was plenty of vegetation to go around.

Marjorie Farabee, who lived in Plantersville, Texas, contacted John. She was director of wild burro affairs for the Wild Horse Freedom Federation. She urged him to join the effort to halt the donkey shooting by writing to Texas Governor Rick Perry. She also invited him to take Smoke to a "March of Mercy" being planned in Austin by the Wild Burro Protection League. John agreed to do what he could, but he declined the trip to Texas. After Smoke's health problems in December, he didn't think another big trip so soon was a good idea.

John and Smoke made good use of the barn that winter. On days that were too cold or snowy for a walk outside, they improvised. John led Smoke into the arena and then raced him back and forth across the large space. Other times they ran up and down the walkway between the two rows of horse stalls. John started out, and Smoke followed the leader—often overtaking his two-legged friend. Once, in his excitement, Smoke instinctively kicked out, just as he did in the pasture with Taffy and Domino, his miniature horse buddies. John, running right behind him, narrowly missed getting kicked in the head. He realized Smoke was just having some donkey fun. But he made it a point after that to let Smoke win their races handily. No photo finishes necessary.

With all the time John spent at the barn, he had learned a little about the skills the horses were working on and wondered whether a donkey could master the same things. He decided to teach Smoke to jump over obstacles. One day when no one was using the arena, he took Smoke in and set up some training equipment. This consisted of an eight-foot-long plastic pipe, four inches in diameter, set two feet above the ground on horse-jumping standards.

With a little encouragement Smoke hopped right over the pipe. But that didn't mean he liked it. No matter how many times John practiced with him, Smoke never made the jump without being coaxed. Sometimes John rushed him up to the pipe, hoping the momentum would lead Smoke to jump. But at the last moment Smoke took a detour, doing an end run around the pipe. Smarter than a horse? You bet.

Winter gave way to spring. The last of the snow melted, and the grass came to life in the pastures. The return of warm weather meant more outdoor walks—and the resumption of Take Flight therapy sessions after their winter break.

Once the ground dried out, Smoke revived one of his favorite pastimes: rolling in the dirt. John could always tell when the donkey was in the mood for a good roll. He would sniff the ground intently, pondering any clues he could inhale. Then, when he found just the right spot, he wheeled to the left, circling once. Then he wheeled to the right, sometimes adding in a happy little half kick. Then he tucked his legs, gently lowered himself to the ground, and rolled on his back from side to side, grunting contentedly as he rubbed the cool dirt into his coat. He had done this for as long as John had known him.

They also played a game in the pasture that they had revived from the old days in Iraq. Smoke took off at a gallop. He ran in a wide, circular pattern, dashing past John and then off again. Once he reached the other end of the pasture, he either made a wide sweeping turn or stopped abruptly, looking around, before turning on his heels and galloping back. One day John took along Belle and Blondie, his two standard poodles. Belle, the older dog, steered well clear of the donkey, remembering an earlier close encounter with Smoke's potentially lethal hooves. Blondie naïvely followed the donkey into the pasture, only to turn and dash back to safety at top speed as Smoke chased her out. Donkeys, after all, are guard animals. To them a poodle looks pretty much like any would-be canine predator.

Smoke set aside his country games temporarily in April, when two special events brought him into the city. First came the International Equestrian Show on April 20 and 21 at the downtown convention center. Lisa had helped spearhead the drive for Omaha to host this Olympic-caliber horse-jumping competition. Riders and their mounts traveled from five continents to compete. The show included an expo with all sorts of horse-related booths and children's activities. A petting zoo featured goats, rabbits, and miniature ponies. Someone suggested that Smoke should have his own booth.

He was a huge hit. Volunteers from the nearby Take Flight booth and a military booth kept an eye on him. He was spoiled by people bringing him apples and carrots and petting him. Children who visited the expo loved him. Some asked if he was the donkey from *Shrek*. No, it's Smoke, the volunteers would explain, and point out the posters about him. "Wow, cool!"

Next up was Black Tie & Tails, a fundraiser for the Nebraska Humane Society. Smoke was to receive the Tina Durham Service Award from the Humane Society's guild, Friends Forever. His history and his work with veterans prompted the honor, which was named after the dog belonging to local philanthropists Margre and Chuck Durham.

John was out of town, so Brenda and Jim Sheets delivered Smoke to the hotel where the event was being held. The honoree's identity was kept secret until the night of the gala affair, and a dramatic entrance was planned. Jim, Brenda, and Smoke were escorted into a back room. At the proper time, they were guided through a hallway to a ramp that led to the stage. But the hallway was dark, and the ramp was curved, and Smoke balked. He didn't like the look of this setup.

Pam Wiese, the Humane Society's vice president of public relations and marketing, was out front mingling with the guests when the sos hit her cell phone. "Smoke is afraid to go up the ramp in the dark! We need a light back here! Can you help?"

Pam called the event coordinator and explained the predicament. After a few minutes the event manager came running up with a desk lamp from her office. "Will this work?"

Just then, Pam's phone rang again. "Never mind. He's moving. Everything is fine."

On stage an honor guard from Offutt Air Force Base stood at parade rest as nearly four hundred guests were seated in the large ballroom. Judy Varner, president of the Humane Society, introduced Sunny Lundgren, the Durhams' daughter. Sunny told the crowd the 2012 award was honoring a veteran who had started off as a starving refugee in war-torn Iraq. A video rolled, describing Smoke's story, his trip to America, and his work with Take Flight.

Then the four-member honor guard turned to face inward, forming two columns. Smoke and his escorts walked out between them, to a roomful of applause. Smoke was presented with a plaque for his stall and a giant basket of carrots and treats. Gale, who was on stage representing Take Flight, didn't think there was a dry eye in the room. Afterward Smoke returned backstage, where members of the honor guard snapped selfies with him, getting a big kick out of meeting "that donkey from Iraq."

Smoke's new plaque added a touch of class to his barn stall. "2012, Nebraska Humane Society, Friends Forever, Tina Durham Service Award," it read. "Smoke, Retired Marine Veteran, Continuing His Work Stateside."

Life settled down considerably after April, and Smoke remained modest in the wake of his growing fame. At the end of May Sandy Spiehs wrote to John. She had taken over as livestock assistant at the state fair and wanted to book Smoke for a return engagement in late August. His appearance would be promoted in the fair's gatebook, which listed special events. John assured her that Smoke would be there.

In June Marjorie once again called on John and Smoke to advocate for a donkey cause. The small town of Van Horn, Texas, was staging Frontier Days later in the month, including "World Championship Donkey Roping." Marjorie and other donkey advocates were up in arms. Donkey roping involves shocking an animal with a cattle prod until it runs off. Then two horseback riders chase down the donkey, rope its neck and its rear legs, and stretch the donkey between the horses. But donkeys aren't built like cattle, and the roping can break their bones, not to mention traumatize these gentle prey animals.

A change.org petition drive was launched, and opponents

inundated the rodeo organizers with phone calls and complaints. Advocates pressed John to get involved because of his visibility and his connection to Smoke. John posted the Frontier Days notice on Smoke's Facebook page to alert his followers. And he contacted community leaders in Van Horn, including an attorney with the local chamber of commerce. John's goal was to defuse the controversy.

He understood that this was a small town simply looking to hold a community event and that the donkey roping was only a small part of Frontier Days. But it wasn't a good idea, and it would do more harm than good to the town's reputation, John told the attorney. He pointed out that Van Horn's residents were being painted as uncaring, unsophisticated yahoos. He told the attorney how outraged the donkey advocacy community was and how damaging and cruel the roping was to donkeys. Community leaders eventually cancelled the roping event. The donkey crisis was averted.

July passed quietly for Smoke. John had a hectic travel schedule, spending much of the time on the road with his nonprofit organization, so he scheduled only one public appearance for Smoke: a low-key visit one weekend to a local farmers' market. John found a shady spot at the market, held outside the Florence Mill, and set up a pen so Smoke could roam around while letting the clusters of children get up close and personal with him.

John drove out to the barn one day in early August, squeezing in one more visit before a weeklong family vacation in Door County, Wisconsin. The weather was hot and humid, and John felt melancholy for some reason. He and Smoke made their way to the south pasture. John walked over to a shady spot in the corner, sat down on a fallen log, and became lost in his thoughts. The donkey watched him for a few minutes and then walked over and stood next to him. Smoke put his head over John's left shoulder, as though to comfort him. John scratched the furry gray head in appreciation. Then he stood up and attached Smoke's lead rope, and the two friends walked back to the barn. He put Smoke back in his stall and headed home to pack.

After a week of camping in Door County, John's family dropped him off in Chicago to rejoin the cross-country trip his nonprofit group organized every summer. He and several volunteers took turns driving a GT500 Mustang, vinyl-wrapped in a patriotic theme, through all forty-eight contiguous states, to raise funds and awareness for combat wounded warriors and their families.

When Brenda stopped by the barn Tuesday evening, August 14, to feed late hay to the horses, she didn't like the way Smoke looked. He was standing in the corner of his stall, ignoring her. She texted John. "Wanted you to know that Smoke is acting a little under the weather today. No temp but he isn't eating and not social at all," she wrote at 8:30. "Looks like he may have a little nasal drainage. One of the other boarders called me and left me a voice mail saying about the same things I had noticed earlier."

John texted back half an hour later. "Do you think he's sad or depressed? I think horses and donkeys have feelings and perhaps get lonely."

Brenda responded about 10 p.m. "Temp was 98.0. Still very lethargic."

John suggested they see how Smoke was acting in the morning, and he would ask Jack to visit Smoke in the afternoon. Brenda thought that sounded reasonable. But when she pulled up to the barn about 8 a.m. Wednesday, she saw him lying on the ground in his run, just outside the door to his stall. She had a sick feeling in her stomach. She jumped out of her truck and rushed over. But it was too late to help him.

Sometime before dawn the little donkey that was tough enough to endure the deprivations of the Iraqi desert had lain down and died. In the end he was not tough enough to win the fight for his life. Ten days short of what would have been the fourth anniversary of the bray heard round the world, and fifteen months after he moved to Nebraska, Smoke the Donkey was gone.

Brenda was devastated. She called John, distraught and crying. John heard the news in shock. He couldn't think, could barely react. How could this be? He had just seen Smoke. Smoke had just been comforting him, the last time they were together. Now he was gone? John left unspoken the horrible, nagging thoughts that flooded his mind. So did Brenda. But inside both were asking themselves the same agonizing questions. What if they hadn't waited? What if they had called the vet the night before? Would Smoke still be alive?

The word of Smoke's death spread quickly. The *World-Herald* posted an obituary, and other news outlets soon followed suit— accounts written by the Associated Press, Reuters, and the *Marine Corps Times* were published widely in newspapers and on television, radio, websites, and blogs.

By that afternoon Smoke lay in state at the Nebraska Humane Society. Judy Varner had authorized Pam to give John whatever support and services he wanted. He hardly knew himself, but his business trip would keep him away from home the rest of the week, so he needed all the help he could get. He was battling feelings of deep grief. He tried to tell himself he shouldn't feel that way, that this was just an animal, just a donkey. But Smoke wasn't just a donkey. "Just donkeys" don't grab headlines and travel the world. "Just donkeys" don't lie in state when they die. "Just donkeys" don't trigger obituaries that flash across the globe.

Randy Garver, the maintenance supervisor at the Humane Society, stayed with Smoke until Gale could get there. A National Guardsman himself, he considered Smoke a true veteran, and he didn't want to leave him without a battle buddy. Pam arranged a viewing area for Smoke, and Jack brought over his halters and other memorabilia. They draped his "Kick Ass" blanket over him.

When Gale arrived, she and Pam began making arrangements for a time when people could stop by to pay their respects to Smoke, to say goodbye, and to share their stories and their grief. Then Gale began phoning people who would want to know right away and who could help her spread the news personally to others who would be especially hard-hit.

The community outpouring that followed surprised Gale. People she assumed wouldn't notice or care about Smoke's death not only sent their condolences but were sobbing when they talked to her. She took call after call from people saying, "I just need to talk." They stayed on the phone for half an hour or more, crying and pouring out their feelings and stories about the little donkey. Many of John's followers took note and sent word of how sorry they were. And he heard from strangers, as well.

"My brother Shaun Brown was in the group stationed at Camp TQ after you and your troops left. He was the Navy Chaplain there," wrote Claire Metzler, a massage therapist in Tranquility, New Jersey. "He would email pictures of Smoke wearing his red Marines blanket and tell me stories about him. . . . I used to send monthly care packages and I would always include a package of Mrs. Pasture's apple & oat horse cookies for Smoke. . . . My condolences on Smoke's passing."

Staff Sgt. Steven Saitta Jr., who had met Smoke while passing through Camp TQ, didn't find out until much later that Smoke had left Iraq to live in Omaha—a great coincidence, since Saitta had grown up in Omaha himself. He was sorry to hear the donkey had died but told John he was glad Smoke ended up getting to Omaha, back to the people who really cared about him.

Terri Crisp was shocked to hear the news and wrote a blog post reflecting on her special time with Smoke. "I could not fathom that this world would no longer have this remarkable donkey in it," she wrote. "Smoke should have lived many more years, continuing to make thousands of people laugh at his antics. . . . I now know what a good friend a donkey can be and Smoke was the best!"

Mary Lou Chapek stopped by Miracle Hills on Thursday morning. It was an overcast, rainy day, which struck her as appropriate. She and Brenda stood in the number-one stall and consoled each other.

Mary Lou had followed Smoke's story ever since reading about him in USA Today during a business trip to Washington

DC in January 2011. She was well aware of the sacrifices made by military families and how difficult their lives were during overseas deployments. Her own father had been killed during World War II in the Battle of the Bulge and was buried at Luxembourg. When she read the story of how John was trying to bring Smoke to America, it touched her heart. "That man loves that donkey," she thought, and she began saving every article she found about Smoke.

The James Sanborn article picked up by USA Today had mentioned that John's eventual goal was for Smoke to work at Take Flight Farms in Omaha. That pleased Mary Lou. Her own horse, Archie, was involved with Take Flight. She had bought the horse several years earlier, on an impulse. Archie had been abused by a previous owner, and he bucked, and he had only one good leg. He couldn't be ridden, and he wasn't especially fond of Mary Lou. But she felt sorry for him and responsible for him, and she continued to pay for his care for years afterward. It was lucky for the Take Flight program that she did. Archie had helped so many people through the equine program that he inspired a children's book, *Straight from the Horse's Mouth*, by regional author Julia Cook.

Mary Lou boarded Archie at Miracle Hills. But she didn't connect the barn with Smoke—she assumed that the Take Flight program operated in multiple locations. She never dreamed that this special Iraqi donkey would soon be living a mile away from her own farm. When Smoke moved in, she was thrilled. She loved how friendly he was, always coming up and sticking his nose over the stall gate. She began stopping by the barn more frequently. If nothing else, she would sometimes swing by stall number one on her way to or from town, greeting him from her truck with a cheerful, "Hi, Smoke!"

Mary Lou had learned about Smoke's death Wednesday morning, when she walked into her office. "I see your donkey died," her assistant said.

"I don't have a donkey," Mary Lou said. Then, with a jolt, she thought of Smoke. "Oh, my gosh!"

She was shaken by the news. She had just seen Smoke a couple of days earlier. All she could think of was how illogical his death was. After surviving in Iraq under such difficult circumstances, Smoke had moved to America, where he was loved and pampered. And now, she thought, now he dies? It didn't make sense.

Once her initial shock subsided, Mary Lou began to worry. Smoke had become such a celebrity, and many people knew where he lived. What if someone had poisoned him or hurt him somehow? The worrisome thoughts kept nagging at her. She knew it was none of her business, but she felt an overwhelming urge to find out: How did Smoke die?

The only way to know was through a necropsy, an autopsy for animals. When Mary Lou went to Brenda's barn the next morning, she brought up the idea. Brenda told her that would have to be the colonel's decision, but she passed along John's phone number. Mary Lou called him immediately. She introduced herself and told John her connections to Smoke. She also told him about her worries. Would he be interested, she asked, in having a necropsy done?

She was sure she could have one arranged. Mary Lou, a microbiologist, owned and operated MVP Laboratories, which manufactured livestock vaccines. Her late husband, Dr. Alex Hogg, had been a respected swine veterinarian for the University of Nebraska Extension Service, and she knew the staff at the university's Veterinary Diagnostic Center.

John took her up on the invitation immediately. He hadn't thought about the possibility of foul play in Smoke's death. But he was wracked with guilt, and like Mary Lou he felt the need to know: What had killed Smoke?

Dr. Alan Doster, head of the diagnostic center, agreed to have his staff conduct a cosmetic necropsy. Brenda picked up Smoke from the Nebraska Humane Society on Friday and took him to Lincoln for the procedure, returning him to the shelter afterward.

Smoke's "visitation" was held the next day. A couple dozen people attended, including Judy Varner and a number of veterans from Take Flight programs. A picture of Smoke was displayed on a large screen in an auditorium. Smoke lay curled up on a table, as if he were sleeping, covered with his red "Kick Ass" blanket. The mourners talked about how shocking his death had been and how sad it was, coming after so many people had done so much to bring him to the United States. They talked about his importance to the Marines in Iraq and their own bonds to him. They talked about what a solace it was to know that the last part of his life had been happy. Mostly they shared feelings of disbelief and sorrow about what might have been.

Sharon was there, both to support veterans she helped through the At Ease program and for herself—she felt as if she had lost a friend. She had contacted members of her support group after Smoke died, including the man who had played with Smoke in their first therapy session. He had later moved to Illinois, but when their support group met that week, she put him on speakerphone so he could participate. At the visitation people talked about how much fun Smoke had been and what a personality he had. An Iraq War veteran speculated about what Smoke could have told them about his life in the war zone, if he could have talked. Sharon left behind a Marine Corps challenge coin for Smoke as her way of saying goodbye.

Mary Lou was there, too. She didn't want Smoke's death to go unnoticed, and she felt the need for some closure. She had been drawn to his story from the beginning. As far as she was concerned, it was a love story, and it wasn't supposed to end like this.

When Gale left the auditorium, she was startled to find a number of people grouped together outside. At the last minute they couldn't bring themselves to go in, unwilling to be confronted so directly with the reality that Smoke was gone. There was something about this little donkey that was so captivating and so endearing—Gale had always been amazed by it. She had worked with a lot of equines, but she had never seen any with those qualities before, and she didn't think she ever would again. Perhaps, she thought, Smoke's final mission was the most important one: she truly believed that he had healed hearts and mended souls.

Lisa was as sad and shocked as everyone else about Smoke's death. But then she thought about the bigger picture—about how well loved Smoke had been and how amazing the last year of his life had been. He could have died alone in the desert, like a lot of other nameless creatures. But instead he had been given a hero's welcome and lived a hero's life for a period of time. Ultimately, she reasoned, the length of time in which an animal benefits from good treatment doesn't determine whether or not helping him was a good idea. And she was incredibly moved by the outpouring of emotions triggered by his death. Despite his short life, Smoke had had a singular and meaningful impact on a lot of people.

Lisa looked back on the Smoke episode with nothing but fondness—and sincere appreciation for John's role in making it happen. Her friend Joe Yoswa, who had helped get things rolling when Smoke was still in Iraq, thought Lisa and John were crazy to take on the task. But the way Lisa looked at it, sometimes the crazier the adventure, the more rational it is. She believed that Smoke's story sent a wonderful message to the world about what matters: taking care of people and helping the creatures around us.

John stopped by the Humane Society after he got back to town, but he didn't want to see Smoke. His feelings were still too raw, and besides, John preferred to hold onto his memories from Smoke's life—and there were many. The old days in Iraq. The major ordeal required to bring him to Nebraska. All their adventures once they were reunited. And their quiet companionship at the barn.

Smoke was moved to Rainbow Bridge, the Humane Society's cremation area. Several sets of clay hoof prints were cast and placed with Smoke to be fired during the cremation. Afterward some of Smoke's ashes were stored in ash lockets for John to distribute.

The Nebraska State Fair was only ten days away when Smoke died. When Kelly heard the news, she burst into tears at the idea of losing her little friend. Sandy, her replacement, had already set up Smoke's pen for this year. Knowing that fairgoers would ask about the donkey since he was a featured attraction, Sandy set up a small tribute to him. She made a sign with a brief description of his life and death and set out a vase with autumn leaves and a U.S. flag. John dropped off a few of Smoke's belongings. The display remained up through Labor Day, when the fair closed.

It was the day after Labor Day when Mary Lou sent John a copy of the final necropsy report. Dr. Bruce Brodersen had performed the procedure, with an assistant and several other pathologists looking on. He concluded quickly that Smoke had died from acute peritonitis as a result of a perforation in his intestines.

He found a significant amount of fluid, mixed with hay, in the donkey's abdominal cavity, where it had spilled after the intestinal wall ruptured. Brodersen couldn't find the perforation, so he couldn't provide more information about it. But he did discover a lot of scarring and fibrous adhesions on the intestinal wall. Those clues told him that Smoke had suffered from peritonitis sometime in the distant past—most likely while he was living on his own in the Iraqi desert.

Peritonitis, an inflammation of the abdominal walls, isn't necessarily fatal unless it reaches the acute stage. But once Smoke's intestines ruptured, the bacteria subsequently released led to systemic toxemia, akin to toxic shock syndrome in humans. Brodersen concluded that although Smoke might have been suffering some discomfort, once the rupture occurred, death had come quickly.

Could it have been prevented? Both Brodersen and Thomassen, who read the pathologist's report later, thought it unlikely. An intestinal perforation is low on the list of diagnoses that would have been considered even if Smoke had gone to the veterinary clinic. Given the amount of fluids found in his abdomen during the necropsy, both considered it highly unlikely that Smoke could have been successfully treated, even with surgery. The damage would have been too massive and the toxic poisoning too rapid to overcome.

The results were difficult to hear, but Mary Lou was relieved to know that no one had intentionally hurt Smoke, that his death was likely unpreventable, and that it had come quickly.

John wanted very much to believe that nothing could have been done to help Smoke. But even after learning the necropsy results, he was still burdened by guilt. Whether or not he could have changed the outcome, the fact remained that he hadn't been with Smoke that night.

Smoke was a tough little donkey, and that very toughness had lulled John and Brenda into thinking he wasn't seriously ill. When the horses had colic, it was obvious. They kicked and stomped and rolled around—they even bit themselves in their attempts to get rid of the pain. Not Smoke. Although Brenda noticed that something was wrong, Smoke displayed no obvious pain or discomfort. Even his temperature was normal. He just stood there, suffering stoically.

When she found him the next morning, he was lying down just outside his stall. Had he been waiting to see John? Smoke often waited there by the fence, his head bobbing up and down whenever he saw John drive up. It was his "Let's go out and play" gesture. But John did not come that night.

As much as he tried to console himself, John kept wondering whether his presence could have helped save the life of his long-eared battle buddy from Iraq. But he tried to believe Brodersen, who had concluded nothing could have been done. And he tried to remember that the doctor had made it clear Smoke's health problems most likely had their origins in Iraq, where a donkey's life is brutal and short.

The air was cool the night Smoke died. Although John would never know the precise hour, he speculated that it was early, perhaps around midnight, when the bacterial toxins had done their worst. Nor would he know how much pain Smoke suffered or what thoughts he had as he lay down to die. Did Smoke wonder where

John had gone? Did he wonder why Brenda didn't return? Was he afraid because he didn't understand what was happening to him?

The only witnesses at the barn were the horses and Oreo the Cat. In the shadow of Brenda's barn and in the stillness of a clear Nebraska night Smoke died with nothing else to comfort him but the silent sentinels of the night: the stars. There was no moon, and by 11 p.m., Mars and Saturn had slipped below the western horizon. But Smoke had other companions.

Riding overhead in that August sky were two special constellations: Pegasus, the flying horse, and Equuleus, the little horse—known by the Arabs as the First Horse, or al-Faras al-Awwal. Also shining down on him was the bright and beautiful Vega, a star regarded by Sargon the Great of ancient Iraq as the Life of Heaven. John thought it appropriate that his special little donkey had such worthy attendants.

After a few days at home John left again to continue his cross-country trip, the High Five Tour. He took along some of Smoke's ashes. John had been corresponding with California author Robin Hutton. She was writing a book, *Sgt. Reckless, America's War Horse*, about the Mongolian mare recruited by the U.S. Marine Corps during the Korean War. The Marines later shipped Reckless to Camp Pendleton, California, but only after fighting the same kind of bureaucratic headaches John had battled in bringing Smoke home.

John's road trip would take him close to Camp Pendleton, a vast Marine Corps facility near Oceanside. Sgt. Reckless was buried there, and John decided it would be fitting to spread some ashes of "America's donkey" at the gravesite of "America's war horse," in honor of their shared Marine Corps service.

The horse's grave lies just outside Stepp Stables, a riding facility at the camp. A stately slab of black marble marking the site bears a photograph of Reckless and an inscription that begins, "In memory of Reckless, Pride of the Marines." John paid his respects and spread Smoke's ashes. He drove up to the Los Angeles area to visit Robin before continuing his tour.

John missed Smoke terribly that fall. Donkey advocates were pressing him to take in another donkey. He wrestled with the idea. He was still grieving for Smoke. But given the work Smoke did with Take Flight, John felt responsible for filling the billet of therapy donkey. Smoke had served a wonderful role with the program, and now there was a gap. Then there was the matter of filling the gap left in his own life.

He finally decided to go for it. Marjorie, the donkey advocate in Texas, told him about some young burros that had been rounded up in California, in the Cibola-Trigo Herd Management Area. The facility is part of a wild burro adoption program run by the U.S. Bureau of Land Management (BLM). The wild burros, or donkeys, which roam several western states, are thought to be descendants of pack animals abandoned in the wake of the 1800s Gold Rush. With Marjorie's encouragement John filed an application to adopt two foals and contacted the BLM office in Ridgecrest, California. But in discussing his plans with them, he learned that the federal agency runs an adoption center much closer to home, in Elm Creek, Nebraska—less than a three-hour drive from Omaha. John wrapped up the High Five Tour and headed for home across Interstate 80, stopping off at the Elm Creek facility on October 5 to visit.

John met with the wrangler. They talked over John's desire to adopt a foal. His adoption application had been accepted, and they walked outside to look around. There in one of the corrals was a filly standing with her mother. John watched as the fuzzy little filly backed up against her mother and playfully tried to kick her. Three times she kicked. And three times her little back hooves cleared the ground by no more than a few inches. It was love at first sight on John's side.

The filly stared at John and the wrangler warily, never taking her big brown eyes off them and never straying from her mother's side. She was far from knowing that this chance meeting, reminiscent of another chance meeting more than four years earlier in the middle of Iraq, would change her life and once again change John's.

The foal was weaned in early December, and John returned to Elm Creek with Smoke's trailer. His heart took a leap when he looked at the adoption papers. He found himself reflecting, as he had one day in Istanbul, that nothing happens in isolation. His deployment to Iraq in 2008 came during the U.S. response to the al Qaeda attacks of September 11, 2001. The reason he met Smoke, in a roundabout way, was 9/11. That's how they began their unforgettable journey. Now here he was, taking in another donkey—one he had stumbled on unexpectedly. He looked at the adoption papers and marveled. Because this little donkey had been born on September 11.

With a birthday like that, the little longears needed a special name. A name worthy of a donkey born in freedom, one destined to teach and heal, one who would provide a reminder of Smoke's own legacy of friendship, connections, and hardships overcome.

Her name: Hope.

30. Smoke's urn.
COURTESY OF
JOHN FOLSOM.

31. Charm the horse meets Hope the Donkey at Miracle Hills Ranch & Stables, in a scene reminiscent of when Smoke was welcomed to Nebraska. COURTESY OF JOHN FOLSOM.

Epilogue

Memories of Smoke have lived on long after his death. His Facebook page continues to attract followers. High school students in an EAGALA program with Take Flight Farms created a grief recovery activity in his honor. Veterans who knew him from equine therapy sessions continue to reminisce about him. And at least one person who posed with Smoke at Bill and Lisa Roskens's party kept the photo on her refrigerator door for years. Smoke's name keeps popping up, among people who knew and loved him, in follow-up news articles, and in curiously random pop culture references.

In March 2013 the *Omaha.com* staff had some fun with March Madness by creating the Tournament of Animals. The bracket featured sixteen entries with animals that had made the local news. Online voting determined who advanced in each round. Smoke won the tourney, beating out Elvis, a lost Schnauzer-poodle mix who uncannily found the church where his owner's funeral had just been held; Melek, a three-legged, globe-trotting homeless dog; and five adorable lion cubs at the Henry Doorly Zoo. In the championship match Smoke prevailed over the formidable Ninja cow, which had eluded captors in southeast Nebraska for three months, hiding by day and foraging by night.

That distinction for Smoke came on the heels of a list of "Seven Famous Military Mascots," published by Mother Nature Network the same month. The special seven ranged from Nils Olav, a King penguin mascot and colonel-in-chief in the Norwegian Royal Guard; to William Windsor, goat mascot of the British Army's Royal Welsh infantry regiment; not to mention Chesty the bulldog, the official Marine Corps mascot. But first on the list was Smoke the Donkey.

Perhaps no reference was more random than the October 19, 2014, broadcast of HBO's irreverent *Last Week Tonight*. British comedian John Oliver was lambasting the complex U.S. process established to grant asylum to military translators from Iraq and Afghanistan. "Our main story tonight," Oliver announced, "is going to end with you getting extremely angry at a donkey."

What donkey? Smoke, of course. Oliver interviewed several interpreters and then showed clips of Smoke and John. He pointed out that while it had taken several months to get Smoke into the country, the process took years for translators who had risked their lives for U.S. troops. "See, I told you this story was going to end with you getting [bleeping bleeped] off at a donkey," Oliver told his audience.

Although Hope was no veteran, she did follow in Smoke's hoof steps in the Take Flight therapy program—once she grew up a little. Hope made a good therapy donkey because she was friendly and curious, yet she was no pushover, as program director Sara Weiss discovered. When a group of high-energy adolescent boys ordered Hope to do their bidding, she refused to comply, compelling them to practice patience and teamwork.

Hope was also perceptive. One weekend about sixty adults from across the country took part in an EAGALA certification session with Take Flight. Lissa Sutton, who followed Gale as Take Flight's executive director in late 2012, helped with the weekend training. She and two other women were role-playing, portraying teenagers who struggled with relationships and responsibilities. When it came to acting like an uncooperative stinker, Lissa nailed it.

Afterward everyone gathered to discuss the results. Without warning Hope marched up and firmly head-butted Lissa out of the group. Everyone's eyes lit up at the "Aha!" moment of the day. Hope knew a brat when she saw one, and she wasn't afraid to point it out. Smoke would have been pleased with the little jenny.

Hope was every bit as smart as Smoke. Take the day of her first snowstorm. Hope was barely three months old when five inches of snow fell in Omaha, a few days before Christmas in 2012. She and John took a walk along the fence that lined her run. Hope walked gingerly in the cold wet snow, tucking her head against the wind—just as Smoke had done a year earlier. When they reached the corner, John kept walking straight ahead, but Hope stopped. She wanted to turn right and keep following the fence line. John walked a few more feet forward, tugging on her rope and coaxing her, but Hope wouldn't budge. John took one more step—and plunged rib-deep into a hole concealed by drifted snow. Hope won the memory challenge, hooves down.

She was just as fond of a treat as Smoke had been and craved attention every bit as much. And she loved John. Whenever he drove up to the barn, there was Hope, waiting at the fence expectantly. The sight brought back fond memories of Smoke. In fact, reminders of Smoke were everywhere. John thought about him whenever he visited the barn. Smoke's urn remained on display in his office. And whenever he wrote on Smoke's Facebook page, thoughts of the little donkey came flooding back.

Meeting Smoke had been a life-changing adventure for John. Nor was his the only life Smoke touched. Who knows how many people had followed the donkey's story and felt attached to him, whether or not they ever met him in person?

When John paused to reflect, he marveled at the amazing turns his life had taken—turns he never anticipated or could have imagined back on August 24, 2008, when he awoke in the middle of Iraq to the insistent braying of a little stray donkey.